LEEDS UNITED

Phil Hay was born in Edinburgh and has been a journalist for over six years. He was promoted to chief soccer writer of the *Yorkshire Evening Post* two years ago. *Leeds United – From Darkness into White* is his first book.

LEEDS UNITED FROM DARKNESS INTO WHITE

The Year of Resurrection

Phil Hay

Foreword by Eddie Gray

MAINSTREAM
PUBLISHING

EDINBURGH AND LONDON

First published in Great Britain in 2008 by
MAINSTREAM PUBLISHING COMPANY
(EDINBURGH) LTD
7 Albany Street
Edinburgh EH1 3UG

ISBN 9781845963934

A catalogue record for this book is available
from the British Library

Typeset in Caslon and Gill Sans

Printed in Great Britain by
Clays Ltd, St Ives plc

3

ACKNOWLEDGEMENTS

THE BASIS OF EVERY STORY IS ITS SUBJECT, AND I AM indebted to Leeds United – their players, their staff and their supporters – for the pleasure of a season which can only be described as an author's dream. No club does plot lines like Leeds United, and no journalist could ask for a more fascinating or unique club to cover. The job is never more satisfying than when players, coaches and supporters excel as they did during the 2007–08 season. Kevin Blackwell, the club's former manager, used to say that nothing rolls with the relentless power of a Leeds United bandwagon. He was not wrong.

I owe considerable thanks to Iain MacGregor, Mainstream's Associate Publisher, for suggesting this project and for the enthusiasm he has shown from the first day of writing to the last. At no stage were his demands anything other than fair and reasonable, and it helped enormously to be working with someone whose interest in the subject matched my own. Further praise is due to Graeme Blaikie, particularly for arranging the photographs for this book, and to everyone else at Mainstream who has been involved in the project. I could not have asked for more professional publishers.

A mention should also be made of my old sports editor at the *Yorkshire Evening Post*, Phil Rostron, who recommended that I take this book on and proved a valuable source of advice in the early days of writing.

I'm extremely grateful to Eddie Gray for providing the excellent foreword for this publication, and also for his friendly and entertaining company at home and away throughout the season. I have never met a more patient and willing autograph-signer, or a man with more inherent passion for football. He is a credit to his sport and his club, and Leeds United will never have a better ambassador.

Football is a game of opinions and your own is never enough, so I valued the chance to chew the fat over the course of the season with other journalists who followed Leeds United: Adam Pope of BBC Radio Leeds, Richard Sutcliffe of the *Yorkshire Post*, Paul Dews of Leeds United, Mark Walker of PA Sport and Tom Kirwin and Michael Weadock of Yorkshire Radio. A view from the terraces is equally useful, and I was pleased that Phil Woodhouse was willing to contribute to this book. Phil is what you can safely call a real fan, and it's always good to get his frank and accurate assessment of all things Leeds United. You can rely on supporters to tell it like it is.

My mother and father would not expect to be listed in this section, but they are anyway – for so many reasons, but above all for treating professional football with the perspective and, on occasions, the contempt it deserves. And finally, of course, a heartfelt nod to my darling girlfriend Fiona, for her encouragement, her support and for biting her lip when she should have bitten my head off. Love always.

CONTENTS

FOREWORD

LEEDS UNITED ARE IN MY BLOOD, AND YOU DON'T HAVE TO ask what my emotions were on the day the club were relegated from the Championship. To say I was disappointed doesn't do it justice. I was caretaker manager when Leeds lost their place in the Premier League in 2004 and that hurt, but the financial problems at Elland Road had become so bad back then that relegation wasn't a huge surprise. I can safely say that nobody saw League One coming. It was almost unbelievable to find the club in that position, but if you've been part of professional football for as long as I have then very little surprises you. The idea of Leeds United being so far down the Football League was actually one I could relate to. When I came to Elland Road as a player in the 1960s, Leeds were a second-division club. A few years earlier, they'd scraped clear of relegation to Division Three and done so by the skin of their teeth. Every club has points in their history where they feel they can get no lower, and Leeds were not the first major team to slip through the leagues. What really worries supporters is the idea that their club might become trapped.

When you're told two days before the start of the season that you'll compete in League One with a 15-point deduction, the automatic reaction is to assume that promotion is out of the question. But funnily enough, I wasn't too despondent. In fact, I still fancied Leeds to win the title. It was understandable that fans were panicking, but League One is not an impossible division in any circumstances. If we'd been talking about the Championship, there would have been no chance of promotion; it's totally unrealistic to think that you could get over that sort of penalty in England's second division. There are too many good teams, and too many good players. But in League One, I was confident that Leeds had the power to go up, even though the summer had been a nightmare.

The 15-point deduction has been the talking point of the whole season, but with hindsight you could argue that the season might have been harder if it hadn't been for that penalty. That sounds like a strange comment, but Dennis Wise was an unpopular manager among the supporters after relegation from the Championship. He didn't have many friends in Leeds and there were plenty of calls for him to go. I'm not saying that he wouldn't have produced the same results without the 15-point punishment, but there's no doubt that the punishment created a sudden and definite siege mentality at Elland Road which hadn't existed before, at least not during Dennis's time with Leeds. The crowd moved behind the club and the players, and the united atmosphere seemed to inspire everyone. Dennis and Gus Poyet played on that siege mentality, and played on it big time. And it worked for them. Dennis himself obviously had something to prove. He can't have been happy about being the manager who took Leeds United into League One.

When you reach a level like this, you realise that something has to change. The decline of Leeds has been going on for some time, and at a very quick rate. I know the club reached the Championship play-off final in 2006, and were that close to getting back into the Premier League, but back then I still had a feeling that things weren't quite right behind the scenes. The club's finances were nowhere near as stable as they seem to be now. Fair enough, promotion to the Premier League would have sorted the problems out – we're talking about a payday of £40 million upwards for promoted teams these days – but there was always that lack of control. When Leeds lost to Watford, the money issues started to bite again, and for the first time in their history, the club were dropped into the third tier of English football. Obviously as an ex-player and manager it saddens me but, as ever, it's the supporters you think about and sympathise with first.

Take, for example, the support we've had this season. I look around at the average attendances in England, and I see a club like Stoke City. They're getting around 17,000 for their home games and they're preparing for the Premiership. Our average attendance is way above that. There aren't many teams in the country who can command gates of over 30,000 – and on a few occasions get almost 40,000. A lot of clubs hope to get to that figure when they reach the Premiership but hardly any of them do. To achieve those figures in League One is incredible, and Leeds United support should not be under-estimated or under-valued.

One of the most important factors during the 2007–08 season was that the fans supported the club from the word go. But you've also got to give credit to the way the players responded to the points deduction. It's easy for me to say that I fancied them to go up, but I couldn't have predicted how positive their attitude was going to be. The manner of their results definitely helped. When I think back to the start of the season, I have to say that a lot of our victories came down to good fortune. Leeds developed this habit of popping up with goals in the last minute, which added to the feeling that the club was on a roll. The game that stands out is our 2–1 win at Nottingham Forest in August. In the second half, Leeds got absolutely battered, and I don't know how Forest missed the chances they missed. Forest should have won that game 5–1 but they didn't, and results like that gave the fans inspiration. I think some of the euphoria came because we were winning games out of the blue, and winning games we perhaps deserved to lose. People started to expect us to score last-minute goals and when you have that expectation, it often happens. I'm sure it played on the minds of the opposition as well.

The advantage that Leeds United undoubtedly have is that the club will always be an attraction to professional footballers, whatever anyone says. If a smaller club had done what Leeds did last summer and said to these players 'we can't offer you contracts at the moment, but come and train with us anyway', some of them might have said 'get stuffed'. A few players said that to Leeds anyway, but I guarantee you that it would have been a million times worse if it hadn't been Leeds who were asking the question. The fact that they were able to bring quality to this league was a huge benefit. Take Dougie Freedman as an example. I doubt whether he really wanted to drop down to League One – and by that I mean he'd have been right in thinking he was better than this level – but he did want to come to Leeds. When this club finally returns to the Championship, as it is bound to do, it will hopefully be the same – assuming, that is, that Leeds have the money to compete. Every time you get to a higher level, the stakes get higher as well. And in the Championship, there are always clubs with money in their pockets.

I still believe that when you talk about Leeds United in the context of the biggest English clubs, you're talking about one of the top eight. I'm not saying they're a top-eight team right now, because there are plenty of better sides in England at the moment, but this club is massive. Truly massive. It's not just about their attendances. Consider as well the number of foreign countries that have registered Leeds United supporters in them. They're everywhere, even now. That's why it's important that our time in League One ends as quickly as possible. When a club is struggling, football moves away quickly, and the financial figures that the Premier League teams are dealing in these days are frightening. Sooner or later – the sooner the better – Leeds have to get back in amongst that money. That's what the club's future depends on.

Given the circumstances, the 2007–08 season has to go down as one of the better seasons in our history. You can only compare like with like, but you can't necessarily argue that getting to the semi-finals of the Champions League is more difficult than getting to League One's play-off final with a 15-point deduction. The 2008 League Two final was between Stockport County and Rochdale, and to Stockport's players, winning promotion will feel like as big an achievement as Manchester United winning the European Cup. The money that Manchester United have makes them potential Champions League winners every season, and the Leeds squad that reached the semi-finals wasn't cheap. They were brilliant, no doubt about that, and went further than most people expected them to, but you can't rate teams on the basis that one trophy is bigger or more lucrative than another. It's all relative. In truth, you'd be hard pressed to pick out a season which was better in terms of results than the one just gone.

Looking at the club in general, I can see that things are on the up again. But we're still a long way short of the pinnacle of the game. For a club like Leeds United, the pinnacle of the game means playing at the highest level. And not just playing at the highest level – competing at the highest level, and winning at the highest level. Gary McAllister played in a great Leeds side who won the league championship and got to the final of the League Cup. There were a couple of disappointments as well, but he still won a major trophy. And that matters. It's what football's about, and especially when you play for a club like Leeds. I can't predict how long it will take the club to get back to that standard, but I know that we're not going to walk it. I also know that once we reach the Championship, as we so nearly did in 2008, the fans will expect promotion to the Premier League immediately. If you support Leeds United, you automatically assume that the club will do well. In fact, you demand it. That's the legacy of Don Revie's team in a way, and I accept that his era can be a noose around the necks of some managers. Every time a team struggles, people say 'it wasn't like this in the 1970s'. But you can't look back in football and maybe we're guilty of doing that too often. You'll never see another situation where 10 or 12 players come to a club at the age of 16 or 17 and stay there for virtually their whole careers, as I and a lot of my team-mates did. I made more than 500 appearances for Leeds and some of the other players made over 700, but those were different days. There's unlikely to be another era where the same squad stays together for more than a decade and wins a load of trophies and medals. Gary Kelly recently passed 500 appearances for Leeds before he retired, but he might be the last guy to do that. If anyone else manages that, I'll be surprised. As much as supporters might like a team to match the one we had in the 1970s, it's not a realistic expectation. Football has changed.

If Don had been alive to see this season, he'd have been delighted – for the simple reason that he'd have approached it in exactly the same way as Dennis Wise did. Can you imagine Don looking at the 15-point deduction and saying: 'Ah well, boys, this season's ruined. We might as well not bother'? No chance. Absolutely none. He'd have said: 'All these people who are having a pop, let's get into them and have a go.' In the 1970s, there was a siege mentality at Leeds, and we knew what was said about us as a team. But when you're winning games week-in, week-out, it doesn't bother you too much. At the end of the day, we were the boys with the medals. With Dennis and his players, it was different. Last summer Leeds were getting taken to the cleaners on all fronts, and things like the 15-point deduction must have created real resentment. If someone says 'you're a bunch of dirty players' and you're holding a league championship medal, you're not bothered. But what can you say to a 15-point deduction? Add that to the fact that Dennis had been under a transfer embargo for months – and that he'd been relegated with Leeds at the end of the previous season – and you can understand why he felt the Football League and the game as a whole were out to get him.

Some people are of the opinion that Dennis deserves no credit for this season. I disagree completely. He's worth every bit of praise he received for the way the club started the season, and had it not been for those results, Gary McAllister wouldn't have had the chance to take Leeds into the play-offs. Gary was terrific as well, but this season has definitely been a story of two managers, and they've both played a part. I understand that people might not like Dennis's character, or his Chelsea connections, but let's not rewrite history. His role was crucial, and it would have been easier for him to walk out of Elland Road six months before he did, when the club's position was dire. I wouldn't have blamed him.

A few times last summer, I heard people saying that Leeds United were on their last legs; that the club might die. But never once did I think that administration or the 15-point deduction would be the end of Leeds United. The club is too big; the city is too big. A team who can pull in an attendance of 38,000 for a League One game has everything going for it, and you can't kill that spirit. One day, the revival was bound to start. It had to happen. The defeat to Doncaster Rovers at Wembley was ultimately a horrible disappointment, but the club have a positive future once more. My only hope is that this season will prove to be the first of many steps forward.

Eddie Gray MBE

PROLOGUE

. . . .

IN DEEPEST, DARKEST LIBEREC

L IBEREC. 21 JULY 2007. THE LIGHT HAS FADED AND THE
mood is dark. Clustered in the silhouette of a stadium they don't
know, in a city they have never heard of, Leeds Uniteds supporters are
seeking solace in litres and half-litres of Gambrinus. It is, according
to those who know, the most refined lager the Czech Republic has
to offer, and on this night of all nights the nations guests deserve
nothing less. The last train to Dresden rolled down the tracks half an
hour earlier; those who should have been among its passengers will
fend for themselves until the light of day returns.

By the blue and rusty gates of Stadion U Nisy – the residence of
FC Slovan Liberec – the undercarriage of a coach is being loaded
with heavy bags. The vehicle carries the banner of Dynamo Dresden,
the deposed powerhouse of East German football, but is charged this
evening with bearing the players and staff of Leeds United back across
the Czech–German border and home to their hotel in Radebeul, a
northern suburb of Dresden.

Carefully, the driver guides his bus through the pockets of drinkers
beside the stadium's primitive beer tents and begins a short, steep
ascent to a car park behind Stadion U Nisy's main stand, the oddity
of an otherwise nondescript venue. An architect worth his salt would

have surveyed the cliff which overhangs the stadium and suggested that Slovan Liberec take their football elsewhere. The club adopted a less defeatist view and hacked the fourth side of their ground into the yellow sandstone. As a result of that pragmatism, Leeds United's squad will leave silently through the back door this evening, far from the madding crowd 100 feet below.

The thick of the congregation of nomadic supporters was not a place for United's players to be. Less so their manager, Dennis Wise. 'I wish the little bastard would come out here,' says a barrel-chested cockney, the severity of his snarl enhanced by the occasional missing tooth. 'He'd get a lively reception from us lot. Very lively. And I'd be right at the front of the fucking queue.' He wasn't joking. Nobody was joking. It was weeks and months since supporters with a healthy interest in Leeds United had shown the inclination to make light of anything. Relegated from the Championship in April and declared insolvent in May, the club could not predict with any certainty that they would be fit and eligible to start the season their players and staff were preparing for when they escaped to central Europe for a brief summer tour on 17 July. A transfer embargo imposed on Leeds by the Football League – an automatic effect of a club's entry into administration – meant Wise was permitted to peruse the transfer market on a look-but-don't-touch basis, a depressing situation made worse by the knowledge that few players were interested in touching an insolvent Leeds United. The 20-man squad which travelled abroad with Wise contained three out-of-contract players, five trialists and five players recently fashioned from the club's youth academy. Quakers went to war with more numbers and more vigour.

In those circumstances, Liberec was an appropriate destination for supporters who had reached the end of their tether. It felt like the ends of the earth. The Czech Republic's sixth-largest metropolis is known to natives as the Bohemian Manchester, but not because it is ready to embrace a cosmopolitan culture. English speakers were few in number, and citizens without a grasp of German conversed solely in the unrecognised language of Czech. The Republic joined the European Union in 2004 but will not implement the Euro as its official currency until 2012 at the earliest. When United's supporters invaded on 21 July, they found that their rolls of Euro notes were essentially worthless in a country which yearns for a wider outlook but continues to display its Eastern European heritage. The supporters who were able to lay their hands on Czech Koruna did a brisk trade in currency exchange around the stadium; others who feared they would be locked out of the ground were reprieved by Slovan Liberec's willingness to accept Euros in exchange for tickets. It is unlikely that the club understood the dark psychological place that the followers of Leeds were in, but their flexibility kept the peace nonetheless.

It was in keeping with so much of the summer that United's presence in Liberec was neither planned nor especially desirable. That scorching Saturday should have been spent playing Dynamo Dresden, the midway point of Leeds' proposed three-match tour which began three days earlier with a 2–0 defeat to Union Berlin in the German capital, and concluded two days later after a 2–1 defeat to FC Energie Cottbus in Dessau. Cottbus were and are a Bundesliga club and represented the most capable team on United's schedule, but Dresden were the draw. More than 1,000 of United's supporters planned to attend the fixture in southern Germany, a pre-season turn-out to dwarf all others. But when local police learned that followers of Dresden planned to provide what could generously be described as a welcoming party, the wheels of authority trampled the friendly into the ground.

Germany has a chronic problem with violence in the name of football and far greater than that of England, the country which is still accused by Europe of having bred and nurtured the hooligan. The issue is accentuated in Dresden, where die Polizei no longer take chances or cut corners. A Regionalliga Nord game between Dynamo and Union Berlin during the 2006–07 season carried such a threat of violence that 1,100 officers were posted to marshal a gathering of 20,000 fans, and the long batons, tough khaki uniforms and ultra-thick helmets carried by police constables do not suggest their idea of crowd control is a subtle concept. Hooliganism in Germany is driven as much by social issues as it is by sporting rivalry, and the gates of Dresden's ground, the Rudolf-Harbig Stadion, carry the ludicrous but necessary warning that supporters are banned from distributing rechtsradikalen propaganda – right-wing propaganda – on the terraces. In England, stewards twitch at the sight of supporters carrying cans of Fanta. In Dresden, they frisk you for Swastikas at the gates. It did not help that on the day of United's friendly with Dynamo, a march with fascist overtones was due to take place in Leipzig, a city which shares the same Bundeslande and police force as Dresden. Twenty-four hours before the kick-off, the plug was pulled.

Thus it was that Leeds and an intrepid portion of their fanbase found themselves in Liberec, a destination beyond the back of beyond. Slovan averted a blank weekend by agreeing at short notice to host a friendly with United, and also adhered to Wise's insistence that their first-team squad be involved. United's tour of Germany – interspersed with their cameo in the Czech Republic – was a valuable break from the overwhelming atmosphere of conflict and controversy which had enveloped the club back home, but Wise was unwilling to allow the trip to mirror a vacation. Had he wanted a holiday, United's manager would have resigned from his post and disappeared to Dubai, the land of riches unimaginable to a club as close to liquidation as Leeds were. A wealthy man in his own right, he did not need their money and he was not obliged to accept the aggravation his job entailed. An icon of Chelsea at the forefront of Leeds United could never expect to command unanimous popularity, but relegation at the end of his first season at Elland Road transformed scepticism of Wise into open hostility. He had been verbally abused by supporters present in Berlin, and would be again when Leeds arrived in Dessau. He did not need to mingle with the moonlit crowd in Liberec to appreciate their volatility and shattered patience. Hundreds of miles from Elland Road, the discord hovered like a persistent fog which the club's pre-season results failed to lift. United, for the record, were beaten 1–0 by Liberec.

The merits of the European tour were difficult to gauge, yet Wise's demand that Slovan Liberec refrain from fobbing him off with a team of reserves confirmed that he at least could see through the smoke and fire of administration, and far enough to visualise the start of the new season. He would later describe United's foreign training camp as the catalyst for the drama which followed, and what Slovan Liberec's co-operative staff could not have realised was the ironically low priority Wise was placing on Leeds' friendly fixtures. In cruel temperatures in the south of Germany, United's coaching team would force their players through hours of exhausting fitness work on the morning of each match, leaving their squad with limited energy for the game which followed in the evening. It left the club susceptible to defeat but allowed their manager to fly back to England with unbridled faith in the condition and mentality of the members of his fragile squad. The supporters who journeyed to the continent were abandoning hope on their return, unaware of the fact that Wise had renewed his. His resolve would be examined again before the start of the season by a punishment which he and his club did not anticipate, but by then the battle lines were comprehensively drawn. The intoxicated antagonist of Liberec would soon be forced to concede that Wise was not for turning – the little bastard with a big heart.

PENNY IN THE POUND

THE SUN CAME UP ON THE MORNING OF 28 APRIL 2007, illuminating the city of Leeds in a tantalising glow. Football takes on a different complexion as the weather changes, and the clear skies over Yorkshire presented an optimistic outlook for the afternoon ahead. By 3 p.m., 31,269 spectators would be crammed into Elland Road, the majority stomaching butterflies but clinging to the promise of salvation that came with glorious sunshine. Leeds United had been backed into a corner and were almost trapped; the Americans would have hung a sign outside Elland Road welcoming travellers to the Last Chance Saloon.

The permutations for Leeds before their last home fixture of the 2006–07 season were potentially complex, yet worryingly simple. The club held 22nd position in the Championship and lay a point adrift of Hull City, their Yorkshire neighbours and by then the only club whose demise would facilitate United's survival. Luton Town had been relegated already; Southend United were certain to follow. With two matches remaining and six points still available, the one outstanding issue was whether Leeds or Hull would become the third and final club to forego their place in the Championship and depart to the outpost that is League One. United's supporters did not appreciate the sight of their club exiled from the Premier League, as Leeds had been since 2004, but a second relegation threatened obscurity on an untold scale. As weary as they were of newspaper articles recalling how six years earlier Leeds United had negotiated a spectacular path to the semi-finals of the Champions League – Europe's most prestigious and affluent club tournament – the comparison exposed in graphic detail the ridiculous nature of the danger they were in.

To the credit of United's squad, they had fought the good fight and railed against the suggestion that relegation was unavoidable. Four victories at Elland Road during March and April and a slight upturn in results away from home kept their noses above water, though the sense of inevitability surrounding their demise was never removed. Of greater resonance than their defiance was a defeat to Colchester United on Easter Monday, when Leeds conceded two goals in the final eight minutes having held a 1–0 lead for most of the second half. The strained look in Dennis Wise's eyes after full-time at Layer Road did not speak of a beaten man but it revealed the concern of one who knew he had lost control of his club's season. 'We were in such a comfortable position', said Wise. 'Then we had a mad 10 minutes.' United's fate in those 10 minutes had been left to hang on the results of other clubs.

It was with that understanding that Leeds welcomed Ipswich Town to Elland Road on 28 April, the penultimate day of the season. Hull City were engaged with Cardiff City on the same afternoon, and it did not take a calculator for Wise to establish the consequences of an away win at Ninian Park combined with a draw at Elland Road. Hull's lead would be three points and their goal difference insurmountable. United's manager was outwardly confident but inwardly concerned. He could rant and he could rave; he could offer his squad every scrap of inspiration he had ever gained. But when the players crossed the whitewash, Wise would be left to cross his fingers and trust to luck. Fortune was all he had left to bank on.

In the days leading up to the game against Ipswich, Wise was drawn into discussing the catastrophic effects of relegation. There would be changes in every department, he warned, and consequences stretching far beyond a squad of players which was already certain to haemorrhage at the end of the season. Staff, in short, would have to be sacked as Leeds revised their levels of expenditure. Exactly how much Wise knew about the holes in United's accounts is difficult to say, but he was clearly aware of trouble behind the scenes. A fortnight after the season finished, his kit manager Shaun Hardy and the club's popular physiotherapist Alan Sutton, an employee at Elland Road for 21 years and a valued part of the furniture, were made redundant by the administrators who had been summoned to deal with the club's unmanageable debts, the first of many painful examples of collateral damage. Leeds were also asked to dispense with Wise's managerial secretary. Do or die, as he had termed the contest with Ipswich, seemed like an apt phrase, and many in England were hoping for the latter. 'An awful lot of people will be rubbing their hands with glee if Leeds take another mighty fall,' wrote Rodney Marsh, the former Manchester City striker, in a national newspaper column before the game. As tactless as the comment may have been, it was not at all inaccurate.

The nervous tension inside Elland Road on 28 April was tangible, and the shiver-inducing noise that met United's players as they stepped from the tunnel in tandem with Ipswich's line-up represented a desperate plea for one last push. The occasion felt decisive. With 12 minutes gone, David Healy drove a shot against the body of Ipswich goalkeeper Shane Supple, and Richard Cresswell threw himself awkwardly at the rebound, bouncing the ball over the goalline with a flick of his head. In those magical seconds, Leeds United felt the surge of invincibility that flows from a goal like Cresswell's. The doubts cleared and the butterflies paused; Elland Road raised two fingers to the rest of the country. He who laughs last . . . But the euphoria couldn't last; Leeds United couldn't last. When news began passing from seat-to-seat that Hull had taken a second-half lead at Cardiff, an advantage they would not relinquish, United's stadium was gripped by a deathly hush, acutely aware of the cost of an Ipswich equaliser. Robbie Blake, the former Leeds striker, admitted in the car park afterwards that the Chinese whispers had seeped through to the players with vivid clarity, bringing with them unbearable pressure. In the 88th minute, Alan Lee delivered the coup de grace Leeds had been evading for weeks by glancing a header beyond the reach of Casper Ankergren, sinking the ball into the Danish goalkeeper's net and a knife into United's gullet. The goal should have brought Elland Road to its knees. Instead, it provoked an uprising. Referee Michael Jones, a late replacement for County Durham's Nigel Miller, whose fractious relationship with Wise made his involvement on 28 April inappropriate, awarded six minutes of injury time but United's supporters had already resigned themselves to a fatal result. As Leeds mounted a final, disjointed attack, a handful of fans broke from the north-east corner of Elland Road and spilled onto the pitch. The invasion began as a trickle but quickly became a flood, and while scores of supporters streamed over the turf, Jones led a frantic dash of players and officials towards the sanctuary of their dressing rooms. Leeds feared an invasion was probable and had hastily planned a post-match presentation to their retiring full-back Gary Kelly, with a warning that it would be scrapped in the event of any unrest on the terraces. The threat did not have the desired effect. Several supporters ran to direct their ire at chairman Ken Bates and United's other board members, who were seated in the directors' box in the centre of the West Stand. The majority moved ominously to the opposite end of the field to crowd around the south-east corner of the stadium, where Ipswich's fans had been housed for the previous hour and a half. A hail of coins launched into the stand left eight wheelchair-bound spectators with cuts and bruises, and the unpalatable scenes would later bring prison sentences and banning orders for a number of the perpetrators. United's active involvement in helping the police identify the majority of those caught on CCTV subsequently spared them from a Football Association charge. Pleas from the club's stadium announcer for the invaders to leave the field were consistently ignored until, to the surprise of everyone, it was confirmed through the public address system that Jones intended to play out the final 45 seconds of a game which had been delayed for half an hour, and which to all intents and purposes was finished as a meaningful sporting event. The announcement had the desired effect and the pitch rapidly cleared. Some supporters were able to retake their seats; others were chased out of the ground by fellow Leeds fans who were incensed by the invasion. The exchange of punches seen on the walkway in the front of Elland Road's Kop, white-on-white violence, was the very essence of a club imploding.

Those final seconds enforced by Jones did not bring a reprieve. Had they done so, the cries of injustice across the country – nowhere more so than Hull – would have been deafening. Hull closed out their 1–0 victory over Cardiff, and as Jones brought a conclusion to a sour afternoon at Elland Road, Hull's chairman, Adam Pearson, was being offered a glass of champagne by his counterpart at Cardiff, Peter Ridsdale, in the bowels of Ninian Park. The insinuation that Ridsdale, a man held in contempt by so many in Leeds, might be toasting the demise of the club he once ran and professed to love did not sit comfortably within the boundaries of Yorkshire. Ridsdale said he had simply been handing his congratulations to a club who had much to celebrate. This gesture had nothing to do with Leeds United's future, he claimed. 'I am saddened by their current plight and have always wished them well as I continue to do.' The offer of sympathy from south Wales was not welcome, nor was it especially relevant. Leeds had a big enough crisis developing on their doorstep without reigniting the debate over the mistakes made by their former chairman, now ensconced in the Principality and hundreds of miles away.

Amid the devastation, it seemed certain that Wise would come out fighting. It is the approach that he knows best. But, to the surprise of many, United's manager held up his hands. At a sombre post-match press conference, Wise accepted responsibility for relegation and accepted that Leeds had deserved to suffer that punishment. In 33 matches under him, United were beaten on 16 occasions. Wise regretted the strength of his squad and the chaotic disposition of the dressing room he had inherited from Kevin Blackwell and John Carver seven months earlier, but Elland Road on 28 April was not the time or the place for excuses. I take full responsibility, Wise admitted: 'I'm not going to blame other people.'

Bates stood in defence of his manager, and in defence of himself. On the Monday after United's draw with Ipswich, he spoke with bullish resistance, knocking back questions over whether relegation constituted a failure by his administration or by Wise. Big clubs rise again, Bates insisted, and he would see to it that 28 April came to represent the very base of United's decline. His conviction was obvious, but the picture he painted of the club's future avoided one crucial detail. At that moment, Bates knew that Leeds United as a business were virtually insolvent.

Administration was first mentioned to me as a possibility after the league game between Leeds and Southend United at Roots Hall stadium in Essex on 17 March. At that juncture it was nothing more than a whisper, a suggestion which could be dismissed as doom-mongering as easily as it was termed a credible threat. Leeds United had debts; that much went without saying. The liabilities first generated by Ridsdale's board had passed through various directors before becoming Bates' problem in 2005, and there was no indication that the bottom line looked any better in April 2007 than it had when his stewardship began more than two years earlier. United's accounts for the financial year running to June 2006 exposed debts of almost £30 million, and Leeds were paying close to £2 million a year for the rent of Elland Road and their splendid training ground at Thorp Arch Grange, an attractive piece of land near Wetherby. Both facilities had been sold to Jacob Adler, a property developer from Manchester, in 2004 by the board headed by former chairman Gerald Krasner, from whom Bates took charge of Leeds. At the time, the sale-and-lease-back agreement with Adler, which also included a buy-back clause allowing Leeds to re-purchase the two properties, had been sanctioned as a result of the pressure that the club's debts were placing on Krasner and his boardroom colleagues. The money raised was said to have met an instalment due on the repayment of a loan given to Leeds by Jack Petchey, then a shareholder of Aston Villa. It bought United time at a point when the ownership of the stadium was the least of their concerns, but the deal with Adler did deprive Leeds of their most valuable assets. In June 2005, the deeds for Elland Road changed hands for a second time when Adler transferred ownership to Teak Commercial Limited, an off-shore company based in the British Virgin Islands (BVI). The individuals behind the BVI firm have remained anonymous, as the tax haven's regulations allow them to do, but they are in possession of a miniature goldmine. United's most recent valuation set the cost of invoking the buy-back clause and repurchasing Elland Road and Thorp Arch Grange at £19,142,806, a figure the present board cannot afford to meet. League One chairmen rarely deal in that sort of money.

The warnings of administration given at Southend were not, therefore, surprising. Clubs whose results fail to satisfy are often the subject of innuendo about their finances, and United's imprudent history encouraged that reaction. But insolvency was indeed on the horizon, and when Leeds visited Southampton on 21 April, the prevalence of discussions about administration suggested the club had begun to seriously consider the possibility. In fact, on the Monday afternoon when Bates sat in his office dissecting the implications of the catastrophic draw with Ipswich Town, administrators from accountancy firm KPMG were already looking through the club's accounts, having been called to Elland Road that very day. KPMG were asked by Bates to instruct him on the best course of action. The only advice they could offer was that any plans to repay United's debts in full or by conventional means should be considered defunct.

The club owed more than £35 million to hundreds of different organisations, companies and individuals. They had nowhere to hide. Leeds declined to comment publicly about the prospect of administration, but on the night of Monday, 30 April, Krasner contacted an impromptu phone-in on BBC Radio Leeds to voice his opinion on the situation at Elland Road. A qualified insolvency practitioner, Krasner declared that he was 90 per cent certain that the company running Leeds United would be declared insolvent by the end of the week. It was, to many, acceptable confirmation that relegation from the Championship was merely the tip of a larger problem. The once-good ship Leeds United would promptly hit the iceberg with full force.

In the days that followed, United made urgent appeals for wealthy parties with a genuine interest in supporting the club financially to declare their interest immediately. The probability of a response was miniscule, and Leeds cannot have expected one. Suspicions about the state of their finances had spread quickly and potential investors with an ounce of business acumen were not about to launch pound notes into what amounted to a black hole. The only advantage of administration was that it would give those interested in presenting funds a clearer picture of the financial landscape inside Elland Road before they made any serious commitment. You don't buy a house that's been chosen for demolition, was how one local businessman put it. United's directors concurred, and the process of administration was promptly set in motion with the assistance of KPMG. The worst-kept secret in Leeds finally became public knowledge at 4 p.m. on Friday, 4 May.

A statement issued by KPMG confirmed that Leeds United had, as expected, been declared insolvent. Richard Fleming, a joint administrator for KPMG, said it was necessary for the club to enter administration as its balance sheet dated 31 March 2007 indicated debts totalling approximately £35 million, with a cash injection of approximately £10 million required to continue trading. The figures were eye-watering, yet not especially shocking. The slow walk to relegation from the Championship, just 12 months after Leeds were competing in the division's play-off final, had, in hindsight, been a veiled hint at the scale of the emergency developing within the club. But the announcement from KPMG came with a twist that caused bewilderment in Leeds. The company controlled by Bates and now declared insolvent Leeds United Association Football Club Limited would be sold immediately by KPMG to a firm called Leeds United Football Club Limited, a firm which listed Bates as a director. United's chief executive Shaun Harvey and their solicitor Mark Taylor, a long-time colleague of Bates, had also been given directorships with the new company. Forty-five minutes after placing Leeds in administration, the sale to Leeds United Football Club Limited had been authorised and confirmed in principle by KPMG. When the dust and the confusion settle, the terms of the deal dawned quickly on the city; by way of KPMG, Bates appeared to be selling to himself.

Leeds United Football Club Limited had the look of what administrators would call a phoenix company, one which takes possession of the assets of an insolvent firm, while retaining some or all of the previous company's directors and continuing to operate in the same sphere of business. The use of phoenix companies is not favoured by all in the business community, but provided certain conditions are met, the process is entirely legal. KPMG's announcement meant in essence that by the beginning of June, Bates was likely to have control of Leeds United through a different firm possessing virtually the same name and registered with Companies House. The only difference in the eyes of the club's supporters was that the debts of £35 million would, in theory, no longer exist. But while Bates believed that a significant portion of the fans were still supportive of his reign, relegation had done as much damage to his reputation as it had Wise's. The sceptical element were no longer convinced that Bates' vision of the future was what they or their club desired.

As KPMG began the administrative work needed to put Bates' proposal to the club's creditors, the doubts thrown up by the rapid sale were growing. Krasner asked why KPMG had been so willing to agree to Bates' offer when a greater degree of patience might have allowed them to find a more attractive and valuable bid. The administrators argued that the speed of the sale was designed to maximise the possibility of survival to minimise uncertainty for all the club's stakeholders and supporters, and to allow the club to plan ahead for next season. Bates had agreed to fund United's day-to-day operating costs during administration but would have been less willing to make that commitment without the assurance that he would eventually receive a solvent business in return. 'The action taken brings to an end the financial legacy left by others that we have spent millions of pounds trying to settle,' Bates said. 'The important thing now is not to view this as the end, but the beginning of a new era.'

The reluctance in Leeds to accept that view was prevalent, an attitude deepened by the release of a document from KPMG to the club's creditors detailing the terms of both the proposed sale to Bates and the Company Voluntary Arrangement (CVA) that would be put in place to settle United's debts. The intricacy of the club's accounts and liabilities were staggering, ranging from almost £13 million due to an off-shore company called Astor Investment Holdings Limited to a £3 bill owed to an insolvent property business in Ferrybridge, West Yorkshire. Leeds City Council were awaiting payment of more than £211,289, and former players of the club were owed a total of £630,000. The most pertinent figure, however, was United's tax bill. According to the CVA document, it stood at just under £8 million, much of that money historic debt, and Her Majesty's Revenue & Customs (HMRC) had served Leeds with a winding-up petition in the High Court of Justice in Bristol on 17 April after agreed monthly repayments of £200,000 from Elland Road went unpaid for two consecutive months. The petition was due to be heard on 27 June, a deadline which KPMG believed justified their urgency in striking a deal with Bates. Bates, meanwhile, was angry that HMRC had failed to treat his club with greater flexibility and compassion. Leeds, he said, had done what they could to meet their responsibilities for repayment of their tax bill, and HMRC were acting with intransigence.

The initial offer from Bates to United's unsecured creditors promised to settle their debts at the rate of a penny in the pound, the lowest sum they could have expected to receive. It meant in effect that the £7.7 million bill owed to HMRC would be cut to £77,000. A local butcher owed a grand would instead receive a tenner. Krasner described the offer as utterly derisory, and promised to use his expertise in insolvency to assist local creditors and force an improved settlement. But the devil of the CVA was in the detail, and the details revealed that Bates' hand contained an unbeatable ace in the form of the unconditional support of United's biggest creditors. It was with their help and their co-operation that he intended to push his takeover through.

By far the largest percentage of the club's debts was owed to three foreign companies, all based off-shore and about whom a limited amount of information could be gleaned. Astor Investment Holdings Limited, based in the tax haven of the BVI, were owed £12,726,687. Krato Trust, a firm located in Nevis in the West Indies, was claiming £2,492,761, and The Forward Sports Fund – registered in the Cayman

Islands, administered in Switzerland, and the vehicle though which Bates had originally assumed control of Leeds United in 2005, a further £2,419,000. At a total approaching £18 million, the liabilities represented close to 50 per cent of the club's entire debt, giving all three companies crucial influence in the vote on Bates' CVA proposal. Astor's position had particular significance. With more than a quarter of the debt due to it, and the fact that insolvency rules entitled creditors to one vote for every pound they were owed, Astor's backing would be crucial in securing the approval from creditors that a successful CVA required by law. Bates needed a 75 per cent vote in his favour, no more and no less. Without public explanation, Astor confirmed to KPMG that it would agree to the terms of the proposal drawn up by Bates, yet vote against any other offer put forward by any other prospective owner. 'Astor always went into it on the basis that they would back Ken,' Mark Taylor told *The Guardian* when asked why the investor was only willing to side with Bates. A total of five rivals bids had been submitted to KPMG, each with proof that they were backed by £10 million worth of funds, and the offers were to be discussed with United's creditors before the crucial CVA ballot on 1 June. Several of the bidders were promising a repayment rate in excess of a penny in the pound, but Astor's stance was rigid, a case of Bates' way or the highway. The company would not be persuaded otherwise. United's chairman was asked whether he was held a direct link to Astor, or whether he knew of any other connection which would have represented a conflict of interest and potentially rule the firm out of the voting. Sworn letters sent to KPMG by Bates and Astor stated that he was not connected. The documents begged the question of what was motivating Astor, who had loaned around £4.2 million to Leeds between June and October in 2006, to fight Bates' corner with such loyalty.

The creditors' meeting held in Elland Road's banqueting suite on the afternoon of Friday, 1 June was a cold affair. Bates was not present at the gathering, leaving Mark Taylor to tackle issues of concern, of which there were many. The involvement of Astor was discussed at length, and Taylor was persuaded into a guarantee that Bates' consortium would pay an extra £5 million to their creditors if Leeds United returned to the Premiership within five years of the date of his takeover. Leeds had worked hard to garner support for their chairman, convincing Leeds City Council among others to stand beside him. At the end of a six-hour meeting, the creditors ballot produced a 75.02 vote in favour of Bates, approving his CVA by the smallest of margins. KPMG assessed the result and brought a heated afternoon to an unsatisfactory end by announcing that the outcome required the surety of a recount.

It left Bates' victory in doubt, but only briefly. Word reached him over the weekend that two recounts were thought to have underlined the initial result, and a reconvened meeting on Monday morning was told that his share of the vote had actually increased to 75.2 per cent, enough to see the CVA carried. 'An awful lot of people voted for it,' said an upbeat Bates. Among those who didn't were the club's striker David Healy, the Football League and HMRC.

The tax authority was not amused, and set about examining the arrangement for legal flaws. The agreement of any CVA is automatically followed by a statutory 28-day period in which creditors are entitled to cool off, consider their position and then challenge the proposal in court. HMRC stood to lose around £7 million and were not prepared to do so willingly. In the interim, the case was taken up by three of Yorkshire's Members of Parliament – Phil Willis, Colin Burgon and George Mudie – who campaigned for answers over the less transparent areas of Bates' takeover, in particular the role and make-up of the off-shore firms who had backed him to the hilt. In an Early Day Motion set down in Westminster on 12 June, Phil Willis asked the Serious Fraud Office to investigate the takeover. Leeds responded by challenging him to repeat the request without the legal protection of absolute privilege provided by Parliament. We will see him in court if he does, said the statement. Behind the vicious scrap played out at arm's length, HMRC were quietly completing their own investigation and at 3 p.m. on 3 July, an hour before the deadline for challenges to Bates' takeover was due to pass, they announced their intention to contest Bates' CVA in court. A late attempt at appeasement by United's chairman, who moved to head off the taxman by raising his offer by 800 per cent to eight pence in the pound and increasing the timescale of the £5 million bonus for promotion to the Premier League to 10 years, was unsuccessful.

The previous day, Bates had discussed the consequences of any creditor placing legal hurdles before him. 'If there is a legal challenge, this football club is finished,' he said. 'We – Leeds United Football Club Limited – have funded the administration period for the last two months, and are not going to do it any longer.' But the reality was less stark, and Leeds United were not finished. A directions hearing over HMRC's challenge was held in Leeds on Friday, 6 July, at which KPMG might have hoped to see the case thrown out. On the contrary, the court ruled that a five-day hearing to decide HMRC's argument should begin on 3 September – three weeks after the start of the 2007–08 League One season. When employees of KPMG convened to consider the implications of the ruling, they soon conceded that their hand had been forced.

The administrators' problem was that Football League rules on insolvency required clubs in administration to return to a solvent position via an approved CVA. The challenge by HMRC would make Bates' CVA impossible to implement, at least until their appeal was thrown out. But United's chairman was deeply reluctant to continue funding the club's operating costs through July and August without a guarantee that the court would approve his takeover, and on the night of 6 July, KPMG abandoned his CVA and put Leeds United up for sale, setting a deadline for offers of 5 p.m. on Monday, 9 July. Rival bidders who believed Bates had already won his war were drawn back to the table. The weekend passed in a scramble of activity as prospective buyers considered how best and how much to bid.

By the 5 p.m. deadline, KPMG had received a handful of offers. Simon Franks, the founder of London-based rescue firm Redbus, and local property developer Simon Morris – a director of Leeds while Krasner was chairman – came together to submit a joint offer, a link-up which was termed as a super-bid but which in reality was thought to be the lowest submitted. The ex-Hull City chairman Adam Pearson, who had recently stepped down from his position at the KC Stadium, also hovered with a much more sizeable bid in his hand. All the while, Bates remained intent on retaining his steely grip on Elland Road. KPMG's handling of the sale failed to satisfy a number of the outside bidders, who were unhappy with what they claimed was a lack of financial information provided by the administrators over the weekend – forcing them, in the words of one interested party, to bid blind. They argued that Bates' intricate knowledge of the finances at Elland Road gave him a considerable advantage at the auction. It subsequently transpired that Bates' proposal had been due to expire at 5 p.m. on 9 July, a factor which appears to have driven KPMG's tight timeframe. Of added significance was the fact that his was the only unconditional offer put forward. But two days later, Bates did what he had promised to do and won back ownership of Leeds United, paying KPMG an undisclosed sum in the process. The sale was ultimately made to Leeds United 2007 Ltd, another company fronted by Bates which had originally been designed to carry the club through administration until their assets could be passed to Leeds United Football Club Limited through a successful CVA. The entire shareholding in Leeds United was placed in the hands of The Forward Sports Fund.

The successful offer amounted to 11 pence in the pound for unsecured creditors – increasing to a maximum settlement of 52.9 pence on United's promotion to the Premier League inside 10 years – with an anti-embarrassment clause included in the contract to prevent Bates from selling the club on inside 12 months without incurring a heavy financial penalty. The sale of Leeds United without a CVA left HMRC's legal challenge redundant, and it was later withdrawn from court. On 11 July, 68 days after KPMG were first called on board, Bates was finally able to re-raise his flag up Elland Road's mast.

United's chairman was typically optimistic and quickly appealed to the mass of supporters who were utterly baffled about where their club had been, where it now stood and where it was headed.

'Part of the reason why were going to succeed is because these Leeds fans are absolutely magnificent,' Bates said. 'Ninety-nine per cent of the letters and e-mails [we've received] are supporting us, and that's not bad. That's as good as Saddam Hussein did and he was fiddling the figures.'

It sounded like victory. It sounded like the turn of a page. 'Never under-estimate the beard,' Bates' ever-supportive wife Susannah told me. But the beard had failed to realise that convincing the Football League to accept his takeover would be like searching for weapons of mass destruction in Iraq.

2

F**K OFF TO THE FOOTBALL LEAGUE

THE FOOTBALL LEAGUE VIEW INSOLVENCY IN THE WAY that national governments view social poverty. In an ideal world, football clubs would have no need for the safety net of administration, just as politicians would prefer to see every one of their citizens above the breadline. But insolvency exists as poverty does, and the Football League have come to live with it in their own practical way. It could not be said that they tolerate clubs in administration, and their penalties for insolvency have become considerably stricter since the turn of the century, but there is only so much tutting an organisation can do when so many of their members have been guilty of swimming beyond their financial depth. For as long as professional football remains a competitive industry, it will also remain a game of risk.

Administration became a buzzword among Football League clubs after the ambitious but ill-conceived existence of ITV Digital came to an abrupt end in 2002. The digital broadcaster had flexed its muscles by agreeing to pay £315 million for the right to televise Football League and English League Cup fixtures, much to the immediate delight of the Football League and the 72 clubs beneath the Premiership. Lower-league matches were less attractive to media groups than the Premier League, which boasted established global appeal, but the sum paid by ITV Digital was more in keeping with the huge commitment made regularly by BSkyB to retain their exclusive right to provide live coverage of England's uppermost division. The agreement with ITV Digital seemed to good to be true, and in essence it was. The broadcaster's business plan quickly unravelled, and on 27 March 2002, it was placed in administration. The millions of pounds promised to individual clubs in television revenue would no longer be paid. In time-honoured tradition, however, much of it had already been spent.

From the moment that the terms of the deal were announced, chairmen across the country began budgeting for the months and years ahead with the lucrative agreement in mind. It influenced the transfer fees they were willing to pay and the wage bills they were willing to support. ITV Digital's money, most directors assumed, was guaranteed income. The effect of the reality was profound, and within 12 months of the broadcaster's insolvency, seven clubs – Notts County, Huddersfield Town, Port Vale, Leicester City, Ipswich Town, Barnsley and York City – had applied to enter administration. The Football League were appalled and their new chairman, Lord Brian Mawhinney, instigated revised regulations which, among other sanctions, enforced a statutory 10-point penalty for any of their members who declared themselves insolvent. The Football League were sympathetic to the plight of chairmen who had been wrong-footed by the broken promises of the deal with ITV Digital, but Mawhinney was also aware that insolvency offered less scrupulous boards a chance to clear their debts at a knockdown price. Why pay £10 million when a carefully constructed Company Voluntary Arrangement (CVA) could cut the amount owed by 99 per cent? Applying sporting sanctions, Mawhinney opined at the time, would make an example of clubs in the only language they understand. His plan was to make administration as unattractive as possible, with the hopeful aim of persuading clubs to do everything they could to avoid it.

Leeds United's declaration of insolvency was therefore a routine occurrence with which the Football League believed they were familiar. By Mawhinney's count, Leeds were the 41st example of a club whose debts had reached irresolvable levels and required the expertise of administrators, and United were subjected to the automatic 10-point deduction stipulated by Football League rules on 4 May, six days after their 1–1 draw with Ipswich Town at Elland Road. Leeds accepted the punishment willingly but the timing of the process bothered Mawhinney. It seemed convenient to him that Ken Bates had waited until United's relegation was realistically unavoidable before applying for insolvency, thus preventing the 10-point deduction from having a punitive effect. Had Leeds been placed in administration after their final match of the Championship season at Derby County, which the club lost 2–0 on 6 May, the sanction would have been applied to their league table for the following season, requiring the club to begin the 2007–08 term with a negative points tally. The Football League could not help asking whether the convenient timing would have been different had Dennis Wise's squad had any chance of avoiding relegation at Pride Park. Leeds United shrugged their shoulders. The date of their entry into administration was coincidental, they claimed, and Football League rules in any case did not prevent them from declaring insolvency at a time of their choosing. The club were right. The process exposed a loophole which seemed to undermine the Football League's policy on administration, and the rules were swiftly rewritten with the agreement of the League's members during the organisation's annual general meeting in Portugal a month later. Clubs who enter administration after the fourth Thursday in March now have their 10-point penalty suspended, to be applied to the season in progress if they avoid relegation, but imposed at the start of the following season in the event that they drop into a lower division. Leeds would be the last club to climb through the loophole.

Their circumnavigation of what Mawhinney considered to be the spirit of the rules did not disguise the fact that Bates' retention of the chairman's seat at Elland Road required the support and blessing of the Football

League. The body is essentially a private members club beneath the masthead of the Football Association, and United's membership had been suspended on the day they entered administration, to be returned only when the Football League were satisfied that their insolvency had been dealt with in accordance with League regulations. Mawhinney, in short, was adamant from the outset that Leeds would be welcomed back into the fold on his terms. Securing ownership of the club was only ever one half of the battle for Bates; the other was persuading Mawhinney and his colleagues to authorise the deal and re-issue United's membership, colloquially known as their golden share.

The Football League were sensibly restrained through United's first month in administration, saying as much in public as was necessary but as little as was decent. As naturally anxious as Mawhinney will have been, news of insolvency at a Championship club was hardly unique. If anything, it was something of an achievement that United's debts had not needed the help of an administrator months or years earlier. Leeds had attempted to trim their liabilities after being relegated from the Premiership, but the historic debt they carried was too great to allow a strategy of recovery in the long-term. Yet the agreement reached between Bates and KPMG on 4 May was proof that at least one person was set on preventing United's extinction, and the possible availability of a club on the scale of Leeds would generate more interested buyers than the average Football League side. Mawhinney is unlikely to have genuinely feared that Leeds United might cease to be; few clubs ever meet that end, however close to the wind they sail. His priority, and that of his board, was to ensure that United played by the rules. To stress the point, a statement released by the Football League in response to the news that Bates' CVA had been accepted by a margin of 0.2 per cent on 4 June read:

> The League has confirmed to the administrator the conditions that must be satisfied before The League Board can consider transferring the club's share in The Football League to the new company. These conditions include the need for all football debts to be settled in full.

The thorny subject of football debts would be central to the chaos that followed.

In amongst the gentle posturing between Mawhinney and Bates, the state of Wise's playing squad was an afterthought. Full-back Gary Kelly had retired in May following the conclusion of his 16th season with Leeds, and a number of other senior players were released by Wise at the end of their contracts, goalkeeper Neil Sullivan and striker Ian Moore among them. Hours before United's first pre-season friendly at York City on 14 July, the club agreed to sell David Healy to Fulham and Robbie Blake to Burnley, stripping two of the more talented forwards in Wise's squad from the pool of professionals at Elland Road. Their sales raised well in excess of £1 million. Leeds were powerless to resist the money being offered, and Wise did not expect them to, but as heavy rain slanted into his face on a miserable night at York's Bootham Crescent, the forces against him felt relentless. In order to fulfil United's summer friendlies, Wise was relying entirely on the dedication of several out-of-contract players who had accepted his vague undertaking of a future deal at Elland Road, if and when the Football League lifted the club's transfer embargo. Certain individuals went without wages; others survived on the severance pay received from the clubs with whom they had parted company earlier that summer. Wise was already estimating that ten potential transfers had been wrecked by United's embargo. Even a supportive letter sent to him in the wake of relegation from an unlikely well-wisher – Sir Alex Ferguson – was providing scant comfort. Wise never disclosed the contents of the letter, but its source revealed the extent of sympathy that existed for him. Ferguson had once described Wise as a man capable of starting a fight in an empty house.

Others held the same opinion of Bates but Leeds' chairman had no interest in fighting the Football League. From the moment his takeover was sanctioned by KPMG, the acquisition of the club's golden share was a job set aside by him for quick completion. There was little value to Leeds in being hesitant, particularly while their transfer embargo was doing so much damage to Wise's strategy for player recruitment, and Bates believed his purchase from KPMG would guarantee the return of the club's Football League membership. It was for that reason that his offer to buy United had been made unconditionally. Other bidders stipulated clearly to KPMG that their tenders for Leeds would only stand if the club's golden share was successfully transferred. The absence of an approved CVA was a contentious problem which the League looked likely to take issue with, but Bates felt confident that the legal contest made by Her Majesty's Revenue & Customs (HMRC) provided a valid excuse. Or, as the Football League might put it, an exceptional circumstance.

The rules of the Football League are stringent about the importance of clubs in administration successfully negotiating a CVA. But they are not entirely watertight. Contained within the regulations is an exceptional circumstances clause, drawn up by the League to allow for the return of a club's golden share in the event that the club in question is unable to obey the standard rules on insolvency for reasons beyond their control. The existence of the clause – which was not common knowledge – had first been confirmed publicly by a League representative during the creditors' meeting at Elland Road on 1 June, and Bates urged Mawhinney to make immediate use of it. United's position, he argued, was the perfect example of why the clause had been necessary in the first place.

There was no question that Leeds had been caught in the crossfire of a wider dispute between the League and HMRC. Since losing its status as a preferential creditor, the tax authority had adopted a policy of applying zero tolerance to professional clubs who attempted to pay their football creditors in full while reimbursing only a tiny percentage of what was owed to the public coffers. It had not always been thus, and HMRC could remember a time very recently when a club's tax bill was met as a priority before all others. The Revenue's unsupportive attitude was confirmed in a letter sent on 10 July 2007 by joint administrator Richard Fleming to Colin Burgon, the Labour Member of Parliament for Elmet who had asked for clarification over the reasons behind United's failure to move forward with a CVA. Fleming wrote:

The joint administrators were not prepared to put forward a further CVA that had no chance of being approved taking into account the policy of HMRC [which] makes it clear they would decline any proposals made by a member of any organisation that requires debts owed to its members to be paid in full, when all other unsecured creditors become bound on the approval of the agreement.

The Revenue's disapproval would be reiterated seven months later when AFC Bournemouth entered administration, again as the result of a winding-up petition submitted in court by HMRC. As with Leeds, the tax authority was not prepared to negotiate with Bournemouth's administrators over a reduced settlement if football creditors were to be paid in full. Given the strict and militant approach of HMRC, it is not inconceivable that the Football League will be forced to reconsider their firm insistence on approved CVAs. Before the 2007–08 season was out, Luton Town and Rotherham United followed Bournemouth into insolvency; the latter confirmed almost immediately that the level of money they owed to HMRC – more than 25 per cent of their total debt – made agreeing a CVA through a vote of creditors impossible from the outset.

The discomfort felt by Mawhinney and his board regarding Bates' takeover stemmed from the complicated and often contentious nature of the sale completed by KPMG. The company was heavily criticised for the way in which it handled United's administration, and the Football League were vocal with their concerns. The League's board gathered to discuss the transaction between Bates and KPMG on 12 July, 24 hours after the completion of the deal. The routine meeting had been scheduled before the takeover, but Leeds United were inevitably prominent on the agenda. Bates had hoped that the club's golden share would be transferred to Leeds United 2007 Ltd there and then, thereby lifting their transfer embargo and bringing a quick conclusion to their summer of discontent, but the League refused to consider the possibility. A statement issued by Mawhinney claimed KPMG had failed to supply the League's board with any documentation detailing the sale of the club to Bates. It also expressed concern that the administrators had failed to attend their meeting, despite agreeing to do so. Additionally, the statement read, the Board expressed concern at the handling of the whole process by the administrators, and the chairman (Mawhinney) was instructed to obtain legal advice in that regard.

There were a number of issues relating to Bates' takeover which caused disquiet. One was the unanimous support given to him by the off-shore companies whose backing had helped to approve his CVA. In the exchange of correspondence between Burgon and Fleming, KPMG's joint administrator stated once again that Astor Investment Holdings Limited would have opposed any CVA other than a sale to Leeds United 2007 Ltd. A second niggle was the meagre amount of time given to outside bidders to present their offers to KPMG after the club was placed on the open market on 6 July. And doubts over the process were strengthened further when it was revealed that Bates had won the creditors' vote with the help of a debt of £480,000 owed to Yorkshire Radio, a digital radio station established by United's chairman in 2006. Bates was listed as one of Yorkshire Radio's directors, as was Mark Taylor. The debt had not been included in the original list of creditors drawn up by KPMG but was approved by the administrator on the advice of Queen's Counsel shortly before the creditors' ballot at Elland Road. The company's debt amounted to 1.3 per cent of the voting rights; Bates' proposal was passed by a margin of 0.2 per cent. The obvious question was how and why Leeds had built up a liability of almost half a million pounds with what was almost an in-house radio station. United explained that the money had been committed to Yorkshire Radio to assist the station's future growth and development. Nevertheless, it was later confirmed that HMRC's legal challenge against the CVA was based on its suspicions over three individual debts authorised by KPMG. The £480,000 owing to Yorkshire Radio was one; debts due to Mark Taylor and Co – Taylor's solicitors firm – and Astor Investment Holdings Limited were also to be queried. The eventual collapse of the CVA and the enforced withdrawal of HMRC's judicial review meant its claim was never ruled upon.

Until KPMG's transfer of shares from Leeds United Association Football Club Limited to Leeds United 2007 Ltd on 11 July, the Football League had been willing to sit passively in the background. The golden share, after all, would only become a relevant issue once United's future was assured. Requests for comments from the press were repeatedly declined, yet the League were aware that their silence was allowing others to speak for them. The organisation were incensed when, midway through the directions hearing into HMRC's legal contest, United's representative suggested strongly that the club would be prevented from starting the 2007–08 season on 11 August if they remained in administration until that day. In an off-the-record briefing given to the media, a League official insisted the allegation was ridiculous. Clubs are entitled to sit in administration for a maximum period of 18 months – few, in reality, would wish to endure such prolonged uncertainty – and United's insolvency would not automatically restrict their involvement in Football League competitions. If Leeds were unable to fulfil any of their forthcoming fixtures, beginning with their opening game against Tranmere Rovers at Prenton Park on 11 August, then that was a different matter, but the League were not inclined to allow presumptions about their rules to be used as bargaining chips in Bates' takeover. Above all, they were not prepared to be told how their own rules should and would work.

Both Bates and Mawhinney understood the importance of time. The sale of United to Leeds United 2007 Ltd had come exactly one month before the start of the new season, and the club were far behind in their preparations. Bates had negotiated a contract with RedKite Group, a Leeds-based company which specialised in financial services, to provide shirt sponsorship for the year ahead, but the contract could not be ratified nor the sponsorship money paid until the existing doubt over the transfer of the club's golden share had been exorcised – and until RedKite were certain that they would indeed have shirts to splash their logo on. The impasse was such that United's squad were forced to re-use old kits throughout their pre-season schedule, some bearing no sponsor at all and others blemished with square patches of fabric hiding the branding of online bookmakers Bet24, whose shirt deal with Leeds had expired at the end of the previous term. The makeshift appearance of Wise and his players was indicative of a club that had lost everything and was struggling through with whatever equipment and resilience they could muster. It is, in these circumstances, the players and coaching staff who merit the most compassion. The flaw of the Football League's insolvency rules, and more specifically their insistence on a 10-point deduction for clubs who enter administration, is that it affects those who – aside from supporters – have least to do with a club's finances. Wise had been manager of Leeds for less than 12 months and could not have been accused of spending recklessly in the January transfer window that preceded United's insolvency. Aside from Tresor Kandol, whose move from Barnet cost Leeds around £200,000, Wise had been restricted to free transfers signed on short-term deals, even after Matthew Kilgallon, a talented centre-back derived from United's academy, was predictably hawked to Sheffield United for £1.75 million. His players were in no way responsible for the club's fractured accounts, and the majority who trained with United during the summer did so without contracts. Points deductions may frustrate chairmen but the effect of the punishment falls directly on a manager and his squad. As his experience of such penalties expanded to a unique and undesirable level, Wise argued with increasing force that United's punishment for any perceived crime connected to their insolvency should have been financial, to correct their financial shortcomings. It was a reasoned hypothesis but an opinion which raised other complications. How sensible was it for the Football League to fine a club whose inherent problem was an inability to pay the bills? Was that not akin to treating a heroin addict by injecting him with smack? As debilitating as a points deduction is, it can at least be described as a meaningful deterrent for professional clubs, or what Mawhinney termed the only language they understand.

Clubs were bound to complain when a 10-point deduction fell in their lap, but the Football League's standard riposte was that their members themselves had voted to implement the sanction. There was no denying that. But the predicament created by Leeds United was different and unprecedented. The Football League were being asked to invoke the 'exceptional circumstances' clause and accept for the first time the emergence of a club from administration without a CVA. The League were deeply reluctant to comply without proving to the other 71 clubs beneath the Premier League that their disapproving attitude towards insolvency was non-negotiable. Communication flew back and forward between Elland Road and the Football League's headquarters on a daily basis, driven in haste by the creeping summer. Wise returned from United's week-long tour of Germany on 24 July to find negotiations in full flow, and Leeds – the city and the club – gripped by a sense of urgency. 'It is important that we receive everybody's support [in] getting the share back,' said chief executive Shaun Harvey, 'which is why I am dismayed that there seems to be a resurgence, fuelled by certain sections of the media, against the consortium led by Ken Bates. This is the time to unite not divide.' On Friday, 27 July, the Football League's board reconvened at an extraordinary meeting to discuss the transfer of United's membership again, and by the middle of the following week, after a series of intense negotiations involving the Football League and members of the Leeds United 2007 Ltd, the club were anticipating a denouement. The answer came with a sting in its tale on the afternoon of 3 August.

During a conference call between the associates of the Football League's board, a decision had been taken to apply the 'exceptional circumstances' clause and return United's golden share, a ruling which instantly lifted the club's transfer embargo. But the price of their membership would be a damaging deduction of 15 points, to be implemented to the League One table from the start of the 2007–08 season. The decision was unparalleled and the damning implications for Leeds were obvious. In effect, it was a sizeable step towards a second successive relegation, something a number of United's fellow clubs may have wanted to see. It also made a mockery of the idea that Leeds would return to the Championship within a year of relinquishing that status – from Wise's perspective, the fitting end to a debilitating summer.

Leeds instantly declared their intention to appeal with the kind of speed that suggested there was a deal to be done. The League were anxious to display their authority but a deduction of 15 points was unquestionably severe. There was, initially, a degree of optimism among the club's supporters that the two parties would meet somewhere close to halfway. The hope was forlorn. The Football League, who were under pressure to settle the matter before the season started on 11 August, set the appeal date for 9 August, 48 hours before their schedule of fixtures was due to begin. United's argument against the penalty was to be heard and voted upon by the other 71 Football League clubs, and Mawhinney distributed letters to all of their members stating his case and the reasons behind the 15-point punishment. United took the same direct approach but with the sorry realisation that their appeal was relying on the support of their competitors. That lack of independence and impartiality, as Bates saw it, would be among a variety of factors which led United and their chairman to bring High Court proceedings against the Football League at the start of 2008.

Mawhinney's letter predicted a landmark decision which will, in effect, create a precedent for the future. Bates' request for support against the penalty stated that such a sanction is wholly unfair and a breach of natural justice. He further asserted that Leeds could not be legitimately accused or found guilty of breaching any of the Football League's rules. Both men were utterly convinced by their own arguments. But a mere six days lay between the announcement of United's 15-point deduction and the date of their appeal, and the idea that club executives across the country would have time to dissect the case fully was fanciful. The chairman of one northern club, who declined to be named and did not attend the appeal hearing personally, admitted: 'Keeping my own club on an even keel financially is enough for me to worry about, never mind thinking about the ins and outs of somebody else's. The appeal was heard two days before the season started and, to be perfectly honest, I had other important matters to attend to as I'm sure a number of my colleagues did. The Football League made their case and the clubs supported the punishment so perhaps Leeds United should have got on with it. But it's not really something I hold too much of an opinion on.'

Bates' sympathisers were few in number but not non-existent. Another Football League club chairman said: 'I did actually sympathise with Ken's situation. He'd put money into Leeds over a period of years and I could understand why he didn't want to let go of the club for nothing.

I also understood the problems he was experiencing with the Revenue, and the club's position was probably a lot more complicated than the average person could grasp. I don't know how many people at the appeal hearing will have genuinely understood it. A lot of the Leeds supporters had turned on Ken and decided they wanted him out and a new man in. But I know and Bates knows that supporters can't always see the ownership of football clubs in accurate terms of black and white.'

Perhaps the most fervent supporter of the Football League was Gillingham's Paul Scally, one of the few chairmen who were latterly willing to speak openly about the case (the vote during United's appeal hearing was, to the satisfaction of most present, a secret ballot). Scally's position was politically problematic. He and Bates had known each other for years, and Gillingham's chairman was also a good friend of Dennis Wise. The roots of their friendship were planted in 1995 when Chelsea – then chaired by Bates – provided the opposition for a pre-season friendly at Priestfield with a team containing Wise. Ruud Gullit's first appearance for Chelsea gave the match national significance, but the Dutchman was not the only debutant on a warm July evening in Kent. The fixture was also Gillingham's first with Scally as their chairman, and the presence of Chelsea to mark the occasion was something of a privilege. Bates might have anticipated that 12 years later he would find Scally on his side of the fence, but conversely found him to be one of the Football League's strongest campaigners. 'I don't need to hide behind anonymity or a secret ballot,' Scally told the *Yorkshire Evening Post*. 'I voted with the League's board and I think I was right to do so. I wasn't responsible for deciding whether Leeds should be punished or what their punishment should be. Neither were any of the clubs. The board took that decision, and we were simply asked to back one party or the other using the evidence in front of us. The League's explanation seemed very convincing to me and, to be honest, I thought Leeds United's case was poor. I asked a couple of questions and got answers from Leeds which I felt were completely unsatisfactory. There wasn't any real doubt about which way I should vote.'

His feelings were shared by many, at least to judge from the outcome of the appeal hearing itself. Representatives of all 72 Football League clubs bar Bury, who failed to attend the meeting, arrived at the five-star Churchill Hotel in London's West End on the morning of Thursday, 9 August to hear the warring factions make a final plea for assistance. Bates did not speak himself, leaving the responsibility for United's argument to a legal representative who addressed the meeting and applied for clemency on his behalf. Several individuals present at the meeting later agreed with Scally that the Football League's presentation had been altogether more convincing, and the backing for the organisation was borne out in the vote. The first question posed asked whether Leeds deserved punishment for the process which had taken the club out of administration. The ballot cast produced a 64–5 result in favour of punishing United, with one spoilt paper. The decision to uphold the 15-point penalty was then made by a smaller but satisfactory majority of 54–16. Mawhinney felt vindicated, and he emerged triumphantly onto the steps of the hotel to meet the gathered media. 'We have an agreement with Leeds, signed by both the League and the club, that they will not take any legal action against us and we will not take any legal action against them,' he said. 'That is a standard part of the agreement that every club signs when it comes out of administration. That has not been generated for the benefit of Leeds United, we've done that in the last 40 administrations and we did in this one as well.' Six months later, the true value of what Mawhinney indicated was a binding agreement would be revealed when Bates ripped it in half and took his fight against the Football League's penalty to the judiciary, claiming the deal had been signed by Leeds under duress. In plain English, Bates contended that Leeds were two days away from the start of the season and in no position to argue with any proposal placed in front of them. It was, after the summer from hell, a low and demoralising ebb that took some comprehending. Even Scally was not immune to the gravity of the penalty. 'It's a shame that the fans at Leeds have had to suffer, and I feel sorry for the players and staff as well,' he said. 'I actually know Dennis well and I'd be very upset if I was in the position he was in at the start of the season. But at the end of the day this was the Football League board's decision, and I don't think Leeds' argument against it was good enough.'

The Football League had created a precedent; they had also created a monster – a monster of Leeds United and a monster of Bates. On one hand, they faced an ignited chairman willing to fight his club's deduction to the death, or at least to the High Court. It was the type of fight he preferred to win, and the type he usually did. On the other, the League had provoked the hostility of a club and a community who, after months of infighting, finally knew their enemy. From the terraces of Prenton Park on 11 August spontaneous chants of 'Fuck off to the Football League' would come to signify the unity that had inadvertently arrived in Leeds. But those cries would come later. Presented with the news of United's unsuccessful appeal, Dennis Wise drew breath and cleared his head. If 9 August had been a dark day for him, his players and his club, it was also the first day of the rest of their lives.

3

THEY'VE CUT ME BALLS
OFF AS WELL

IN THE DEEP SHADE OF ADMINISTRATION, DENNIS WISE cut an ethereal figure who slipped in and out of public consciousness. He and his assistant manager, Gustavo Poyet, began the summer with a holiday in Dubai, reasonably expecting that the mess at Elland Road would be cleaned up on their return, and Wise was not seen by the media until the end of June, when he agreed to open a new football facility at Hunslet Boys and Girls Club in Leeds, constructed with the aid of Barclays Bank. The event was a vivid reminder of the delightful simplicity of jumpers-for-goalposts, and of football played without a care in the world. As pre-season rolled into motion, Wise's involvement with the press remained sporadic, as it would throughout his tenure, and his deepest thoughts were something of a mystery. In truth, there was little for Wise to say. He wanted to sign players but couldn't. He knew his position was desperate but utterly beyond his control. He recognised also that the chaos of the summer was ruining his chance of convincing Leeds United's supporters that his heart was in the right place – in the same place as theirs. The season ahead was supposed to belong to Wise and him alone, untouched by the thoughts, tactics and signings of his predecessors; a season, in short, on which he believed he could be accurately judged. With negativity so prevalent, Wise saw sense in silence and the left the soundbites to his chairman. But on 9 August, Leeds United's manager rediscovered his tongue.

It went without saying that Ken Bates' response to his club's failed appeal against their 15-point deduction would be venomous, but it was clear to everyone that the most serious victims of the Football League's disciplinary arm were Wise and his players. Wise had come to accept that his transfer strategy had been decimated and that his signings might consist of the last paint colours in the shop. This, as he would so often say, is the way it is, chaps. But the loss of 15 points two days before the start of the season caught Wise off balance. He had expected United's appeal to work; expected that chairmen and chief executives across the country would come to the club's aid at what was now the eleventh hour. A transfer embargo he could grudgingly accept, but a penalty which sent bookmakers scurrying to produce odds on Leeds' relegation was a different matter altogether. In an instant, Wise was ready to hold court.

The local and national media were summoned late in the afternoon of 9 August to a press conference at Thorp Arch Grange, the sight of United's immaculate training ground. The briefing was staged in their medical room towards the rear of the facility, which for several years has served as the club's press area in its free time. The room overlooks a large swimming pool and a huge indoor Astroturf pitch, and on this particular occasion the venue was packed. Journalists from every conceivable medium had responded to the invitation, aware that Wise's fuse was likely to blow. They were not disappointed, and nor was United's manager. His comments had been intended for widespread consumption.

Wise was incandescent, to an extreme which surprised even those who had dealt with him regularly and knew the excesses of his temperament. His eyes were fixed in a fierce, piercing gaze, and his shoulders forced back behind his tightly crossed arms. Wise looked ready to explode and Poyet, sat alongside him, looked equally short-tempered. Lying on the table in front of Wise was a pile of cuttings drawn from *Yorkshire Evening Post*, most of which contained articles documenting United's passage through administration. Much of the coverage had reflected negatively on Bates and, for several weeks, Wise had refused to talk to the newspaper, a display of staunch support for his chairman. As the *YEP*'s chief soccer writer, I was directly – and unsurprisingly – in his crosshairs as the press conference began. He brandished the bundle of photocopies and delivered an irate assessment of the trail of stories that had documented his and Leeds United's torturous summer. 'It's all rubbish, mate,' he said. 'Your behaviour's been a disgrace.' It is not Wise's style to pull punches and his criticism was ferocious, but it was difficult to agree with colleagues who suggested afterwards that his behaviour had been unacceptable. He, like us, was permitted the right to speak his mind, and his outburst was not especially vindictive. If anything, it proved to everyone present that Leeds United mattered to him and that, on the subject of the club's chronic problems, he genuinely cared. It was difficult not to sympathise. He was, on that scorching afternoon, embattled beyond belief but not to the point where his fight had gone. The *YEP*'s scribe was, in any case, hors d'oeuvre: Wise's main duty was to serve up the Football League, and his cut was made with a razor-sharp knife.

'It's laughable,' he said, without a smile. 'They've not only taken my arms and legs off, they've cut me balls off as well. It's not funny at all. You need to be fair, and I think a lot of [club chairmen] will go home knowing deep down inside that they haven't been. Some will have [voted against Leeds] for their own reasons and probably not the right reasons. Everyone wants to get a head start, and 23 teams in our league have got a very good head start on us. We have to get 106 points to win the league, 92 points to get in the play-offs, and 70 points to stay up. Thank you very much. But these players and these fans are going to stick together and are going to be strong. There's a massive point to prove – for everyone. A lot of people want to see us fall flat on our faces and they haven't helped the situation. We've got to fight against it.

'The supporters don't like Batesy, and they don't particularly like me.

But they've got us. We're part of this football club. Because of your background and where you come from, they find it very difficult to accept. It takes them a bit of time to get used to you and I've got to give them that time. So has Ken Bates. But how many people would take this on? We will take it on, and we love it – we love the challenge and we need the supporters behind us. It's that simple. In time, Bates has turned other things round and so have I. Hopefully we can do it for the fans, ourselves and this football club. It's time to march on.'

With hindsight, it is possible to identify the seeds of resolution sown by Wise's unscripted and impassioned speech. Leeds United, as a club and an institution, were apparently on their last legs, but the defiance shown by their manager indicated that he and his players were willing to run another mile, in spite of the blisters all over Elland Road. And the news was not all negative. The signing from Norwich City of Andrew Hughes, an energetic midfielder with combat in his blood, had been completed shortly after the announcement of the failed appeal to the Football League, following on from the one-year contract given to club captain Alan Thompson earlier in the day. Wise had a squad ready to start the season and capable of starting the season in competitive fashion. Among the biggest dangers hanging over Leeds through the summer months was the stark possibility that their transfer embargo would create a squad of meagre strength and insufficient quality to mix confidently in League One. But two days before the season kicked off, Wise looked at his work and saw that it was good, or as good as he could realistically have expected. Unlike his first season in Leeds, the squad beneath him was his creation and crowded with players he trusted implicitly – free from 'shitbags', as Wise would eloquently put it. Not all were journeymen or cast-offs. Thompson was a former England international, albeit with a single cap to his name, and recently renowned for his contribution to Celtic's most sustained period of dominance over Rangers for more than a decade. The left-footed Geordie had been a general in Martin ONeill's Glaswegian ranks (Glaswegian in spirit, if not in the origin of the club's players) and seemed suited to the annual conflict between the Old Firm which so many players found excessively intense. League One held fewer surprises and, at the age of 34, the effect of time was a potentially bigger enemy of Thompson's. In Casper Ankergren, meanwhile, Wise had a goalkeeper on the fringes of the Danish national team, and Angolan centre-back Rui Marques brought international quality to his defence. He had played in the 2006 World Cup and would participate in the African Cup of Nations on the back of his contribution at Leeds. The list went on: Jonathan Douglas was a Republic of Ireland international, and David Prutton had played in the Premiership for a sustained period with Southampton. Less than three months earlier, Nottingham Forest's qualification for League One's play-offs was achieved with Prutton in their squad. Hughes, meanwhile, had more than 350 senior appearances behind him for a variety of clubs including Norwich and Reading. And up front, the potential jewel in Wise's crown was Jermaine Beckford, a striker of non-league history but Football League stock who had scored eight goals in eighteen matches while on loan with Scunthorpe United at the end of the 2006–07 season. Once a youth-team player at Chelsea, Beckford stepped into professional football in his early 20s and had found himself in a sporting sense at Glanford Park. Scunthorpe's manager, Nigel Adkins, was interested in signing him permanently, but Wise was never tempted to do business. 'We had an offer for Becks from Scunthorpe for £75,000,' he revealed, 'and some silly managers might have taken it.' Thirteen goals from Beckford before Christmas would vindicate Wise's decision not to sell. His squad also contained the ageing Tore Andre Flo, whose reputation as a clinical striker had been built solidly at Chelsea in the late 1990s, and Wise's one disappointment was that Leon Constantine – the scorer of 26 goals for Port Vale during the 2006–07 term – had broken his ankle during United's pre-season tour of Germany and the Czech Republic. He was nevertheless signed to a two-year contract, a weapon in storage for later down the line, and the arsenal available to Wise was reassuringly potent. Unlike Lieutenant George in *Blackadder Goes Forth*, he was not being asked to defend himself from howling machine guns with a plain wooden stick. And his managerial colleagues in League One knew it; none would have asked to inherit Wise's problems, but most admitted that they wouldn't mind the use of his squad. Names on paper, however, did not alter the demoralising portent of bookmakers offering United's relegation at the slender price of 2–1.

It was those odds, rather than the more fanciful permutations on offer, that dominated the agenda as United's supporters traversed along the M62 towards an overcast Prenton Park on 11 August. The fears were endless: Was the pool of players constructed in haste by Wise strong enough for the task ahead? Would Wise receive the support he needed from the terraces to carry him and his squad through the season? And was it possible for any club to overcome a penalty on the colossal scale of United's? The questions were rhetorical, as so many are on the first day of a new season, when expectation is coupled with doubt. Tranmere Rovers had justifiably been talked up as promotion candidates by their manager Ronnie Moore, and the prickle of optimism on the Wirral was modestly tangible. Tranmere's butterflies spoke of a club who knew mid-table mediocrity should be beneath them; the stress on United was more akin to the pregnant pause which grips the passengers of a rollercoaster in the seconds before it flies free down the tracks. There would be no one there to catch Leeds in the event of an accident. Asked before kick-off about United's predicament, Moore said: 'A lot of people have got the violins out for Leeds, and we've got to get our thoughts completely away from that. Leeds are going to be sending a team here on Saturday with a lot of quality in it. People say they have lost this player and that player, but there are still a lot of good players in the side. And they've signed a dozen players this week. My lads are ready and if they can't be up for a game like this, there's something wrong.'

The team chosen by Wise for the first leg of United's League One marathon was unsurprising: Ankergren in goal, a back-four of Frazer Richardson, Rui Marques, Matt Heath and Eddie Lewis, a four-man midfield containing Hughes, Thompson, Ian Westlake and Curtis Weston, and Beckford paired with Tresor Kandol in attack. With the exception of Beckford, a shortage of pace was evident throughout the list of 11 players but the balance and experience of the team was satisfying, not least because six of the individuals starting had been signed less than seven days before kick-off. For 45 minutes, however, Wise's players operated like the strangers that so many of them were, stumbling through the first half with desperate ineptitude. Tranmere made effective use of their two lively wingers, Chris Shuker and Steve Davies, and Shuker's low cross to the back post set up the opening goal from Chris Greenacre in the 22nd minute. United's defence had been cut to shreds in the build-up, and not for the first time; two earlier saves from Ankergren had warned that Tranmere's goal was in the post. Wise started the game perched in the stands, giving him an overview of the field below, but he abandoned his detached position and descended to the dug-out as soon as Greenacre's side-footed finished stretched the net behind Ankergren. His anxiety was understandable. A positive start to the season was imperative for Leeds, both in terms of tackling the threat of relegation and creating the opportunity to achieve something greater. It was also necessary to prevent the fans who had been pushed to the point of revolution three months earlier from sharpening their pitchforks once more. A workable coalition between Wise and the supporters had been established hesitantly, created on the condition that United's manager prove himself worthy of the job, and the Cowshed Stand at Prenton Park was said to have witnessed widespread infighting as half-time arrived, between those who believed Wise deserved their backing and those who feared the 1–0 scoreline after 45 minutes was an extension of the failure experience over the previous 12 months, and a sign of things to come. The sceptics would have been satisfied to know that Wise was as angry as them, and in the heart of Prenton Park the walls of United's dressing room echoed to an exchange of harsh opinions at the interval. A repeat of the first 45 minutes would see Leeds beaten, and it did not take a man of great wisdom to know how quickly and easily the truce agreed between the establishment and the hoi polloi of Leeds United would disintegrate beneath the pressure of poor results. 'We didn't play well in the first half and we had a little argument at half-time,' Wise said afterwards. 'That sorted a few things out.'

The most worrying aspect of the first half had been the re-appearance of the less agreeable habits shown by Leeds during the previous season.

Their tactics were direct but without direction, and their inability to retain the ball was inviting Tranmere to run riot. Moore's players accepted the invitation with glee but at the cost to Leeds of a single goal, and against that shambolic backdrop, the second half would come to stand as a positive indictment of Wise's motivational skills. United's energy levels soared, the chests of the players expanded by an extra inch, and ten minutes into the second half Thompson's deep free-kick was driven past Tranmere goalkeeper Danny Coyne by the forehead of Heath. The set-piece was wonderfully inventive and clearly rehearsed, providing evidence that Wise's summer had not been wasted or idly spent. Heath was mobbed by his team-mates in front of United's aroused supporters while Moore's players bemoaned the outcome of United's first serious opportunity on goal. Their hackles raised, Tranmere punched Leeds to the point of senselessness. Two shots from Greenacre struck stray legs in United's crowded box before they could reach the goalmouth, and Calvin Zola was thwarted by Ankergren's save in the twilight of the second half. Moore could see another goal in the game for Tranmere, but the decisive strike which arrived in the 89th minute caught him unsighted and his team off-duty. Hughes collected a throw-in from Richardson and looped a cross into Tranmere's box, where Kandol crouched to meet the ball and divert a header through Coyne's legs. The Cowshed froze for a second before exploding in a chaotic wave of bouncing bodies and a sea of arms punching the air. Kandol sprinted towards the corner flag to the left of Coyne's goal and threw himself into a glorious back-flip, the start of riotous celebrations that gripped a quarter of Prenton Park through five minutes of injury time. As the match referee, Lee Mason, sounded the final whistle, Wise turned to the main stand and raised his index finger to the sky, a show of delight which might have doubled as a disguised insult to all who had questioned him. He, his players and his staff gathered in a huddle in the centre of the field, milking the exhilaration of their supporters who had come to Prenton Park expecting nothing and were now leaving with a straw to clutch. Wise had spoken of the importance of unity two days earlier, but in the confines of Leeds' training ground his comments were merely words. He had no clear idea how quickly or how willingly the supporters would rally to his banner.

A number were with him, that much he knew, and a shift in attitude – however small – had been evident a week earlier during Leeds' final pre-season game at nearby non-league club Guiseley on 6 August. Wise was applauded by United's supporters as he crossed the pitch at half-time of the low-key friendly, and the following day's *Yorkshire Evening Post* published a comical picture of him wearing a look of jovial surprise as he listened to the crowd's reaction. Whether an instinctive pose or a deliberate one, acceptance was not what he was used to. The accord of Guiseley was multiplied immeasurably at Prenton Park, where Wise and his club became one entity, aligned against what the majority of supporters believed was a personal and vindictive attack on Leeds United by the Football League and every club who had worked to uphold their 15-point punishment. Wise had earned his moment of release, and so had Leeds. 'That's a Dick Turpin job if ever I've seen one,' said Ronnie Moore, who had good cause to talk of daylight robbery. His team had deserved better, without question. But this was one day when fate had fought United's corner. It would not be the last.

Leeds had been drawn away to Macclesfield Town in the first round of the League Cup, scheduled for the Tuesday immediately after their pulsating victory at Tranmere. A night game at the primitive Moss Rose epitomised the level of English football that United had been reduced to, but the low-key surroundings of Macclesfield's stadium gave Wise and his players a chance to escape the heat of Prenton Park and settle into their stride. There were no Sky cameras, a scattering of journalists and a crowd of less than 3,500, still big enough to provide Macclesfield's second-largest attendance of the season. A sweetly-struck volley from Ian Westlake, though late in the game, advanced United into the second round with the minimum of fuss. 'Hopefully we can get a nice draw – a home draw and carry on,' Wise said. 'I don't care who we take but we'll take them at home.' The reward, if he could have called it that, was a tie away at Portsmouth, a bind of a draw which heightened Wise's suspicion that cup competitions would not be his primary concern.

* * *

A bigger and more immediate priority was United's first home game of the season against Southend United on 18 August, a re-run of the exact fixture that began Wise's tenure as manager 10 months earlier. Southend had been relegated from the Championship alongside Leeds, and the summer had not been especially kind to their manager Steve Tilson. Freddy Eastwood, his immensely talented striker, had been sold to Wolverhampton Wanderers with the inevitability which drags highly-rated players from relegated clubs, and new signings of note were scarce. But his team were still expected to impose themselves on the higher reaches of League One, and not least by Wise's staff. 'It's going to be a massive game on Saturday,' said his assistant, Gus Poyet. 'For both of us.'

Before the season started, there was a strong likelihood that the attendance drawn in for United's home match would be indicative of the disillusionment and apathy created in the city by the sight of the club on their knees. But the result at Tranmere, and more particularly its dramatic nature, had turned many heads. The morbid trek to Elland Road which so many supporters had endured during the previous season – the same sensation, joked one fan, as approaching the gallows – suddenly became an intriguing march into the unknown. The performance at Prenton Park had been deeply ordinary, but the outcome and the resulting celebrations had been magical. Word of the experience had spread quickly. Disharmony still existed and grudges were held as firmly as ever; one group of supporters had hired a small aircraft to fly over Elland Road shortly before kick-off against Southend, carrying a banner protesting against Bates' takeover. But for all the effort and money spent, it went largely unnoticed. The crowd had not come to Elland Road for a fight; half of them, in any event, were busily engaged in a scramble for tickets.

The attendance at Elland Road was officially declared as 24,005, but there were far fewer spectators than that in the ground when referee Neil Swarbrick set the game rolling. As a result of administration, United's facilities for accepting credit card payments had been withdrawn, denying the club the ability to take advanced bookings, and late arrivals at Elland Road were met by the extraordinary sight of queues snaking back and forward through the car park behind the West Stand towards the besieged ticket office. Hundreds were still waiting to hand over their cash when a sharp rise in decibels inside the stadium confirmed to the massed, ostracised ranks that Leeds had drawn first blood.

The match was three minutes old when Thompson curled a free-kick from 30 yards across the body of Darryl Flahavan and into the top corner of the goalkeeper's net, the type of finish on which Thompson's reputation had latterly been built. The goal harnessed the crowd in the way that Wise intended, but the dawn was apparently false. Southend struck the post 11 minutes later and performed with a level of dominance which was convincing enough to leave Tilson shaking his head at the scoreline as he left the field at half-time. Leeds were content to sit on their narrow lead but lacked the conviction to defend it. With 69 minutes gone, Ankergren was left prostrate by a shot from Lee Bradbury which the Danish keeper parried brilliantly, and Adam Barrett stole in to head the rebound into an empty net. Southend were worth their goal, and Wise knew it. But he was not prepared to accept four points from two games when a second goal would leave his team on minus nine points and counting. He surveyed his bench and handed his missive to Flo, the one experienced option among his substitutes. Flo was in the final stages of recovering from a broken foot and he was patently short of match fitness. It had surprised everyone to see him included in the squad at Tranmere seven days earlier. But with five minutes remaining, Sebastien Carole's cross sat up nicely in front of the Norwegian, who threw himself into a volley that Flahavan had no chance of repelling. United's lead re-established, the rain on Southend's parade came through the floodgates. Marques headed home Carole's corner in the 89th minute, and Beckford ran through Tilson's despondent defence in injury time to sweep a low shot past Flahavan. Leeds were showboating, to the amusement of their players and the delight of their crowd. Only a pedant could find the energy to argue that the 4–1 win had flattered them or that a period of reflection was necessary, but Wise was that pedant. 'It's an important time for us,' he said. 'We need to try and clear these points as quickly as possible and I don't want them to get carried away because we've done nothing at the present moment. It's a bit disappointing because we should be top of the league.'

Leeds, of course, were not top of the league or anywhere near it. On 18 August, they were still 15 points behind Leyton Orient and Huddersfield Town. They were nine short of Southend, who had dropped to 23rd place, the lowest of the clubs whose playing field was level. It was, therefore, in Wise's interest to keep United's disparity in the public eye. He and his players had already taken their penalty to heart and taken it personally. The atmosphere created at the end of their first two league matches demonstrated to Wise that United's supporters were doing the same, and that a club with a common cause would go further than a collection of warring factions. The 40-year-old was understandably indignant; he also knew how to work a crowd. Leeds United are generally at their most pugnacious when the world is breathing down their neck.

Wise was right, however. Back-to-back wins courtesy of goals in the final minutes were suggestive of nothing in particular. The common belief before the season started was that, in spite of their 15-point penalty, Leeds would find four clubs worse off than themselves by the final day, thus avoiding relegation. Their first two results gave credibility to that train of thought. But promotion or, better still, the title? That was more difficult to predict. Wise privately considered both to be realistic possibilities, but was loathe to say so publicly. All he would admit to was a target stored in his head which, it seemed fair to presume, was set higher than the total of points needed to remain in League One. But the subject of promotion was suddenly topical; seven days after their victory over Southend United, Leeds were scheduled to visit a club for whom nothing else would suffice.

Nottingham Forest started the season as the bookmakers' favourites for the title. Forest, in League One, always did. Their supporters can argue with United's about the respective size, stature and history of their clubs, but they have much in common, particularly the fact that both institutions look badly out of place in England's third division.

Their stock is far higher, and the reality of decline had bitten Forest hard. This was their third season in League One and potentially the last chance for their manager, Colin Calderwood, to retain his position at the City Ground. His team had lost in the play-off semi-finals at the end of the previous season, which was no disgrace but a vital step short of where Forest expected – demanded – to be. Calderwood did not enjoy unanimous support among the club's fans, a problematic situation that Wise could empathise with, and the mediocrity of goalless draws in Forest's first two matches were a catalyst for early criticism. In his pre-match press conference, Wise was unforgiving. 'They haven't won yet and they haven't scored yet, but they're favourites to go up,' he said. 'Everyone knows that, and there is pressure – pressure on Colin, because he needs to produce for Nottingham Forest. He's had 15 months in the job and it's a big year for them. They were favourites last year and didn't make it, so this year they're under even more pressure. Their wage bill is probably the highest in the division. We're looking forward to upsetting them.' Wise could have been accused of playing cheap mind games, but his appraisal was fairly accurate. Calderwood was indeed under pressure. His club had staggered into League One under different management in 2005 and were now beginning to wallow in it. Even the cleaners at the City Ground were despondent. 'I don't expect anything any more,' a middle-aged lady by the press box said to me, her duster in hand. 'At least then there's a chance you might get a pleasant surprise. But I'm not holding my breath.' Beating Leeds United would put strength in Calderwood's corner, albeit momentarily.

The city of Nottingham was baked in sunlight for United's arrival, and the crowd of 25,237 at the City Ground fell just a touch short of its capacity. Forest's stadium has a parochial feel to it, lacking the grand design and prestige of homes owned by other clubs with European status to rival their own, but the massed ranks of white at one end of the ground offset by swathes of crimson in the other three stands gave the fixture the important context it deserved.

The view from the touchline looked better for Wise than it did for Calderwood. Leeds opened the scoring in the 17th minute when Kandol anticipated Beckford's through-ball and drilled a low shot past

Paul Smith in Forest's goal, and the 1–0 scoreline at the interval seemed ample reward for a quiet first half which had caused United limited discomfort. It was the perfect scenario imagined by Wise. United's victories over Tranmere and Southend were credible, but neither was especially deserved nor particularly likely to shake the rest of their division. A win over Forest – away to Forest – would be different. Leeds were unlikely to face a more expensively-constructed squad at any stage of the season, and the sound of Forest being jeered off the pitch was music to Wise's ears. But in the changing room down the hall from him, Calderwood was plotting a response, and it came quickly and ferociously. Kris Commons equalised after five minutes of the second half when his free-kick bounced through a crowded box and beyond the reach of Ankergren, to nestle lazily in the back of the net. Wise knew a soft goal when he saw one, and he was soon faced by the sight of Forest rampant. But the slick attacks concocted by Calderwood's players were repeatedly stunted by a grim display of finishing. James Perch sliced a shot wide of an open goal from four yards out, and Commons and Felix Bastians were equally profligate from positions where missing the net took some talent. If Calderwood expected the pressure to tell, he was also aware of the scripts written for Southend and Tranmere during the previous fortnight, and the counter-punch which landed on his chin in the 89th minute seemed strangely inevitable. A scuffed shot from Carole bobbled weakly to the far reaches of Smith's six-yard box, where Beckford slid in to drive the ball into the roof of the net with the pocket-picking skills for which Nottingham had become famous. Ronnie Moore had invoked the name of Dick Turpin at Prenton Park; in Beckford, Calderwood saw Robin Hood reincarnated. As 3,483 visiting supporters made the City Ground shudder, Calderwood stood motionless in his technical area, trapped in the isolated wilderness that every manager despises. Six feet away, the reaction was delirious. 'It hurts,' said Wise, with all the sympathy he had afforded Calderwood before kick-off. 'Or it will for them anyway. There was a lot of pressure put on us and in the second half we didn't play at all well, but it was difficult at times. It was lovely to see the goal go in. We won't ever say die.' Wise beamed beneath the bright sky with a rare look of satisfaction. He had smiled as United's manager before, of course, but usually in defiance of the criticism that was hurled at his face. His grin at the City Ground was the smile of a coach with everything going his way. 'We won't ever say die.' The words lingered as Wise stepped out of the stadium, leaving behind the impression that this man once despised by so much of Leeds United's family might just save them.

WASH YOUR MOUTH OUT, SON

THERE IS A SONG POPULAR AMONG LEEDS UNITED'S SUPPORTERS which, to the tune of Doris Day's *Que Sera*, goes:

> When I was just a little boy,
> I asked my mother What should I be?
> Should I be Chelsea? Should I be Leeds?
> Here's what she said to me:
> Wash your mouth out, son, and go get your father's gun,
> And shoot the Chelsea scum.
> Shoot the Chelsea scum.
> We hate Chelsea! We hate Chelsea!

The chant existed long before Ken Bates or Dennis Wise made strides towards Elland Road, but its relevance was heightened by the involvement of both men at Leeds United. The idea of the club being run by a raft of former Chelsea employees did not sit well with portions of the Leeds fanbase and during Bates' stewardship, a small migration had taken place from Stamford Bridge to Elland Road. On the day that Wise was first presented to the media as United's new manager – 26 October 2006 – the top table at the press conference consisted of four men with strong ties to a club that Leeds supporters detested: Bates, Chelsea's ex-chairman, was sat centrally alongside Wise, formerly a captain at Stamford Bridge; assistant manager Gustavo Poyet, the ex-Chelsea midfielder, was positioned at one end of the table, with Gwyn Williams, United's technical director and previously a long-serving chief scout in West London, at the other. The claim that the quartet had come to Leeds with ulterior motives beyond the success of the club was unfair and intolerant, but the more paranoid fans could see shades of a Trojan Horse in the gang of four. 'They say keep your friends close and your enemies closer,' said Bates with a mischievous smile. 'Well I've got the buggers at the top table.' There were many in Leeds who agreed wholeheartedly, without seeing the joke.

A delicate relationship existed between the dug-out, the directors' box and the terraces at Elland Road, and the talk of shooting Chelsea scum was for Wise's benefit as much as Bates'. United's chairman is a resolute individual and a man whose judgement is rarely swayed by dissent in the ranks. Furthermore, the more level-headed fans could not ignore the fact that Bates had taken Leeds on at a time when the club were on their knees financially and with few other willing saviours in sight. They had that to thank him for, however many grievances they had developed since. But Wise was protected by no such history, and his leap into the unknown of Elland Road was made without a safety net. The problem was not simply his strong Chelsea connections; Wise's fiery and controversial reputation preceded him, and not in an endearing way. The quality of his managerial record was also open to debate. He had taken Millwall to an FA Cup final while player-manager at the New Den between 2003 and 2005, and his move to Leeds had come after a spell of just six months in charge of Swindon Town. The Wiltshire club made an eye-catching start to the 2006–07 season, winning nine of their first 15 matches, but a short period of success in League Two was not enough to convince the masses in Leeds that Wise was suitably qualified for the manager's position at Elland Road. The overriding feeling was that his appointment had been facilitated by his long and friendly relationship with Bates rather than his managerial credentials, and it is certainly true that few other men in Bates' position would have risked such a selection. As a permanent replacement for Kevin Blackwell, the fans were receiving precisely the individual they didn't want, and one whose Curriculum Vitae appeared to fall short of the requirements of their club. Had Wise enjoyed their unanimous support, the chant against Chelsea would have been less vociferous and less meaningful. But with doubts aplenty, it was a warning that his every step would be watched in search – and, at times, in hope – of a false move. The firing squad had itchy trigger fingers and would take their first opportunity to shoot. The former Scotland international Craig Burley, once a colleague of Wise's at Chelsea, analysed the situation perfectly. 'If Leeds achieve success, Dennis will be the best thing since sliced bread,' he told the *Yorkshire Evening Post*. 'But if it all goes wrong, he'll be hung, drawn and quartered.' He could well imagine which eventuality was more likely.

Wise's position was unenviable from the off, and it was not entirely clear why he had walked into such an obvious trap. As he would argue constantly, money was not his issue or his motivation. Wise's playing career had blossomed during the Premier League's boom, and the remuneration provided by 11 seasons with Chelsea, one of the country's most wealthy clubs, was easy enough to estimate. The salary being paid to him by Leeds – some £400,000, according to documents released during administration – was hardly insignificant, but nor was it a sum beyond his wildest dreams. The same went for Poyet. Wise's claim that he had come to Leeds to assist Bates, an old friend, in a time of great need was more credible – their relationship had developed to such an extent at Stamford Bridge that Bates was chosen as the godfather of Wise's first two children. But as an absolute explanation for involving himself in a crisis at Elland Road that bordered on and later became civil war, it seemed implausible. Wise might have owed Bates but not to the extent that he would offer himself up for crucifixion without a second thought. The more he discussed his position, the more it became apparent that he had accepted the summons to Leeds United because he wanted to be there, engulfed in the chaos. To understand why is to understand the personality of Dennis Wise, the player, the coach and the man.

The story of Wise's first meeting with Bates, far back in 1990, is a comical tale worth telling in full. Wise, who was then 23 years old, had been lined up to sign for Chelsea from the sadly disbanded Wimbledon FC on the same day that Chelsea expected to recruit Andy Townsend from Norwich City. Both players were stood in Bates' office, Townsend appropriately dressed in an immaculate suit and Wise bedecked in a scruffy tracksuit. The transfer fee agreed between Chelsea and Wimbledon was not inconsiderable, and Bates was understandably bemused by the aloof appearance of the character in front of his desk. 'Is this it for £1.6 million?' Bates asked with forthright force. 'Yes,' replied Wise, tapping his chest with a fist. 'But I've got a big heart so you'll be OK.' Bates is said to have laughed out loud, caught off guard by Wise's self-assurance, and their initial encounter was the start of a unique friendship. Wise has never has referred to his elder as Ken Bates or Mr Chairman but as Batesy, a gentle liberty that few others are allowed to take. Bates is a formal operator whose insistence on staff at Elland Road wearing shirts and ties to work is non-negotiable. His employees knew better than to follow Wise's lead and belittle Bates with nicknames. 'Because I called him Batesy that day – and because it was a natural thing for me to do – he lets me call him it now,' Wise said. 'No one else does. He tells people off if they do. I can do it but they can't. We're very close.'

That is Wise in microcosm – arrogant, provocative and difficult to intimidate. An individual, in short, who delights in operating close to the bone and is utterly impermeable to attacks on his personality and mannerisms. It is unsurprising, when such a picture is painted, that he might see potential where others would fear to tread, and there was no bigger minefield open to him than Elland Road in the final months of 2006. From the outset, it seemed to me that he had taken the job for exactly that reason, to discover – and, ultimately, to prove – that he was big enough and talented enough to turn the swell of a damaging tide. Swindon Town had been too simple in comparison. 'I was in a better position at Swindon,' he said, speaking on his first and only anniversary as United's manager. 'I was 45 minutes from my house, and it was all quite simple – I seemed to have a job there for as long as it wanted it, I got a percentage of the gate and all sorts of other things. But Batesy gave me a call and asked if I would want to come to Leeds. I said of course. There were two reasons – firstly because it's a massive football club but also because of my relationship with Ken Bates. We're close and it wasn't looking too fantastic for him. I knew the financial side of the club wasn't great and I knew the dressing room wasn't great. Why did I do it? Because I'll have a go. I don't shirk. I'm thick-skinned and I've taken abuse all my life. I once had a situation where I was playing for Millwall and I had 5,000 West Ham fans singing "he's five-foot-four and his wife's a whore". I laughed. Why? Because people get carried away. They read the papers, they want to slaughter you and that's what happens in football. It doesn't bother me.'

It was no secret that when Wise took over as United's manager there was division and conflict within his dressing room. His style of management was not immediately popular, and rumours of an acute lack of unity told in the club's performances and, more significantly, their results. Wise was convinced that certain players were set on undermining him, deciding on his first morning in the job that he was operating on borrowed time and would bow quickly to the pressure put on him by militant supporters who opposed his appointment for all manner of reasons. 'There were a lot of strong personalities and they thought my days were numbered,' Wise said. 'They basically said let's do him. They didn't think I'd be here a year later. But I was always going to be here. Maybe they thought sod him, he'll be gone, but I knew differently. It was no good me going in a cupboard and hiding, and I wasn't going to walk away just because it was a bad time. No chance, and not in a million years.' The changes came quickly, and Paul Butler and Sean Gregan – two of the most experienced defenders in United's squad – were informed they were free to leave the club within weeks of Wise's arrival. New players appeared on loan, and the January transfer window saw plenty of movement, but the crisis was deeper than he had imagined and too complex to be solved by changing personnel. His first season at Elland Road was a disaster, both in a sporting sense and politically. In February of 2007, Wise accused one of his players of leaking his team to a member of Crystal Palace's squad 24 hours before the clubs were due to play each other at Elland Road. The individual, he warned, would never play for Leeds under his management again, but having spoken with the conviction of a man who had identified his Judas, Wise was forced to backtrack quickly amid much finger-pointing and innuendo after the club confessed they could not apportion blame with 100 per cent certainty. It was a public-relations disaster brought on by their manager. The frustration, however, was tenfold at beginning of March when Wise announced to a press conference at Elland Road that his captain, Kevin Nicholls, had attempted to extricate himself from United's relegation fight and was requesting a transfer on loan to Luton Town. The development was remarkable and an unseemly distraction from the pressing priority of maintaining Leeds' position in the Championship. Wise maintained that he wanted Nicholls to be involved in the final weeks of the season; Nicholls subsequently described Wise and Bates as bullies. Against that divisive backdrop, relegation was probably inevitable in spite of the fact that Leeds were still kicking and screaming on the penultimate weekend of the season.

Relegation was an obvious cue for Wise to walk away, but as the dust settled, something strange happened – he offered to take a pay cut, to ensure that Leeds could afford to employ him in League One. There was no indication from Bates that Wise's job was in danger, but there was every possibility that Wise would declare United's problems impossible, his own position untenable, and react by tendering his resignation. He was not attempting to pretend that his initial experience of Leeds had been at all successful or positively memorable. 'The first six months were a real nightmare,' he said. 'The easy option was to say sod this, why would I want to be here next year? The reason is that we want to change it. We haven't come here for the short term, we've come here to make something happen. I needed to do this for my own purpose and my own challenge. This was about fighting something. I've enjoyed it from the start in a funny way – a strange and warped kind of way. I enjoyed the battle with people and I enjoyed the slaughtering because it makes you stronger. You see if you can stand up to it. I knew I would take dogs' abuse. But if you can stand up to it then you can stand up to a lot of things. I needed to find that out.'

Choosing to remain *in situ* was a freedom that Wise would have so long as Bates retained control of Leeds United at the end of the club's insolvency in the summer of 2007. New owners would have their own strategies, and they were unlikely to involve a manager whose popularity in Leeds had started badly and declined from there. Wise did not believe he deserved the sack but he was honest enough to realise that showing him the door would be a quick and easy way to earn brownie points from the city. Until the deal allowing Bates to repurchase the club from KPMG was completed, he was one unfavourable turn of events away from becoming the archetypal dead man walking, waiting for a very public execution. 'If someone else had taken over the club in the summer, I knew I was gone,' Wise admitted candidly. 'The perfect situation for them would have been to get rid of me. They'd have thought the crowd hates him, everyone hates him. And they'd have been the cult hero because people would say thank God you got rid of that idiot. I knew what was coming to me if anyone else took over. I'd have gone away on holiday and taken it easy. But the other thing I knew was that I had a fighter behind me, and that's Batesy. The supporters' first thought when I came to Leeds will have been what is he doing here? I needed a chance and in the first six months I never had it. I got battered all over the place – by the papers, by the fans. But I knew it was going to get better. You might not believe me but I knew it couldn't get any worse. That was it. I realised that I'd dealt with it all, mentally and physically. I never cracked.'

The deduction of 15 points a mere eight days before the start of the season was perhaps as close as he came to losing faith, but the irony of the punishment was that it placed Wise in a predicament that called on his greatest strengths. Whether deserved or not, he had dealt for years with victimisation and the feeling that people delighted in seeing his darker moments: the string of red cards he received as a player; the incident at Leicester City which left his team-mate Callum Davidson with a broken jaw and brought about his departure from the club; and now the slow assassination of his reputation which was taking place at Elland Road. But it was on the subject of victimisation that Leeds United and Dennis Wise found common ground, and a battlefield on which they could assist one another. The jokes being made at Wise's expense were only as cutting as the general contempt being directed at Leeds, a club who had never been relegated beneath England's second division in more than eight decades as a professional entity. In defence of their honour stood their supporters, their players and their embattled manager. And if the contest from United's point of view was us-against-the-world, it begged the question of who better to lead the club than a man who had built a profitable career in virtual isolation. Not everyone disliked Wise but the balance of opinion was very clear. 'I've taken abuse all my life,' he would say. 'Except from the people I've played for.' It was a subtle point, but a point well made.

Relegation had not surprised Wise. When he and Poyet first took on their jobs at Leeds, they accurately concluded that the margin by which survival was won or lost would be extremely tight, as the final Championship table without United's 10-point deduction for entering administration proved. One train of thought argued that Wise and Poyet as a management team were simply out of their depth, lacking the tactical nous and man-management skills to allow a club like Leeds United to prosper. Wise argued differently. On his arrival, he claimed, the veins of the club and their dressing room were irrevocably ruptured; the squad had aged rapidly in the lead up to the 2006 play-off final, and United's accounts were broken beyond the point of repair. As much as his first task had been to avoid relegation, Wise insisted he had implemented a long-term strategy that could still be achieved from the starting point of League One. 'When I first came here, I wasn't popular,' he said. 'But there were a lot of problems at this football club, and it needed to be cleaned out – completely cleaned out [Bates described United's dressing room as the Augean Stables, after the fifth labour of Hercules in Greek mythology]. It's taken time to do it and it opened my eyes to a lot of things that I've not been involved with before. There was a lot of dead wood here. We needed fresh people who weren't coming here just to have a job, to get some money and to be happy with that. When I first walked into this place, I felt very uncomfortable. People didn't know me, I didn't know them and they judged you on what they've heard, not on what you're actually about. It takes them a bit of time to get used to you. The ones who can do that will get on with you. The ones that you don't see eye-to-eye with don't. There were problems that I had to sort out, but the public never see what's inside the circle, only the outside. They never knew what was really happening. When a manager has spent a lot of money and it hasn't worked over eight months or so then maybe they deserve to go. When a manager hasn't spent money and you know the club's in a bit of a mess – a financial mess – you have to give the person a little bit more time to try and change the situation and to do his own thing.' Wise conceded that if his plans for League One proved to be an unmitigated disaster then he would happily take the bullet from Bates, but he was not prepared to accept that his first six months in the job were reason enough to hang him.

Others were less sure. As Wise walked into Elland Road for the final pre-season fixture arranged for United's first-team on 4 August 2007, he was confronted by a supporter who explained in explicit terms that he was not welcome at the club, and never had been. Wise advised the fan to get used to the sight of him in the dug-out. 'I suppose that seems hard to take,' Wise said, 'but I'm used to it.' The subsequent performance against Wigan Athletic, a Premier League club who had sent a strong line-up to Elland Road for the friendly, improved Wise's optimism and also gave the first serious hint that the squad he had built with unavoidable haste would do more than make up the numbers in League One. United lost 2–1 to Wigan but were deserving of a draw. Outside the stadium, a banner hung on the iconic statue of Billy Bremner and directed squarely at the Football League read: *You can take our points but you'll never take our heart.* To judge by the endeavour that day, the sentiment applied to Wise's players just as it did to United's supporters. It was a start, if only a small one. 'At least the players look like they're going to fight this,' said one fan as he left the ground. 'I'm not convinced about Wise but if I was him I probably wouldn't be here. It's a hell of a job. Maybe he fancies it, and if he does then fair play to him.'

Solidarity was Wise's bunker of protection, and few clubs do siege mentalities like Leeds United. Millwall's supporters coined the phrase 'no one likes us, we don't care', but their claim makes the assumption that enough people take an interest in Millwall to dislike the club en masse. Millwall were feared because their more volatile fans were capable, historically, of starting a riot at the flick of the switch. The furthest reaches of England truly hate Leeds United, and not simply because sections of their support would willingly take part in any riot provoked by Millwall. In his book *Guvnors*, Mickey Francis – a now-retired member of Manchester City's hooligan firm – wrote:

> One of the most popular football songs goes, to the tune of *The Dam Busters*, like this: We all hate Leeds and Leeds and Leeds, Leeds and Leeds and Leeds, Leeds and Leeds and Leeds, we all fucking hate Leeds.

They're not the most imaginative lyrics, but you get the picture. The attitude is endemic. Those with long enough memories resent the combative and ruthless approach of the Leeds United team constructed by the late Don Revie in the 1960s and '70s, an exceptional collection of players who have been collectively and unacceptably slandered through three decades. Revie's players deserve to be celebrated as one of the finest English teams ever produced, and in West Yorkshire they are. It is still the club's most sustained period of success. Others speak only of Dirty Leeds. The reputation of United's supporters also goes before them, as the stringent policing methods applied to their first season in League One would show. The remaining protagonists, meanwhile, simply jump on the bandwagon. It is fashionable to hate Leeds, so in Leeds it is fashionable to be hated. United do not count on friends; they never have, and never will. Nor do they seek acceptance. If you hate Leeds United, have a go.

The trick for Wise was to work his way into that inner circle, and convince the mob who doubted him that he was prepared to fight their corner – that it was, in fact, his *raison d'être*. As results began to swing in his favour, Wise played the solidarity card to increasingly good effect. He poured regular praise on the punters, as he liked to call them, aware after three straight wins over useful opposition in Tranmere, Southend and Nottingham Forest that the distrust of him and Poyet was weakening. When Luton Town visited Elland Road on the first day of September, the final whistle provoked a scuffle on the touchline between Wise and Kevin Blackwell, the Luton manager who had thrown so much time and energy into his stint as United's boss between 2004 and 2006. Blackwell cared deeply about Leeds United, but this was Wise's time and the club were Wise's concern; the present incumbent was only too willing to reiterate that fact in full view of the crowd. At the end of the month, Wise involved himself in a more unseemly tangle with Danny McDermid, a young referee from London whose misfortune it was to be at the centre of a 1–1 draw between Leeds and Gillingham on 29 September. It was, incredibly, the first time that United had dropped points in a league fixture, and Wise blamed McDermid directly, striking a chord with the supporters who had chased the referee from the field at Priestfield with a hail of missiles. A mutual wavelength slowly developed, and what mattered to the supporters was seen to matter to Wise. The 10th anniversary of Billy Bremner's death fell on 7 December 2007, and a minute's applause was held immediately before the Yorkshire derby between Leeds and Huddersfield Town kicked off at noon the following day. On the eve of the match, Bremner's statue – a wonderfully iconic symbol on the south-east corner of Elland Road – was defaced by spray paint showing the letters HYC, an apparent reference to the Huddersfield Young Casuals, a group of hooligans connected in name at least to Huddersfield Town. Bremner's statue was built in 1999 and has become a focal point for the club's followers in times of crisis. It is to Leeds United what the Shankly Gates are to Liverpool, and the statue ought to have been sacred ground. The vandalism was discussed in United's changing room before kick-off, and Huddersfield were subsequently routed 4–0. Wise said: 'I have a message for whoever did it. I'd just like to say up yours. You deserved everything you got today. You don't disrespect a player of that calibre and it's disappointing that some idiot can decide to do that. They are idiots, people like that, and they're better off away from football.' The city of Leeds nodded in agreement, content that their manager was speaking for them. It had not always been so. Four short months had passed since Wise was caught on the steps of Elland Road being told to go forth and multiply. The change had been rapid and Wise gave the distinct impression of a former outcast who was starting to feel at home. 'This could be my last job,' he said. 'It really could. I'm being totally honest.'

That prediction would ring incredibly hollow in January when, with 28 games of the season gone and Leeds a point short of second position, Wise tendered his resignation and accepted a job with Newcastle United. At the time, however, there was no question that he meant what he said, and that his positive comments were given for more than effect. But talk is cheap, as the old saying goes, because supply exceeds demand. The romantic notion of dragging a famous club from the pits of obscurity was easier to imagine than to actually realise. Elland Road was not the scene of Wise's last job in football and, at the age of 41, it was never likely to be.

His premature exit was seen by some as a sign of weakness, something he is not prone to showing. Wise possesses elephant hide where others possess thick skin, and he always maintained that insults and criticism washed over him without leaving a trace. But in private, he was conscious of United's supporters – conscious of their thoughts, and of their mood. He was not reticent enough to deny that he could survive in the long-term without their assistance. 'I just hope they stay with us when we have a bad patch,' he said to me once, shortly after the start of the season. 'I'll see how they are with me then. Because we can't stay unbeaten for ever, and we can't win games for ever.' There was no arguing with that. Leeds, for all their defiance, were not invulnerable, and they could not realistically expect to finish the season with 46 league victories to their name. Try telling that to the supporters. Dashing wins over Tranmere, Southend and Forest were leading United into their meeting with Luton on 1 September, and the crackle of anticipation in Leeds was immune to the power of home truths.

Wise, however, could not resist pelting the Football League whenever the opportunity presented itself, and it was with unfortunate coincidence that the organisation were required to bestow him with the first manager of the month award of the League One season. How happy the Football League were to find themselves rewarding their most fervent critic – Ken Bates aside – is a matter for conjecture, but the fact that Wise deserved the prize was beyond dispute. Only one other club – Leyton Orient – had produced a perfect set of results during August, and the difference in circumstances between Elland Road and Brisbane Road was apparent to anyone who had followed United's summer from hell. Leeds, furthermore, had enhanced their reputation by producing a competitive performance during a 3–0 defeat to Portsmouth in the second round of the Carling Cup. Most likely, the eye-catching victory at Nottingham Forest on 25 August had swung the vote in Wise's favour. But he was not prepared to accept his award graciously. It is standard practice for managers who receive the monthly prize to pose for promotional photographs with the trophy, for the benefit of the Football League and, to a degree, themselves. The League's request for Wise's co-operation was swiftly rebuffed, as they knew it was likely to be. 'After what they've done to us, this is like a little tap on the back saying "we do apologise, here's the manager of the month award",' he said. 'I'd rather have my 15 points back than get manager of the month. It means not too much to me, to be honest. Nothing from the Football League this year will be going near my mantelpiece or any of the trophies I've got on my mantelpiece. I just can't accept what they've done to us.' Leeds suspected that Wise might dispose of the trophy by handing it to a young supporter outside Elland Road, or perhaps by tossing it carelessly into the stadium's Kop. Either way, they were sure that it would not be going home with him. The decision to discard the award was eventually taken out of his hands, and the trophy tucked away in a quiet corner of Elland Road. United's administration were reluctant to lose a trinket which would stand in years to come as a small example of their success in adversity. As it happened, a second manager of the month accolade would be added to the pile by the end of September.

* * *

Against that productive backdrop, the fixture between Leeds and Luton Town at Elland Road on 1 September did not require the hard sell. The club's first home game of the season against Southend United had drawn in a crowd of 24,036, but the opening date of the calendar is traditionally effective at pulling supporters through the turnstiles. The fans who parted with their money on that afternoon had no idea whether their first glimpse of Leeds would be a joy to behold or a demoralising indication of a horrible season ahead. By the end of August that question had been answered, and tickets flew out the door ahead of Luton's arrival. To add to the sense of intrigue, the occasion involved a fascinating side-issue which was largely unconnected with United's struggle. In the opposite dug-out to Wise would be Kevin Blackwell, the Luton Town boss and a man who had been sacked abruptly by Ken Bates 12 months earlier. Elland Road was home to Blackwell for more than four years, initially as the club's assistant and later as their manager, and it was a period of his career he was deeply proud of, not least because he had taken charge of the club immediately after their relegation from the Premier League in 2004 and, in his words, built it up from scratch. On 21 May 2006, Leeds competed in the Championship play-off final at the Millennium Stadium in Cardiff – the pinnacle of his tenure – but a day which promised so much delivered abject disappointment. United were routed 3–0 by Watford – managed by Aidy Boothroyd, a former coach under Blackwell at Elland Road – and having signed a three-year contract with Leeds two months before the play-off final, Blackwell was removed from his position on the instruction of Bates eight games into the 2006–07 season. Leeds, at that point in their increasingly nervous history, were sitting second from bottom in the Championship table. The parting of ways was far from amicable, and Blackwell subsequently instigated legal action over his dismissal. In the interim between his sacking and his arrival in Yorkshire with Luton Town, there had been no obvious reason for him to return to Elland Road. He did not expect to be invited back. His appearance at the stadium on 1 September was, therefore, his first since his acrimonious exit, and an opportunity in Blackwell's eyes to acknowledge the supporters who had stood patiently by him for more than two years. 'It'll be an emotional occasion for me,' Blackwell said in the days leading up to the game. 'Leeds United were a massive part of my life and a very proud part of my life. Everyone knew how much managing that club meant to me and still means to me. I've never hidden the fact that I thought the job was taken from me too soon, but you accept people's decisions and move on. This is a chance for me to say thank you to the fans and to the people who worked so hard for me behind the scenes. I've never really had that opportunity.'

Blackwell's style of management was not to everyone's liking, but his commitment to the job had been beyond reproach. The attention he paid to the club and to his position bordered on the obsessional, and he operated with the single-mindedness of a workaholic. In the summer before he was sacked, Blackwell was able to count the days he spent on holiday on one hand, occupied as he was by the process of reorganising United's squad and an untimely stint of jury service. There were times in the build up to the start of the 2006–07 season when he looked visibly exhausted, and the false dawn of the play-off final had left many at the club in need of revitalisation. When his reign turned sour, there were many in Leeds who felt the time was right for a change of manager. But there was no disputing that Blackwell had put his soul into a job that he had genuinely loved, and for that the city of Leeds should have been grateful. Few in football were willing to champion the merits of Leeds United with the passion of their former manager. 'It's the biggest club in Yorkshire by a country mile – and in the north of England,' he once said, with a sly nod towards Manchester United. 'Forget about the mob over the Pennines – they can't touch you.'

Dennis Wise had been the eventual beneficiary of Blackwell's departure, and he was reluctant to see the return of his predecessor thieve attention from United's immediate priorities. Luton's coaching team also contained other links to Elland Road in Sam Ellis and John Carver, both of whom had at one time been assistant manager at Leeds. Carver had later endured a horrible spell as United's caretaker, in the short period between Blackwell's departure and Wise's appointment.

'I'm sure Mr Blackwell, Mr Carver and Mr Ellis will be paying more attention to this game than the others,' Wise said. 'They would love to shove it down our throats and beat us. But this isn't about Blackwell and him being the ex-manager. It's about Leeds versus Luton and us getting three points.' Wise's single-mindedness did not suggest that Blackwell would be welcomed home with open arms by the regime at Leeds. There was clearly little chance of Blackwell sharing a pint with Bates and, reading between the lines, the two managers did not appear to possess particular admiration for each other. As a gauge of United's indifferent attitude, their ex-employee was not afforded a single mention in the matchday programme. But Wise gave Blackwell his moment by allowing Luton's manager to walk from the tunnel first and receive the recognition of the crowd at Elland Road. He applauded the West Stand then raised an arm towards the Kop, standing in the touchline for a few second before settling into his seat. Wise, on contrast, nipped quietly into his dug-out as the applause died down, happy to leave the limelight vacant. Perhaps inevitably, the spectacle that followed was unspectacular in its entirety.

The match was settled by a goal from Tresor Kandol, just as Blackwell believed his side had completed the first half unscathed. Jermaine Beckford won possession on the left wing and fed a pass into the box, meeting Kandol's run perfectly. The Congolese striker was slightly off balance but kept his feet long enough to hook the ball across Luton's goalkeeper, David Forde, with his left foot and find the corner of the net. With a minute of the half remaining and little in the way of chances before Kandol's goal, the timing of his strike was as important to Wise's tactics as it was crippling to Blackwell's. Luton's players tested United's nerve after the interval and found it to be solid. An offside flag disallowed a header from Paul Furlong, and a shot from David Bell shaved the crossbar on the hour, but Leeds could not have been accused of surviving on the ropes. For all the hype surrounding Blackwell's return, the game had passed off with a competitive spirit that was mild-mannered and respectful, and the behaviour of the club's respective managers was impeccable until the sound of Clive Oliver's final whistle reached their ears. Wise walked from his technical area and marched directly towards Blackwell, who looked his counterpart square in the eye before exchanging a cold handshake. Wise put his arm around Blackwell and pulled their foreheads together, provoking an incensed reaction from Carver, who threw himself at United's manager with a finger pointing at Wise's face. Carver was quickly restrained by a steward, and alert security staff separated the two backroom teams; while Blackwell took his leave of the field, Wise cracked a smile and headed for the centre circle, his fist raised in the air. The arguments and scuffling continued inside the tunnel, and Luton's squad wasted as little time as necessary in boarding their bus and rolling onto the M621, away from Elland Road. It had, perhaps, been too much to expect that the reunion between Blackwell and Leeds would pass off peacefully, and the drama on touchline spoke of bad blood that was simmering as fiercely as it had on the day of his sacking. Blackwell made as little as possible of the touchline incident at his press conference afterwards, and attempted to lighten the mood. 'Our relationship's terrific,' he joked when asked about Wise. 'He'll be round for dinner tomorrow.' Carver described the scuffle as 'handbags', and he and Wise soon smoothed the choppy waters during an amicable phone call. But where Blackwell was concerned, Wise was less forgiving. 'Sometimes people are bitter,' he said. 'I can't help that bitterness. I don't think Kevin wanted to shake my hand, and he told me to eff-off. He was obviously upset that they'd lost because this was probably the biggest game of his career. The game was built up because of Kevin coming back and he tried to put a bit of pressure on me. He's quite clever with his words. But he didn't get the happy return he wanted. These are different times now – his is over and he's gone. Obviously he thinks he did a fantastic job here and he's entitled to think that.'

The exchange became the talking point of the match, largely because the game itself had been a subdued exhibition of competitive football. But it detracted from a result which had placed Leeds within one victory of crossing the 15-point penalty. As one newspaper headline put it, the temperature at Elland Road is minus three and rising. And so it was. Leeds had produced their best start to a league season since 1984 and a stringent penalty which had seemed custom-designed to relegate United was being swept aside with haste. What was all the more surprising was the relaxed aura that had filtered through Wise's squad. On the Tuesday after their win over Luton, BSkyB sent cameras to Thorp Arch to film United's players taking part in the Crossbar Challenge for *Soccer AM*, the satellite broadcaster's popular Saturday morning show. The training ground was awash with glorious sunshine and devoid of a single furrowed brow. The healthy atmosphere was understandable on the back of four straight victories, but the league table still presented problems. Though three points below zero, Leeds remained 13 adrift of the top of the division and 10 away from the final play-off position. Their progress was commendable, yet the gaps illustrated why Wise insisted on preaching caution when asked about promotion. His assessment of the league was simply that it looked better than it might have done, and better than it had on 9 August. But the buzzing morale of his squad – which on the final day of the summer transfer window had been strengthened by the signing of young goalkeeper Alan Martin from Motherwell, Portuguese winger Felipe Da Costa from Greek club Ionikos, and centre-back Paul Huntington from Newcastle United – illustrated how happily they were warming to the task. Smiles had been difficult to find at Thorp Arch when Wise first sat behind his desk. Collectively, the squad's attempt at the Crossbar Challenge – a game in which players attempt to strike the woodwork with a single kick of the ball from the halfway line – was feeble, and not one effort succeeded in hitting the frame of the goal. The squad shrugged their shoulders and mocked their own failure; they had bigger fish to fry, and United's eyes were already set on the forthcoming delivery from Hartlepool, the seaside town where monkeys fear to tread.

Hartlepool United are a club of rich heritage but not a club with many honours to show for a century of professionalism. Though in existence for years before Leeds United were founded in 1919, the clubs had not contested a single league fixture before Hartlepool's arrival at Elland Road on 8 September 2007. In 2001, when Leeds finished fourth in the Premiership, Hartlepool were competing in Division Three's play-offs, some 67 places further down England's pyramid of leagues. But their recruitment of Danny Wilson as manager in June 2006 was an astute appointment, and Hartlepool had been promoted from League Two within 12 months of declaring him gaffer. The club appeared to be moving forward while the decline of Leeds became ever more steep.

Wilson came from good stock, in a managerial sense. He had coached in the Premiership with Barnsley and Sheffield Wednesday, and had fought repeatedly, if unsuccessfully, for promotion from the second division for four years with Bristol City. Wilson knew League One inside out, and was more qualified than most managers to analyse Leeds United's form. 'Promotion contenders?' he replied, when asked whether Wise's players deserved such a description. 'I don't know if that's the right phrase. If Leeds keep this form going then they'll win the league. There won't be much contending involved.' It sounded like mind games but Hartlepool's boss was not the type to involve himself in needless psychology. A considered and affable man, Wilson does his job and leaves others to do theirs. His opinion was given honestly, and though Wise was taking every chance to highlight the yawning gap between Leeds – on minus three points – and the highest reach of the division, he was fighting a losing battle. The optimism that was rife in Leeds had translated into pensive acceptance among League One's managerial fraternity that United would not be pigeonholed as also-rans by their points deduction. 'There was never any doubt in my mind that Leeds would have a chance of promotion this season,' Wilson said. 'But we've gone past that. It's obvious now that they're going to be up there.'

The eighth day of September promised to be a momentous day for Leeds – the day on which their preliminary skirmish with the Football League would be won. Such was the club's momentum that a fifth straight victory and their arrival on nought at the bottom of League One felt like a formality. What was inevitable was the appearance at Elland Road of the stadium's biggest crowd of the season, with some 26,877 supporters crushing through the turnstiles. Elsewhere in League One, the other nine matches played that weekend produced an average attendance of less than 6,000. There were none that exceeded 8,000.

United's results thus far had been exceptional; in the third tier of English football, the loyalty of their supporters and the scale of their crowds was a phenomenon. The confusing paradox was that visiting teams seemed unperturbed by an atmosphere which classed itself as intimidating.

Wilson will never be able to truly explain how Hartlepool came to suffer a 2–0 defeat at Elland Road on 8 September, save to admit that United's goal was more charmed than his. His team struck the woodwork on three occasions and allowed the simplest of opportunities to slip through their fingers. Hartlepool were reluctant to play the role of lambs in the abattoir, but suicidal finishing saw their slaughter ensue anyway, and a goal in either half allowed Wise to celebrate a telling fifth league victory. Wilson could only lay claim to a moral victory.

United's cause was helped by the fact that Hartlepool came to Elland Road hidden in their shell, and refused to emerge from it until they fell a goal behind with 20 minutes gone. Jonathan Howson knocked a diagonal pass into the path of Frazer Richardson, who dropped a cross onto the head of Kandol and left the striker to apply the crucial touch. But it took a outstanding save from Casper Ankergren – scraping a header from Richie Barker onto the crossbar with his fingertips – to defend the slender lead given to United by Kandol before half-time, and the advantage of a single goal appeared to be insufficient protection. Five minutes into the second half, a moment of brilliance conjured by the feet of Jermaine Beckford ensured that Leeds would smash through the surface of a Football League penalty which had threatened to drown them. Michael Nelson, Hartlepool's central defender, misjudged a hooked clearance from Sebastien Carole, and the bouncing ball looped over his head and dropped to Beckford. The striker controlled the ball with one touch and, from the most ridiculous of positions on the left wing, stabbed a delicious chip over goalkeeper Jan Budtz and inches beneath the crossbar. It was a sublime goal on a day of sublime celebration, and the animated crowd were oblivious to the onslaught that came from an aggrieved Hartlepool team in the final half-hour. James Brown hit the post, and Ian Moore did likewise; Barker and Godwin Antwi saw shots repelled from the goalline, denied on two occasions when United's clean sheet appeared to have drawn its last breath. Such was Hartlepool's dominance that Wise was inclined to take issue with the performance of his players, even as he basked in a story of redemption that was capturing the country's attention. 'There's a buzz about the place because we've been put on the floor by the Football League,' he said. 'It made us closer – very close – and there's something we need to achieve because of everything they've bunged at us. You try to use that to your advantage and we are. But the players have still got to perform.'

His realism was lost in the clamour at Elland Road, in Leeds and beyond. On Monday morning, the exorcism of their 15 points was acclaimed by Chris Moyles, the BBC Radio One presenter, who acknowledged the achievement of his hometown club on his breakfast show with an alternative rendition of Enrique Iglesias's song 'Hero'. *'We have got to zero, baby. Minus points have now all gone. We can now start from the bottom. We might make the play-offs in May.'* There was a strong temptation to replace 'might' with 'will', and the talk in Leeds was of possible records in the making. Wise's players were two victories away from equalling the run of seven successive league wins produced by Don Revie's team at the start of the 1973–74 season, and three victories from eclipsing it. Wise found a correlation between Revie's squad and his own difficult to accept with a straight face. The players managed by Revie, after all, had walked through Tottenham, Arsenal and Everton in reaching their magnificent seven, and Wise's Leeds were engaged in a different league, literally-speaking. Scalping Hartlepool United did not necessarily compare. But Wise could argue legitimately that the quality of the squad available to him at Elland Road was far beneath what it had been in Revie's pomp. And indulging the possibility of eight straight victories was preferable to dealing with the reporters and fans who were now asking whether Leeds were talented enough and dominant enough to finish the season unbeaten.

As ludicrous as the question may have sounded, it demonstrated to Wise and his players how easily they might become victims of their own success. Avoiding relegation was not a foregone conclusion, but it seemed probable after five matches which had banked 15 points.

Survival was already being seen as a mundane outcome when the other possibilities created by United's form were considered. As Wise reflected on the 2–0 victory over Hartlepool, he was asked whether avoiding relegation during the next 41 games would be enough in itself to satisfy his personal ambition. 'I want to get safe first, and then I'll answer that question,' he said. 'Deep down inside I know my feelings but I'm not going to express those feelings. We need to do a job first of all, then I might open my mouth.' It was his way of saying no.

Ambition also oozed from the pores of United's squad. The players toed the party line in public and talked of survival before promotion, but their language on the field spoke differently. The following Friday, Leeds made the long journey to Bristol Rovers and collected a 3–0 victory, a scoreline which was again more conclusive than their performance. Jermaine Beckford opened the scoring with a flicked header in the ninth minute, and finished off Rovers with a sweet overhead kick in the last. In between, Tresor Kandol's close-range volley had put the result beyond reasonable doubt. Kandol's goal was his fifth of the season, on a par with the tally produced by Beckford, and their contribution to the win at the Memorial Stadium was financially timely. Just days earlier, Wise had instigated contract talks with both players in response to their early-season form. Their importance to United was so great initially that discussions over new deals seemed unlikely to depend on intense negotiations; they were more a case of Beckford and Kandol naming their price. It constituted a strange turn of events. Kandol had become a constant target of criticism from United's supporters, especially at Elland Road, during the 2006–07 season, and his lack of popularity was influenced by his record of one goal in 18 matches. It was not what strikers were paid for. Beckford finished the same season on loan at Scunthorpe United, away from the implosion that was taking place in Leeds. According to Scunthorpe's manager, Nigel Adkins, Beckford had been 'desperate' to relocate to Glanford Park permanently in the summer of 2007, but Wise decided not only to retain both players but to implement them as his first-choice strikers. By the middle of September, Wise was recommending to Ken Bates that Leeds extended their contracts, and the decision met with the approval of both the club's chairman and supporters. In a short space of time, the forwards had proved their worth in a way which had seemed improbable a month and a half earlier. To stress the point further, Beckford scored the first of United's goals against Swansea City at Elland Road on 22 September, generating a 2–0 win that was sealed by David Prutton's 20-yard finish and which extended United's spotless sequence of results into a seventh game. Wise, as he hoped he would, had drawn level with Revie, whose 34-year-old record was starting to look vulnerable.

The fact that Gillingham were next in line meant the idea that Leeds might fall short of an eighth straight victory was scarcely considered. Gillingham were ranked 20th in the division, two positions below Leeds, who were by now six points in credit. On the weekend that United beat Hartlepool, Ronnie Jepson had walked out of Priestfield after deciding the manager's job at Gillingham was beyond him. A 3–0 defeat to Southend United was the final straw. Jepson had held the position for two years but did not feel that the club were making satisfactory progress under him. Assistant boss Mick Docherty and first-team coach Iffy Onuora were named as joint caretaker-managers, but having beaten Brighton 1–0 in their first match in charge, Gillingham were hammered 4–0 at Nottingham Forest a week before Leeds descended on Kent on 29 September. The capitulation did not bode well, and United scented blood. The bookmakers confidently stretched a home win out to 5–2.

Previous squabbles dictated that Paul Scally would play the role of the pantomime villain at Priestfield, largely because of comments made by Gillingham's chairman in support of the points deduction imposed on Leeds by the Football League. United's supporters were not impressed by Scally's stance, and peppered the directors' box with unrepeatable chants about him and his wife. But the ire of the visiting fans massed together in Priestfield's temporary and uncovered stand – the type of stand which tells away supporters that their comfort is no more than an afterthought – was soon directed elsewhere. A close-range header from Sebastien Carole after 28 minutes put United a goal ahead and set their afternoon in motion, but the sense of inevitability was reversed four minutes before half-time when Tresor Kandol was sent off for a second bookable offence. His first crime had been to describe a decision from referee Danny McDermid as 'crap', and the red card was drawn after Kandol sarcastically applauded a call from the match official in his favour. United negotiated the final minutes of the first half safely, but Wise weaved his way swiftly to the door of McDermid's dressing room. After voicing his dissatisfaction in frank terms – 'How could you fucking send someone off for saying "well done" to you?' – United's manager was instructed by McDermid to stay away from the visitors' dug-out during the second half, and to watch the remainder of the match from the press box high towards the rear of Priestfield's main stand. It was the start of a conflict which would lead both Wise and McDermid to the door of the Football Association's disciplinary department. With Kandol already dismissed, Jermaine Beckford complicated Wise's tactics further by bringing about his own dismissal in the 57th minute with a ill-judged lunge at Gillingham full-back Sean Clohessy. Once again, United's striker had cause to dispute an earlier yellow card shown to him after he drove a shot into Gillingham's net seconds after McDermid had halted the game with a blow of his whistle. The inexperienced Londoner was not making friends among the travelling contingent from Yorkshire. Yet, for the bulk of the second half, Wise sat impassively beside the watching media, speaking occasionally through his mobile phone to assistant Gus Poyet, who stood animated but alone in the technical area in front of United's dug-out. Leeds had only nine players, but Gillingham were struggling to exploit their advantage, and when they found a route through to Casper Ankergren, the goalkeeper was immovable. As the match entered injury time Leeds seemed to have dodged a bullet, but their resistance finally broke when Ian Cox headed a corner above the leap of Rui Marques, who was charged with protecting one post, and into the roof of Ankergren's net. The equaliser stoked Wise's volcanic temper, and he leapt from his seat to begin screaming instructions at Poyet. In the crescendo of noise spilling from three sides of Priestfield, it is doubtful whether Poyet could have understood a single word of the conversation, and their frantic connection was broken when Wise's phone dropped from his hand and scattered in pieces on the concrete steps beneath him. At that surreal moment, he looked hopelessly detached from his team's plight. He also looked like a man who was about to pick a fight.

The design of Priestfield is unusual, in as much as the stadium's tunnel is placed in one corner of the ground, between the main stand and the temporary seating erected for visiting supporters. After sounding the final whistle, McDermid was therefore required to make his exit at close proximity to a collection of United's fans who were ready to riot. He started his walk slowly, surrounded by security officials, but McDermid and his linesman broke into a run once missiles began flying from the away end. Chased into the tunnel, he was immediately confronted by Wise, who told him: 'That's what happens when you make decisions like that.' United's manager alleged that McDermid responded by telling him to 'fuck off', a claim supported by several of Gillingham's stewards and a number of the security staff from Leeds who had travelled south from Elland Road that morning to help manage the crowd at Priestfield. The exchange left Wise in a fiery mood at the end of a game in which the perfect record constructed by his team had gone up in smoke. 'The players were fantastic but unfortunately this fella has got the headlines,' Wise said, referring to McDermid. 'Well done to him. But when a referee tells a manager to eff-off after a game, it's not acceptable. I've got five witnesses, and three security guards heard him say it. There was no need. I'll be reporting him. He sent me off at half-time, but I need to report him for what he did at the end of the game.' Wise carried out his threat and reported McDermid to the Football Association, while McDermid ensured that a complaint about Wise also landed on the relevant desk at Soho Square. Predictably, United's manager came off worst. The FA summoned him to a disciplinary hearing in late October and punished him with a £5,000 fine and a two-match touchline ban. The punishment also activated a suspended penalty from a previous offence committed by Wise, extending his suspension to three games. To the surprise of no one at Elland Road, and least of all Wise, the charge brought against

McDermid – a charge which the referee denied – was found to be 'not proven' by an independent regulatory commission set up by the FA. A not-guilty verdict would have been decisive; not proven sounded more like a whitewash, especially since so many independent people were said to have heard McDermid's comments. The thoughts of the FA's commission were never made public, but it was interesting to note that McDermid refereed only four more matches before Christmas.

To inadvertently lighten the mood, Wise was named as League One's manager of the month for September, his second such award in as many months and another trophy that would be left to gather cobwebs in a dark cupboard. But on this occasion, he was happy to accept the tribute as deserved recognition of the squad who had worked tirelessly beneath him. 'If you get a group like this who'll die for the club, you can take a lot of stick,' Wise said. 'It's not that other players [at Leeds] before didn't want to achieve something, but when this club was on the floor, who stuck around?'

6

NO PROBLEM, GAFFER

THE NEWS THAT LEEDS UNITED'S APPEAL TO THE Football League on 9 August had been rejected – and rejected out of hand – swept across the Elland Road grapevine like a disease in summer heat. As Dennis Wise digested the implications of the conclusive ballot against his club, an unavoidable itch reminded him of the most pressing phone call he had to make. He scarcely dared to dial the number, for fear that the recipient of his call would hang-up immediately or, at the very least, make the same predictable excuses given to him many times before. It had been like that throughout the close-season for a manager who was being asked to bargain with imaginary chips. Would you like to sign for Leeds United, he would enquire of professional after professional. Yes, they often replied. Can you wait until August for a contract? The line of communication soon went dead. When his hands were at last freed from the handcuffs of a transfer embargo, Wise's task was to dress up a League One club with a 15-point deduction as a sensible career move. The men who sold tickets for the *Titanic* at least had the benefit of marketing their product before it sank.

The player in question was Andrew Hughes, a midfielder on the books of Norwich City, and it was clear from Wise's subsequent comments that he was genuinely concerned about Hughes' most likely response to the offer of a contract at Elland Road. Players had the right to expect security, and the right to decline transfers that either failed to meet their needs or threatened to. Hughes had 12 months remaining on his deal at Carrow Road, and it would not have surprised Wise to hear his plea to the 29-year-old declined with token gratitude. It might, however, have broken his heart, the one vital organ that the Football League's penal system had left undamaged thus far. He needed players and he needed them instantaneously. After Hughes, the cupboard that housed the transfer market was virtually bare.

'Andrew,' he said, as the call connected, 'we're minus 15.' The confirmation travelled from phone to phone and sank in immediately. 'No problem, gaffer,' came the reply. 'Let's brush ourselves down and get on with it.' For Wise, it was a moment of reassurance and defiance. He had worked skilfully and tactfully to persuade other players to commit themselves to his club, but Hughes was the first to forego a contract already in his possession in order to sign for Leeds. He was also the first to do so in the knowledge that United's 15-point deduction would not be lifted. Norwich sanctioned his transfer willingly but with great regret; they had not planned on losing Hughes, and certainly not to a club who had driven up a cul-de-sac without a reverse gear. His friends and relatives were similarly perplexed. 'People told me not to do it,' Hughes said. 'Almost everyone I spoke to said I'd be making a mistake. They saw the 15 points, and their attitude was "why join a club that's going to be relegated?" I suppose I can see where they were coming from but I never saw it like that. It wasn't me being pig-headed – the fact that Leeds United could be relegated again just didn't enter my mind. It didn't seem possible. OK, I couldn't say with 100 per cent certainty that we'd be promoted either but I was pretty confident. You can smell ambition among players in the same way that you can smell fear, and I could feel the ambition in the dressing room. I signed on the Thursday night [9 August] and came up to train with the squad the next day, the day before the first game of the season. When I met the lads, I was counting good player after good player. I already had the buzz of signing for a new club but that got the excitement flowing.

People outside the club were going on and on about relegation and I thought you're joking, aren't you? Take a look at what we've got on the inside."I couldn't have been more positive.' Wise warmed immediately to Hughes' attitude; it reminded him of his own. He wanted players with a passion for trench warfare and players who would invest in the idea that a club with a negative points tally as great as United's could lose that specific battle while winning their wider war. 'He doesn't care,' said Wise. 'He wants to give it a real go. So does every player here. I've got the utmost respect for every single player who's still at this club. They've all been fanatics.' Fanatics was an apt description. As you enter the front doors of United's training ground at Thorp Arch and pass into the complex's inner sanctum – the site of numerous dressing rooms and a mammoth gymnasium – a bright yellow sign displays the message:

'Team work is to keep working together, even when things don't go your way.'

United's players were not merely embracing that doctrine. They were signing it in blood.

Hughes' rationale for joining Leeds was commendable but it did not alter the probability that for every player who nodded to Wise's proposal, ten others would have shaken their heads and disappeared into the night. The conservative sections of football's community might have considered his decision reckless; those with a superficial attitude towards the sport – and, more particularly, the valuable business football entails – would have questioned his sanity. Far better, surely, to float through a steady contract with a middle-of-the-road Championship club than to give your career to an unpredictable project which sounded ambitious in principle but could easily have been disregarded as whimsical. In Wise's mind's eye, Leeds would be promoted. Back in the real world, retaining the club's place in League One would constitute a satisfactory season. And that in itself was the problem: the majority of clubs begin each season with a sense of ambition, realistic or otherwise. Very few see their season effectively written off 48 hours before their first game. Though disappointed by the potential signings who had turned their backs in him, Wise was not naive enough to take them to task. 'I've spent a lot of time on the phone, but that's about it,' he explained. 'I've had a lot of chats with a lot of players but you can't do anything. You just chat to them. Then they go, unfortunately.' The magnet of Elland Road had grown a layer of rust, thick enough to make the average player think twice about giving in to Leeds United's pull. Hughes was not blind to the presence or the smell of iron oxide; he simply believed that the clean-up job was one he could contribute to. With all around him losing their heads over the merits of a transfer to Yorkshire, Hughes sought the considered view of his wife, the one opinion he could not do without. He was rapidly approaching his 30th birthday and was deep into his professional career. To Leeds or not to Leeds? That was the question. 'I said to her we've got an option here that I really want to take,' Hughes recalled. 'She told me I should grab it, which was exactly how I felt. That was the only confirmation I needed. The manager made the effort to sell the club to me, but he didn't need to bother. What could he tell me that I couldn't see in this club already? It's everything you look, and all you ask is where do I sign? That night, I went to Leeds and signed my contract." Swift his relocation may have been, but impulsive it was not.

In Hughes, Wise had acquired a player of immense loyalty and a player devoted to his trade. He does not drink alcohol and can probably never picture himself being overweight. It is difficult, in fact, to imagine him doing anything to excess, with the exception of the amount of time he commits to his conditioning and fitness. Hughes enjoys the smell of battle and, when circumstances require it, the taste of blood. On one occasion at Norwich, he shattered his cheekbone during a 3–1 win over Southampton, prompting the medical staff at Carrow Road to enforce a minimum absence of six weeks upon him. Hughes returned in four. When his head was cut open by an elbow in the early stages of a game between Leeds United and Tranmere Rovers on 2 February 2008, leaving a crimson smear across one side of his face, he sprinted down the tunnel at Elland Road before reappearing five minutes later with the gash wrapped in thick bandages. Hughes fits the model of the midfield enforcer, the trooper to Alan Thompson's general, you might say. But to categorise him as a player for whom the term 'combative' was invented is to misinterpret his appreciation of football, his range of talent and his outlook on life.

When Hughes completes his final game as a professional player, he does not expect an invite to the celebrity circuit to land on his doormat, and nor would he be interested if it did. He might, in fact, apply to become a teacher of physical education at a school in Greater Manchester, the region where he was born. As Hughes set out on his career at Leeds, he was reaching the conclusion of a university course he had taken up on the advice of Steve Coppell, a former manager of his at Reading. A footballer with a degree is not unique, but qualified players are still extremely rare. Coppell is among their number, trained in economic history, and at the time this book was published Hughes was in the final throes of a sports science programme at Manchester Metropolitan University, a course which was destined to redefine him as a Batchelor of Science. PlayStations and snooker tables are the domains of a vast proportion of footballers, many of whom are oblivious to higher education. The most sought-after qualifications among ex-professionals are coaching badges, and none more so than the UEFA Pro Licence. For most of the past decade, the UEFA Pro badge has been a mandatory requirement for any coach who wishes to manage a top-level club in Europe. Those promoted to managerial positions without the necessary paperwork are required to twist numerous arms in order to retain their jobs. According to many retired pros, a surplus of men are now competing for coaching jobs that exist in too small a number to accommodate them all. Badges and certificates are only as valuable as the employment market allows them to be. In returning to school, Hughes had broadened his horizons. A sports science degree would potentially open the door to physiotherapy; it would also qualify him for the role of a fitness coach or similar positions. Even PE would be an option. Players are constantly told to plan for their future – the nervous day when their boots are cleaned for the last time – but there is more to later life than merely saving money, especially for the scores of professionals outside the Premier League. 'I'm never going to be comfortable in life, not like some of the big boys are money-wise,' said Hughes. 'So I looked at a sports science degree. It's something to do when I'm finished, whether that means staying in the game, taking warm-ups, gym sessions or pre-seasons, or even being a PE teacher. It's hard work and I'm not the brightest, but I spoke to Steve Coppell because he's got a degree, and he said that if I do the work, I'll get the diploma. You've got to grind through it.'

It is not necessarily true to describe Hughes as a man who is easily bored, but he is undoubtedly someone who makes a deliberate attempt to keep himself interested. By his own admission he is hyperactive, and inclined to beat his hotel room-mates – Jonathan Douglas or David Prutton – out of bed on the morning of a game. Of more fascination to the general public is the unique pre-match warm-up which became synonymous with Hughes' first season at Elland Road. He is routinely first to appear on the pitch wherever Leeds are playing, typically 10 minutes ahead of the club's other outfield players. Even United's goalkeepers – traditionally the first people to emerge from the tunnel in their training kit – find Hughes' schedule impossible to pre-empt. On his own and in front of rows of empty seats, the midfielder's process of activity is virtually identical week after week. He sets out by jogging the breadth of the pitch, flicking his feet up to catch his hands behind his back. From there, his programme moves quickly in a range of stretches and exercises – a gentle run with his knees raised high into the air; side steps across the field, each leg flicking behind the other with the poise of a dancer; jump after jump into pretend headers; and, finally, short, sharp sprints where his feet hammer into the ground. It is a 30-page warm-up manual condensed into 10 minutes of activity, and a routine which runs like clockwork. At first it seemed that the display of commitment might be a way of scoring brownie points – like the kid who catapults purposely to the front of the race during school sports – but Hughes has carried out his lonely preparation for years. Far from seeking attention, he is normally the picture of studious concentration, lost in his own world until the collective warm-up begins. So concerned was Dennis

Wise that the midfielder might waste precious energy that he asked Hughes to rein himself in and limit the length of his private routine. 'I'm quite a hyperactive person and when I'm sitting in the changing room, personally I like to get out there, suck a bit of fresh air in and get a few strides in to get me going,' he told the *Yorkshire Evening Post*. 'I just like getting my head on the game. Fans get up and they probably go to certain cafes and chippies on their way to the game. I'm like that. It's just a little routine I have. It's nice to see the crowd come in and the atmosphere build up. You look around, thinking this is going to be full with 30,000 soon.' After weeks of watching Hughes' habitual nature, it became clear that his attitude was that of a player intent on maximising his potential. There are inevitable confines to a professional's talent, and boundaries of ability that few can cross, but there is no such restriction on commitment and no automatic limit on passion. Players are born with skill; how well they utilise it is entirely a matter of character and personality. There were players in England more gifted than Hughes, but Wise was not convinced that many were more proud or protective of the ability they were blessed with. 'One thing I'd been told about Leeds was that they value players who play for the shirt,' said Hughes. 'If you stick in and fight for the club like it matters to you and you care about it, then the supporters will accept that. Not every player is blessed with unbelievable ability and I don't think there are any outstanding players in League One. There are very good players, and players who should be playing in the Championship, but I'd say that playing for Leeds United is about more than ability alone. It's a passionate club and a passionate place to live in terms of its sport. If you want the easy life or want to duck under the radar, so to speak, then you don't come here. You need quality players at Leeds but I think you also have to look for certain characters – the right type of characters. It's not easy playing for Leeds and it's not a club where you can cruise through your contract. The bottom line in football is who can get the best out of themselves and out of each other. Every season, people act surprised because unfancied clubs are up in the play-offs, but if they've got their preparation and their tactics right then where else would they be? You're as good as your performances and your results, and that's nothing to do with the name on your badge or the names on your teamsheet. It's maybe easy at a club like Leeds to think that your reputation does the hard work for you, but that couldn't be further from the truth.'

Wise shared his philosophy. If his first six months at Elland Road had taught him anything, it was that the reputation of Leeds United was no longer the guarantor of success. He also accepted that any attempt to bring a player to Elland Road could not be made under false pretences or through dubious predictions. New signings had the right to know what they were getting themselves into; it was inappropriate for Wise to state categorically that his club would be promoted nine months later, simply because they were Leeds United. What he could promise was that his strategy for the season and his intermittent targets would be set with promotion in mind. Proof of his sensible projections was found in the fact that, by New Year's Day, United had gathered 52 points. Before the start of the season, Wise had predicted that his squad would reach the turn of the year with 53, an amazingly astute estimation. It was also an example of one of the reasons why United's season exploded into life with the force that it did – their squad were never fed with pie in the sky; instead, Wise made sure that the bulk of his pledges were achievable. Professional players in any case are trained to sniff for bullshit, and the trials of insolvency and a transfer embargo had taught Wise that honesty was his most agreeable policy.

United's first pre-season friendly of 2007 had taken place against Shelbourne in Dublin on 7 July, 24 hours after KPMG unexpectedly announced that the club were up for sale. Wise was restricted at that stage from making any signings, so the squad which crossed the Irish Sea was riddled with trialists. In total they numbered eight, not counting those players who had returned to Thorp Arch after reaching the end of their previous contracts at the conclusion of the 2006–07 season. The trialists included David Prutton, Leon Constantine, Paul Boertien and Graham Coughlan, players of considerable stature who were unattached and potentially interested in moving to Leeds. Boertien and Coughlan played against Shelbourne but by the end of the July they had signed for

Walsall and Rotherham United respectively, unsure of the true nature of the circumstances at Elland Road. For Prutton and Constantine, their commitment was surprisingly unconditional. Both took part in the pre-season tour of Germany and the Czech Republic, as part of a squad which could only tenuously have been described as United's property. A large number of players involved in the tour had gone for weeks without pay and were still to receive contracts at Elland Road. Prutton's finally arrived in the form of a one-year deal – plus the offer of a year's extension after his 15th league appearance for the club – on 7 August, 31 days after his debut in Shelbourne and 81 after parting company with Southampton. Prutton's career at St Mary's had ground to a gradual halt but when it came to clubs interested in signing him, he would not have been found wanting. The question, then, was why a player with an much easier route to financial and professional stability would look to the most unstable club in England for his next opportunity. What was it about Wise's vision that inspired such a gamble, and such immediate loyalty? Doesn't the house always win?

'It wasn't a straightforward situation by any means,' said Prutton. 'But from my point of view, I tried to be as realistic as possible about the position we were in. I suppose it was case of thinking about the club's problems as much as was necessary but not letting those problems distract you to the point where they overwhelmed you or frightened you away. Players are pretty good an insulating themselves from things they've got no control over and I can't remember any of us talking too much about administration or what might happen in the future. It was a pretty pointless discussion because none of us really knew what we were talking about. Every time I picked up a newspaper, it sounded like the club were jumping from one crisis to another, but the reality for us was very different. The players and the staff were pretty relaxed on a day-to-day basis, and the things we were being told by the chairman and the manager were much more positive than that. But you needed to be slightly realistic because there was only so much they could promise you. Personally, I didn't let the summer worry me, which isn't the same as saying I was blasé about the trouble the club was in. You've got to protect your future and think carefully about your career, but if you were prepared to be open-minded and actually listen to what the management were telling you then it was easy enough to feel confident that the situation would sort itself out. It wasn't as if we were being told things that were totally unrealistic. I wanted to come here, and because the promises I was hearing were genuine ones it didn't really cross my mind that I might go somewhere else. I'd have known if people were lying to me but there was never any bullshit – just people promising to do the best that they could for you, as soon as possible.' The image of players biting their nails and trawling through tabloids for the latest speculation about Elland Road was indeed mistaken. On the final night of their summer camp in Dresden, Wise's squad were holed up in an Italian hotel in the northern suburb of Radebeul, reflecting on a tour which had been of immense value. Walking past the eatery, the raucous laughter coming from inside did not give passers-by the impression of a panic-stricken group. It sounded instead like the pragmatic mood of content and faithful individuals. Bullshit, as Prutton said, was never on the menu.

Prutton found Wise an agreeable coach to work under, but United's manager was something of an acquired taste. Not every player who said no to Leeds United allowed insolvency to rule his head. Wise approached Rob Kozluk, the Sheffield United defender, during the close-season with a view to bringing him 30 miles north to West Yorkshire and Leeds. Kozluk's response was unusually candid. 'Leeds United, yes,' he was quoted as saying, 'but Dennis Wise, no.' An alternative stance was adopted by players like Prutton, who were unwilling to back out of Elland Road until they had no other option. If a transfer to Leeds was ultimately impossible then so be it. They were willing to hang around at Thorp Arch for as long as it took to find out. But at certain points of the summer, United's slow crawl out of insolvency and back into the fold of the Football League must have felt like creeping death.

Towards the end of his first season with Leeds, Prutton earned the nickname 'Jesus' from the club's supporters. With his long, dark hair, his thick stubble and his sizeable sideburns, the likeness was striking; Prutton might also have contended that a number of his performances were divine, though he was too modest to talk himself up. 'There are worse role models around than the son of God,' Prutton would joke, even though the comparison struck him as bizarre. There were also worse places to pursue a career in football than Elland Road, the church where so many in Leeds practised their religion. When Prutton collected the player of the year trophy from the *Yorkshire Evening Post* before United's last home game of the 2007–08 term, it was a personal reward for a player whose excellence had been consistent, but also a collective acknowledgement of the individual squad members who had taken the time to look at the bigger picture while the claws of administration were wrapped around Leeds. 'They say you get rewarded for hard decisions,' Prutton said. 'I think a lot of us have been.'

The late arrival of Hughes at Elland Road, two days before United's opening game of the season against Tranmere Rovers, spared him from the full exposure to the club's near-collapse which the likes of Prutton had experienced, but his attitude was derived from the same open-mindedness that Wise had nurtured in his camp. I met Hughes for the first time outside the dressing rooms at Prenton Park on 11 August, the carpet beneath him indented with stud-marks and strewn with chunks of mud. With their tight corridors and low ceilings, the bowels of Tranmere's stadium are more than a little claustrophobic. There was nothing flash about his immediate surroundings, and nothing flash about the job he had accepted. But Hughes was unequivocal about the thought process that had brought him to Prenton Park as an employee of Elland Road. 'We're in a bad situation but I don't think the club can go any lower than this,' he said. 'It's at a low point. But the decision I've made . . . well, it's just Leeds. If you'd turned round to me when I was 11 years old and said you're going to play for Leeds United, I'd have snatched your hand off. One hundred thousand kids in Leeds would. I just felt it was right to give it a go and have a fight. That's the attitude I'm used to. Sometimes you can go through your career and just be happy. I felt that this was a challenge that people seemed to be walking away from, and if I've been seen to come here for a fight, that's what I want.'

Nine months later, shortly before the League One play-off semi-finals began, Hughes was able to proffer his opinion on the season behind him and assess the true nature of his transfer. It had been a good year. Leeds had banked a top-six finish courtesy of a victory at

Yeovil Town on 25 April, and Hughes' wife was pregnant with their first child. He was preparing to become a father at the age of 30. 'I think being around this city and being happy has helped,' he said with absolute honesty. Football is allegedly capable of having that effect. Research carried out in Germany indicated that the birth-rate in certain parts of the country rose by as much as 15 per cent nine months after their national team reached the semi-finals of the 2006 World Cup. In Scotland, that figure is more likely to show a marked increase nine months after the group stages (and these days, not at all). It pays to be happy, and it pays to feel content. Nothing good ever came of negativity, and especially not at Elland Road. 'Sometimes it seems fashionable to be negative about Leeds,' Hughes said. 'It's just the way some people are. Maybe this year the negative publicity has had a positive effect on the players. Criticism can drag you down but that depends on the character of the group of players who are getting hammered left, right and centre. Some teams buckle when the heat's on. I get the feeling that we're at our best when our backs are against the wall.'

The was clear irony in the fact that the shambolic nature of Wise's summer recruitment had brought together a balanced squad with such natural unity – ironic because, in hypothetical circumstances, he would perhaps have recruited different players. But as his first season at Elland Road had proved, when 44 different players – a virtual cast of thousands – wore Leeds United's shirt, there was a fundamental difference between talent and hunger. Even Diego Maradona could see that. Asked once about Real Madrid, the Argentinian icon said: 'The problem is that they're all stars at Madrid. You need someone to carry the water to the well.' Maradona was the archetypal prima donna, but his understanding of the intricacy of football is wonderfully precise. The value of a team, in essence, is the sum of its individual parts, and how willing they are to commit to the cause. His comments bring to mind another of the motivational signs plastered to the walls Thorp Arch:

> 'There are two options regarding commitment. You're either in or you're out. There is no such thing as a life in between.'

7

STREETS PAVED WITH GOLD

BEHIND EVERY GOOD MANAGER IS A LOYAL AND TRUSTWORTHY assistant, and at a club as volatile as Leeds United, Dennis Wise needed the support of a man who displayed both traits in abundance. Elland Road was Wise's stamping ground on which he would have the final say, but he could not have tackled the project alone. In recruiting Gustavo Poyet – the former Chelsea and Tottenham Hotspur midfielder – as his assistant, United's manager ensured from his first day in the job that he would have at least one ally in the camp at Leeds. If all else turned against him, Poyet would still be there to watch his back. Managers can be flexible over the identity of their second in command, but Wise was particular about the involvement of Poyet. He respected him and trusted him, and their relationship was much as it had been as players. Accepting the chance to manage Leeds would always have been made easier for Wise by the fact that Poyet was willing follow him north.

The pair had become friends at Chelsea in the late 1990s when, with both Wise and Poyet in their squad, the club enjoyed a period of qualified but palpable success. Poyet and Wise won the defunct European Cup Winners' Cup together in 1998, and the FA Cup together in 2000. The following year they went their separate ways,

Wise to Leicester City and Poyet to Tottenham Hotspur, where the Uruguayan remained until his retirement in 2004. Wise was managing Millwall when Poyet announced that he was ending his playing career, and attempted to convince his former team-mate to take up a final contract at the New Den. Poyet considered the offer seriously but declined Millwall's terms just as it seemed a deal had been struck, returning instead to his homeland with his family. His only request was that Wise remain in touch and pick up the phone if ever he required Poyet's service again.

The call came in the summer of 2006 after Swindon Town made an ambitious attempt to appoint Wise as their manager and the full-time replacement for Iffy Onuora. Wise was open to the idea of working in League Two but wanted Poyet to step in as his assistant. Having favoured a relaxing stint in Uruguay over an extension of his career as a player at Millwall, it was not guaranteed that the less-than-bright lights of Wiltshire would whet Poyet's appetite, but Wise found him willing and ready to enlist at the County Ground. Their tenure there was short and sweet – little over five months in total – but Wise and Poyet complemented each other well, and Swindon were positioned fourth in League Two on the day that Leeds United came calling for their management team. If Wise was happy to relocate to Elland Road, it went without saying that Swindon would lose Poyet, too.

Few assistant managers are as publicly visible as Poyet became at Leeds, but Wise was happy to delegate responsibility to his number two. Poyet was regularly assigned to deal with press conferences, before and after games, and was free to speak openly about relevant issues, controversial or not. Sending out Poyet was not a means by which Wise could duck awkward questions; Poyet was always likely to address them as honestly as his manager. It was very much the Dennis and Gus show, and Poyet's affable personality was valued on the training ground. He had kept in shape and was as fit as the average professional footballer. In their first season at Elland Road, Wise and Poyet took the club's squad and staff to HMP Doncaster for an exhibition match at the prison. The word from the players who took part in and witnessed the game was that Poyet had not lost his touch; he was, in fact, the star of the show. But he and Wise did not allow romantic notions to cloud their vision, and they were never registered as player by Leeds.

Wise welcomed Poyet's input, and he welcomed his support. There were times when he needed it badly. 'We're good friends,' Wise said. 'We talk the same kind of way, and we understand each other very well. He's knows what I want and we're on the same wavelength. It's good to be like that. He will argue with me and I will argue with him, but it doesn't fester. We walk out the door and it's gone. You don't want an assistant who just nods his head and says yes, yes, yes.' Poyet was not a yes-man, but nor would he seek to slip a knife into Wise's back. They had walked into Elland Road together and Wise expected that they would walk out together, whenever the time came. It was not an exit that he envisaged making any day soon.

In the aftermath of United's 1–1 draw at Gillingham on 29 September, his phone was never silent. The loss of two points and the end of the club's winning streak was an irritation, but the consequences of the fractious match ran deeper. Tresor Kandol and Jermaine Beckford had incurred one-match bans after their controversial red cards, and Leeds were due to visit Oldham Athletic for a Tuesday night fixture little over 72 hours later. Both strikers would serve their suspensions while United turned out at Boundary Park. Kandol and Beckford had started every league match until then, and while their return of goals had justified Wise's selection policy, there were few other alternatives open to him. Leon Constantine had a broken ankle and would not be fit until the end of October, and Tore Andre Flo was beset by perpetual injury problems. Neither player had any chance of making the squad selected to play Oldham, and Wise's only available strikers were the green and raw products of United's academy. He took out his contacts book and began flicking through the pages, learning the true meaning of the Football League's emergency loan market. The loan system in England's lower leagues is rarely used in emergencies and has become a means of bypassing FIFA's unpopular system of transfer windows. But Wise's squad was in distress, with limited time to uncover a solution, and it was two of his former clubs who came to his aid – Coventry City and Leicester City. Coventry agreed to allow their striker, Wayne Andrews, to join Leeds on a month's loan, and signed the necessary documents on Monday morning. A short while later, Leicester confirmed that Mark De Vries, the Dutch forward, would also move to Elland Road for a month. Both players were lined up to make their full debuts at Boundary Park the following evening, which, from Wise's perspective, was not ideal. But it was better to walk into battle with unfamiliar weapons than it was to charge with no weapons at all. For the help given by Coventry and Leicester, Wise was thankful.

Located within the boundaries of Greater Manchester and on the edge of the Pennines, Oldham's Boundary Park is a hostile environment. The stadium has the reputation of being one of the coldest grounds in the country; precisely the sort of location where visiting teams worry more about their results than their performances. Wise could certainly not afford to be precious. The legs of his players had been strained by the task of playing against Gillingham without Kandol for an hour and Beckford for half an hour, and his team was being headed by the makeshift strikeforce of Andrews and De Vries. Predictably, neither striker made any significant contribution to the match, save to keep the home defence occupied and honest. Oldham had relied on two goals in the final seven minutes to magic a 3–2 victory against Crewe while Leeds were re-enacting the Alamo at Gillingham, and the demeanour of both sets of players was jaded. The teams negated each other effectively, and it was slightly ironic that the most impressive player on the field was a player who Wise had disposed of within weeks of becoming manager at Leeds. Sean Gregan had, in effect, been the first casualty of the Wise era, sent on loan to Oldham within a fortnight of the latter's appointment. The defender's contract at Elland Road was then terminated completely, giving him the freedom to agree permanent terms at Boundary Park, and though prominent in the season that saw Leeds reach the Championship play-off final, the release of Gregan at the age of 32 appeared to make sense. On the evidence of his performance at Boundary Park, it seemed more like a mistake. Wise came as close as he ever would to admitting as much when asked about Gregan afterwards. 'Last year I knew that I needed to make a load of changes,' he said. 'I saw Sean after and shook his hand. I said no hard feelings, and he was fine. When I came in there was something I had to deal with, and I wanted hungrier people – people who want to die for this club. That's what I've got.' Gregan's appetite on that October evening had been striking, giving United's forwards nothing to feed on. But in the fourth minute of injury time, both he and his defensive colleagues went missing. Sebastien Carole received a throw-in from Andrew Hughes on the left-wing and curled a cross to the back post where Ian Westlake – on the field as a substitute for a matter of seconds – applied a volley with the instep of his foot which flew like a bullet into the net of Oldham goalkeeper Mark Crossley. More than 3,700 of United's supporters had journeyed across the Pennines, and the routine was wonderfully familiar – as Westlake provided the finishing touch, the stand housing the away contingent went up as one, ignited by the last kick of the game. Among United's fans that night, a song was coined which would come to epitomise the club's belligerent mentality, and their refusal to accept the limitations of their 15-point deduction: *Fifteen points, who gives a fuck? We're super Leeds and we're going up!* Wise was ecstatic on the touchline, but appeared more sheepish in the tunnel. 'Bloody hell,' he said, puffing his cheeks out in an admission that a 1–0 victory had slightly flattered Leeds. Still, the events of Gillingham were fresh in his mind and Oldham's injustice was their problem. What goes around comes around.

United's season was beginning to take shape, assisted by the meandering form of so many teams in League One. Leeds had amassed 25 points from their first nine matches, and were 10 points in credit. Leyton Orient stood on 19, but the gap to Tranmere Rovers in second place was a mere six, while the advantage held by Swansea City in sixth was just four. However consistent their own results were, Leeds could not legislate for the form of other clubs, and there was little they could have done to halt the runaway trains had a handful of teams streaked clear at the top of the division. That was one of Wise's biggest fears – that the 15-point deficit would be unassailable unless results elsewhere ran repeatedly in United's favour. He need not have worried. Points were being spilled at every stop of the 300-mile stretch from Carlisle to Yeovil, and the clubs inside or within touching distance of the top six were falling over each other in the stampede. Yeovil were a good example. Their manager, Russell Slade, had guided the club into seventh position, but their progress was sporadic. Away from home, the club had won three of their four matches. At Huish Park, they had taken maximum points from one of five games. Most managers had the same complaint over inconsistency as Slade, and Wise was a rare exception. But as the next visitors to Elland Road, Yeovil's away form caught his eye.

The Somerset club were among the more progressive outfits in the lower leagues, having lived outside the Football League for most of their existence. Their success as a non-league club was impressive, but the Conference became a brick wall which Yeovil were unable to scale. They were almost elected to the Football League in 1976, denied entry by a handful of votes, and it would be 27 years before Yeovil were accepted into the third division as Conference champions in 2003. Their promotion was something of a watershed and, under the inspired management of Gary Johnson, they won promotion from League Two at the second time of asking. In May of 2007, meanwhile, Yeovil appeared in the League One play-off final at Wembley, where they lost to Blackpool but came within one victory of stepping from the Conference to the Championship in the space of four years. At least one member of Leeds United's squad knew enough about Yeovil to be wary of Slade's team. David Prutton had been part of the Nottingham Forest side which lost to the Huish Park club over two legs in the play-off semi-finals. It took a 5–2 victory at the City Ground to drag Yeovil to Wembley after the first leg left them trailing 2–0, and the exhausting battle in Nottingham ended early for Prutton, who was sent off shortly before the match spilled into extra time. Yeovil's performance at the City Ground was exceptional, though somewhat under-rated and under-appreciated. The public were more struck by the realisation that Forest – twice winners of the European Cup – had come up short, again.

Wise, though, was beginning to feel confident. The list of beaten clubs was stacking up, and the catalogue of scalps was valuable: Tranmere Rovers, Southend United, Nottingham Forest, Luton Town, Hartlepool United, Bristol Rovers, Swansea City and Oldham Athletic. A who's who, Wise believed, of teams with the depth and quality of squad needed to qualify for a play-off position at the end of the season. It was slightly bizarre that the only comparative failure – their draw at Gillingham – had come against the team that Wise expected nothing of. 'I think we've seen the best teams in there – the teams that we've played against,' he said. 'Of the teams so far, six or seven of them are going to be very close to the play-offs, and maybe winning the league as well. But football does kick you in the goolies, and last Saturday at Gillingham gave us a little reminder of what can happen.' Slade was ready to stick his boot where it hurt. The natives of Somerset had been mildly insulted to hear that the club shop at Elland Road was selling a line of clothing bearing the slogan 'Where's Yeovil?', a light-hearted jibe inspired by United's foray into what was for them the unknown territory of League One. 'We'll try to make life difficult for them, and hopefully an element of frustration will set in,' he said.

His plan could not have been more perfectly hatched, and the patience of Elland Road wore thin more quickly than he had imagined. Anthony Barry, Yeovil's young Liverpudlian midfielder, should have scored the opening goal midway through the first half when he drove a shot against Casper Ankergren's body, and a full-stretch save from the goalkeeper repelled a shot from Paul Warne, one of Slade's older heads. Set against their visitors, and with Jermaine Beckford and Tresor Kandol reinstated after suspension, United looked ordinary, and it was Yeovil striker Marcus Stewart who would shoulder the burden for the 1–0 defeat which befell his unfortunate side. Stewart was presented with a pass across goal from Kevin Betsy but swiped his foot at the ball and, from six yards out, sliced it wide of a goal which Ankergren was unable to cover. With 17 minutes remaining, the chance might have settled the match, and Slade mdust have known what was coming. The match was creeping towards added time when Jonathan Douglas's floated cross reached Mark De Vries, and the striker directed a glancing header past Yeovil's Romain Larrieu, who had otherwise been the more idle of the two keepers on display. It was the fifth time in 10 league fixtures that Leeds had settled a game with a goal in the final five minutes, a Midas touch worthy of any superlative. At the end of another priceless result it was scarcely relevant to argue that Yeovil's display had been the more creditable, though Wise's claim that the second half had been 'one-way traffic' in the direction of the visitors' goal was slightly disingenuous. 'We had one or two outrageously good chances to make life extra difficult for Leeds,' said Slade. 'But if they didn't know where Yeovil was before, maybe they do now.'

United deserved that riposte, but Wise was not listening. Everything about Elland Road was relentless in its productivity. Now 12th in their division, Leeds travelled to County Durham on 9 October for a Football League Trophy second-round tie at Darlington, who they beat 1–0 through a header at the start of the second half from young centre-back Paul Huntington. The competition, which had for years been known as the LDV Vans Trophy and was now sponsored by Johnstone's Paint, was a tournament open exclusively to teams in Leagues One and Two and, as such, Leeds had never competed for the prize before. The club were given a bye through the first round and it was Wise's prerogative to rest as many of his senior players as possible at Darlington. The competition was a low priority in the grand scheme of United's season, and their starting line-up contained nine changes from the team named against Yeovil. Alan Thompson, who had missed most of the schedule through September through injury, was the significant face included, and Huntington's header added Leeds to the draw for the last eight of the Trophy's Northern Section. The lure for every manager, Wise included, was an appearance in the final, which would be played at Wembley, but promotion was a more palatable prize for Leeds and, after 10 league games unbeaten, just as realistic an aim. More satisfying for Wise than the win at Darlington was the announcement two days later that Jermaine Beckford had signed a new contract at Elland Road. Tresor Kandol's negotiations were dragging their heels slightly, but they would also be concluded successfully before the end of the month. Wise made sure that neither deal contained clauses allowing the strikers to leave Elland Road for a specific price. Beckford, especially, was a player who United's manager expected other clubs to sniff around when the transfer window opened in January.

Not everything was satisfactory, however. The list of match official appointments released by the Football League for their fixtures over the weekend of 13 October confirmed that United's game at home to Leyton Orient would be refereed by County Durham's Nigel Miller, a man who had been expunged from the Christmas card lists of Wise and Poyet. United's management team blamed Miller specifically for the club's 1–1 draw at Southend seven months earlier, a result which contributed to the club's relegation from the Championship. The official had overlooked an apparent handball inside Southend's box, which appeared more blatant and obvious with every replay; in injury time, the award of a penalty would have given Leeds the chance to steal a priceless win at Roots Hall, and Wise was angered more by the fact that Miller appeared to point to the penalty spot before apparently reversing his decision. He did not hold back. (Wise is liable to speak his mind, and inventive when it comes to making his point. After a game between Leeds and Ipswich Town at Portman Road in December 2006, he surprised the media by presenting them with video replays of a particularly contentious decision on a laptop owned by United. Most of the journalists present had never seen a press conference like it.) Naturally, disciplinary charges against him followed, and the Football League had the good sense to prevent unnecessary conflict by removing Miller from United's penultimate game of the same season, the day on which the club's relegation from the Championship was confirmed. With Orient lying second in the division, Wise hoped to instigate another alteration and bring about a change of official. 'I can't believe the Football League have given us Nigel Miller,' he said. 'People at this club know what happened last season with him, and what happened with me and him. I hope he doesn't hold grudges and referees very professionally. We asked them to change it, but I don't think they will.' His hunch was correct. The Professional Game Match Officials Board, the body responsible for appointing referees to individual fixtures, rejected United's request, arguing that there was no good reason to withdraw Miller from the game. But by the end of Orient's outing at Elland Road, it was Martin Ling rather than Wise who had reason to question the clarity of Miller's vision.

Orient did what so many teams had already done at Elland Road, and took the game to Leeds with confidence. But unlike the five teams who had already been beaten in West Yorkshire, they succeeded in scoring first. Their goal in the ninth minute was incredibly soft, a free-kick from Sean Thornton that looped tamely over Casper Ankergren and nestled in the net without the need for a goalwards touch, but it was the peak of a brief shift for Thornton, which ended 23 minutes later. The midfielder caught Sebastien Carole with an elbow as the players competed for the ball in the air, and Miller issued a straight red card in the blink of an eye. The dismissal gave Leeds the advantage of numbers, and though Wise's players were strangely reserved in attack, they exploited Orient's shortage of players 10 minutes after half-time. Carole and Alan Thompson exchanged a short corner, and Orient's lack of markers allowed the French winger to burst into the box and launch a sharp strike beyond goalkeeper Stuart Nelson. Carole's influence had been telling throughout the game, and when Paul Terry – the brother of Chelsea and England captain John – climbed on him needlessly inside the box with 10 minutes remaining, Miller was compelled to award a penalty. The noise of the crowd revved in anticipation, but the supporters sank back into their seats as Tresor Kandol leaned back and slashed the set-piece high into the Kop. The striker had laid claim to the ball as soon as Miller's whistle sounded, but Wise's experience of Kandol on the training field had taught him that penalties were not his forte. United's manager rebuked himself afterwards for failing to insist on a different volunteer, and Beckford was rapidly appointed as the club's designated penalty-taker. But the horse by then had bolted, and Kandol's miss was quickly forgotten amid a moment of chaos in the 86th minute. A shot from Adam Boyd bounced directly towards Ankergren, but the keeper allowed the ball to slip through his grasp and bounce towards the goalline, clawed back only by a desperate swipe of his arm. Miller looked to his linesman, who decided that Ankergren's fingertips had averted a goal. Those in the furthest reaches of the North Stand, however, could see that the ball had crossed the line, and television evidence confirmed that the assistant referee, William Smallwood, had misjudged a relatively clear incident. Without his help, United's first league defeat of the season would have been placed on their record at full-time. As Ling reflected on a 1–1 draw, which represented a solid result for Orient, he denounced Miller as 'biased' and claimed that an unhealthy amount of attention had been given to the official's involvement before kick-off. Whether the attention had affected Miller's performance was a moot point, but Boyd certainly thought so. 'It was on Teletext about Dennis Wise having a go at him beforehand, and it worked,' he said. 'That's what he was trying to do – get him on side. I think he did it and decisions went against us.' Orient felt grouchy, and Wise was not much happier. His team had failed to win at Elland Road for the first time and, despite the get-out-of-jail-relatively-free card handed to them by Miller and his assistant, Kandol's penalty rankled. 'It's all very well people moaning about them deserving a second goal,' Wise said, 'but what they forget is that if Tres scores the penalty, it's game over. Tres isn't our penalty-taker but he wanted to take it. I don't think he'll be taking them again.'

It was churlish to blame Kandol, however, for an afternoon when Leeds made hard work of a team of 10 players, and over the next few days, Wise and Poyet worked to restore the striker's confidence. Drop your head, they told him jovially, and we'll beat you up. It was not the most inspired of motivational speeches, but it proved effective. At Brighton's Withdean Stadium on 20 October, a game which could be most charitably described as nondescript was settled in the 79th minute by Kandol's tap-in. The only goal of the match – Kandol's sixth of the season – stemmed from a costly mistake by Adam El-Abd, who sliced a lazy clearance across his own goal and gifted Kandol a chance three yards from the line. Leeds would have viewed a goalless draw as a fair result, and an acceptable one at the end of a drab match. The theft of a win was a considerable bonus. 'We got the lucky goal that sometimes you need,' said Poyet, with his usual brand of honesty.

'Sometimes you just have to get the result but I'd like to see us play better.' Unbeknownst to everyone – and perhaps himself – he would not see United from the touchline again.

By the end of October, Martin Jol's reign as manager of Tottenham Hotspur was reaching a sorry conclusion. For some time previously, it had been common knowledge that his jacket was hanging on a shaky peg, and manoeuvres in the background at White Hart Lane served only to undermine the Dutchman. Spurs seemed to be waiting for the most opportune moment to sack him. Jol was supported in public by the club's board and their chairman, Daniel Levy, but each vote of confidence was less convincing. It did not help the credibility of Levy and his directors when news broke of an approach made by representatives of Spurs to the Sevilla manager, Juande Ramos, while Jol was still in position. The 51-year-old was the proverbial dead man walking, and his final hours were a farce. English football had developed healthy respect for Jol, and the general feeling was that he deserved better.

The decision to jettison Jol was taken on Thursday, 25 October, hours before Tottenham were due to play Spanish club Getafe in a UEFA Cup group match. Though effectively in possession of their P45s, Jol and Chris Hughton, his first-team coach, took to the dug-out for the fixture, a final hurrah and an apparent attempt to mask the fact that the axe had already beheaded both men. The plan was as ill-conceived as it sounded, and while the match was in progress, word filtered through to the press and the supporters present at White Hart Lane that Jol and Hughton would be gone in the morning. The crowd sang Jol's name relentlessly in a show of appreciation and support that was broadcast live across the country. Sympathy for Jol came from all quarters, and sympathy for Spurs from few. Leeds United's supporters could not really have cared less. But as the match wore on, a second announcement made by Sky Sports caused the city of Leeds to sit up rigid. Juande Ramos would be Jol's replacement, Sky said, confirming the worst-kept secret in English football. Then came the bombshell: his assistant manager would be Gustavo Poyet.

The Uruguayan had been at Thorp Arch on the morning of 25 October, as lively and cheerful a presence as ever he was. His wife and two sons had travelled up to Yorkshire from the south of England, and Poyet was making the final arrangements for them to stay at a nearby hotel before the start of training. Shortly after, a taxi whisked his family away and Poyet retreated into the rear of United's training complex to change into his training kit. Nothing in Poyet's face or behaviour betrayed the fact that change was in the air, and Wise was equally unreadable. The next day – 26 October – would be the first anniversary of his appointment as manager, and he conducted interviews with the media for half an hour, discussing 12 complex months in minute detail. With the anniversary approaching, he had asked Joe Allon, a member of his backroom team, to define the year in a sentence. 'Last year you were Osama Bin Laden,' said Allon. 'Now you're Elvis.' The analogy raised a smile and, to a point, Allon was right. Though never as unpopular as Bin Laden or as revered as Elvis Presley, Wise had succeeded in swaying public opinion in his favour. It was in those interviews that Wise said: 'This could be my last job. It really could. I'm being totally honest.' If he knew then that Poyet was preparing to bail out, Wise's poker face was incredibly convincing.

By the Friday morning, there was no hiding from the issue. With Tottenham's interest plain, Wise spoke with Poyet and found that his assistant was intent on talking to Spurs. United were due to play Millwall at Elland Road in 24 hours' time, and it was agreed that Leeds would prepare for the match without their assistant, in part to maintain the focus of their players and in part because Poyet's departure seemed unstoppable. Spurs were already satisfied that a deal would be done. Poyet stayed away from Thorp Arch during Friday's training session, and did not appear at Elland Road on Saturday afternoon. Leeds and Tottenham were still haggling over compensation for Poyet, and Ken Bates was angry that their intentions had been revealed to the media before him. A fax from White Hart Lane requesting permission to speak to Poyet was sent to Elland Road's general fax number at 11.39 p.m. on 25 October, almost two hours after the conclusion of Spurs' game against Getafe and long after the lights in Leeds had been turned out.

Bates would have preferred a call direct to his mobile, and made his feelings clear. 'The most unfortunate thing about the whole business is the way Tottenham Hotspur have behaved,' said Bates. But business was business, and Poyet's mind was made up. Negotiations continued over the weekend, and compensation was agreed on the evening of 28 October. Sir Alan Sugar, Tottenham's ex-chairman, is believed to have helped to smooth the waters.

Leeds were saddened by the loss of Poyet, but refused to pine. 'He will be missed,' said Alan Thompson, 'but I would think he'd be replaceable.' In the absence of their outgoing assistant, Leeds beat Millwall 4–2 in front of an attendance of more than 30,000, having led by four goals after an hour. Outside Elland Road, supporters of the two clubs confronted each other in a running battle which left numerous bus windows shattered and a number of fans under arrest. Life moved on as swiftly as Poyet. But the celebratory post-match huddle involving United's players was unusually subdued, as if it were lacking a certain *je ne sais quoi*. Something seemed to be missing. For Poyet's services, Leeds would be paid £565,000 by Tottenham. Whether the handsome sum would compensate them fully for the ramifications of his departure was a different matter altogether.

NOVEMBER RAIN

IT WAS NOT IMMEDIATELY OBVIOUS HOW LEEDS UNITED – THEIR players or their supporters – were supposed to react to the sight of Tottenham Hotspur poaching Gustavo Poyet. His desertion was not an insurmountable problem, but it was eminently bad news. Poyet had been half of a partnership to which United's fans had slowly warmed, and a partnership that United's players were finally beginning to understand. If the results produced on the playing field were an accurate translation of the work completed on the club's training ground, the tactics drawn up by Dennis Wise and Poyet were making perfect sense to their squad. Yet Poyet had decided to walk at the most productive point of his relationship with Leeds, and at the first opportunity. It had, until then, been an uphill trudge. But United's victory over Millwall – achieved in spite of their loss of personnel – resulted in the club's appearance in League One's play-off positions for the first time, four points shy of Carlisle United, who were setting the pace at the start of November. If Poyet's departure was the cue for Leeds to derail, the club had missed their initial prompt.

The attitude among their squad was pragmatic, as it was with Wise and Ken Bates. During a telephone conversation with Poyet, United's chairman joked that the respective positions of Leeds and Tottenham, who were toiling in the depths of the Premier League, would allow the Uruguayan and Wise to cross swords with one another in the Championship before long. There were no grudges to be held. Wise's feeling of disappointment was more evident, but his assessment of Poyet's exit was made without bitterness. 'I love Gus to bits,' he said. 'We're good friends and we always will be. I don't blame him – you have to do what is right for yourself.' David Prutton, meanwhile, was even less inclined to place excessive importance on the management structure at Elland Road. 'The only important things are winning games and playing well,' Prutton said. 'They're the only things the fans are bothered about. Players never know too much about what's going on. The only person you answer to is the manager, and he answers to whoever's above him. The day-to-day stuff doesn't change. As a player you can bury your head in the sand and get on with what you're doing. I don't know if that sounds selfish, but it's just the way it is.' The strain on Wise was intense, however, as he considered how best to fill a vacancy which could not stand empty for long.

When Swindon Town made their beeline for Wise, his choice of assistant was based on personal experience rather than reputation alone. Poyet was a well-respected individual, but he was also someone that Wise knew he could work with and rely on. In the wake of his lieutenant's defection, United's manager looked again to his network of contacts and old friends; he contacted Dave Bassett, and requested his help. Bassett could certainly be classed as an old friend. He had celebrated his 63rd birthday two months earlier, and had not worked in a managerial role since his short stint as Southampton's caretaker in 2005. Over the course of almost three decades, he had contributed enough to professional football to merit retirement five times over. But since leaving Southampton, he had kept his hand in the game, operating as a scout for various managers and taking in matches whenever possible. The irresistible drug still had a hold. The role of assistant manager that Wise was offering him did not come without its problems, the biggest of which was the need for him to commute to Leeds from London on a regular basis and commit to rising at 5 a.m. But Bassett said yes. Wise must have known that he would. The two

UNITED WE STAND: Supporters queue round the block for tickets ahead of Leeds United's first home match of the season against Southend United.

IN FULL FLO: Frazer Richardson (left) and Tresor Kandol (arm raised) celebrate Tore Andre Flo's crucial goal against Southend United.

HEAD TO HEAD: Dennis Wise holds a 'frank discussion' with Luton Town head coach and ex-United caretaker John Carver on the first day of September.

JER-MAINE MAN: Beckford celebrates his sublime goal in Leeds United's 2–0 win over Hartlepool.

FIFTEEN POINTS, WHO GIVES A F**K?: Back to zero points on 8 September.

FAREWELL POYET: Alan Thompson and Joe Allon (arm raised) stand in for United's outgoing assistant, but Leeds don't miss a beat as Millwall are routed 4–2.

HONORING A LEGEND: A minute's applause for the late, great Billy Bremner on 8 December.

HONORING A LEGEND: This is followed by a fitting 4–0 hammering of Huddersfield Town, inspired by Jonathan Douglas's brace.

HAPPY NEW YEAR?:
1 January arrives – but
United are left behind
by Oldham Athletic.

DON OVER: Dennis Wise's final home game
– ruined by Doncaster Rovers.

HOMECOMING: Gary McAllister, back at Elland Road.

SPOT ON: A maiden win eludes McAllister but Beckford's penalty earns a point against Nottingham Forest.

FLY IN MACCA'S OINTMENT: Cheltenham win at Elland Road.

THROUGH THE EYE OF A NEEDLE: Beckford hits the net against Walsall.

FREE SPIRIT: Dougie Freedman volleys home against Carlisle as Leeds close in on the play-offs.

NOT A SEAT IN THE HOUSE: A crowd of 38,256 pack Elland Road for the final home game of the season against Gillingham.

LIFELINE: Dougie Freedman scores in the sixth minute of injury time to drag Leeds United back into their play-off semi-final against Carlisle United.

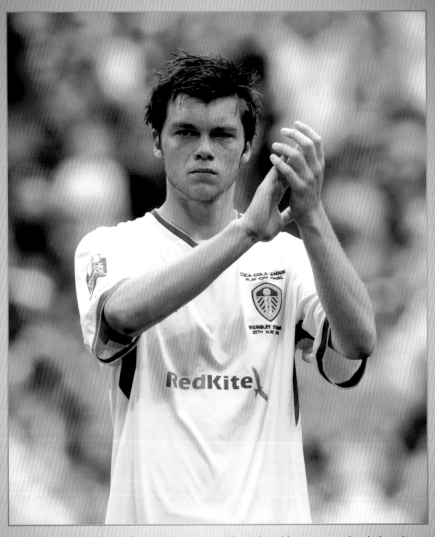

SO NEAR, YET SO FAR: A devastated Jonathan Howson applauds Leeds United's supporters after the club's promotion dream fades at Wembley.

men had come to know each other well in the 1980s at Wimbledon, where Bassett achieved unprecedented success as a manager and Wise fostered his feisty reputation as a player, and they had worked together subsequently – at Leicester City and Southampton. It did not seem unnatural to either of them that Bassett was preparing to take orders from a retired player he had once managed and, at the age of 63, it seemed unlikely that Bassett would demand or desire a more dominant position. His contract was valid only until the end of the season.

Bassett has always enjoyed – and actively maintained – a healthy relationship with the media, and he has a good understanding of how the press work. At his first press conference, he was naturally anxious to reiterate the structure of the hierarchy at Elland Road and to confirm that he was required and happy to be subservient. The cliché of the second fiddle applied. 'Let's get it right,' Bassett said. 'Dennis is the manager and I'll do what he wants. I've not come here to say we've got to do this or we can't do that. Yes, we might have discussions about things we might consider, but Dennis is here and I won't be laying down any foundations. I will conform.' There was no pressure on him to do anything more. Before his appointment, United had bulldozed 11 clubs and completed 13 league matches without defeat, and Bassett was being asked to help maintain a watertight vessel. 'The club is buzzing, which is nothing to do with me,' he admitted, though not without the sober reflection of how demanding it would be to sustain the standards set by the managerial partnership of Wise and Poyet. Bassett and his predecessor were different men with different personalities, and contrasting ideas of how football should be played. Poyet was seen as the flamboyant entertainer, Bassett the long-ball merchant who had graduated from the old school of English tacticians. Wise believed the latter's reputation for an overtly direct philosophy was unfair, but from the outset it was clear that Bassett would be damned by public opinion. United's promotion was bound to be seen as the result of foundations laid with the help of Poyet, but their failure to climb out of League One would leave supporters thinking back to the day of Tottenham's approach and asking whether their season was irreparably damaged at that juncture. Football, said

Bassett dismissively, has always been thus. 'There's going to be the odd hiccup,' he said. 'It would be a tremendous feat if we could get through the season without losing a game, but Dennis is not stupid enough to think there won't be a setback around the corner. It's how we respond to it that's important. If some people think that if Leeds United lose on Saturday it's down to me, that's nonsense. As Dennis said, had Leeds lost (to Millwall), it wasn't down to Gus Poyet.' Nevertheless, it would have suited Bassett better had fate allowed his first game to pass with no more than a modicum of attention.

The fixture list for 3 November had, by chance, thrown together Leeds and Carlisle in what represented the most intriguing League One contest of the weekend. No team other than Leeds had been more consistent than Carlisle during the first three months of the season, but the Cumbrian club had been fallible enough to allow Wise's players to creep to within four points of themselves and the summit of the division. Carlisle were desperate to slow the pace of Elland Road's bandwagon, but Wise saw huge potential in the game at Brunton Park; a game which, with the help of favourable results across the country, could elevate his side into one of League One's top two positions, another compelling step back from the precipice his squad had been pushed towards by the Football League. Bassett was forced to miss training on the morning before the game in Cumbria by a commitment made before his appointment at Elland Road, but he appeared as promised at Brunton Park, bedecked in a short leather jacket and visibly comfortable with the view from the touchline. Also present in United's dug-out was John Gannon, another of Bassett's former players at Wimbledon who had been recruited that week as Wise's first-team coach. The absence of Poyet, who had dominated the technical area with his energetic display of expressive mannerisms, still felt peculiar, but Wise sought safety in greater numbers with Bassett and Gannon on either side of him.

For an hour and a minute, their introduction was as passive as it could possibly have been. By the end of the season Brunton Park would become statistically the most unforgiving stadium for away teams in League One, with a record which surpassed that of Elland Road, but through two-thirds of their game against Leeds, the division's leaders looked like impostors. Jermaine Beckford separated the teams with a tidy finish in the 28th minute, slipping a shot past goalkeeper Keiren Westwood after finding himself in the path of a deflected strike from Jonathan Douglas, and a single goal was the least that United deserved at half-time. An earlier header from Sebastien Carole had been cleared off the line, and Westwood made two alert saves to repel shots from Douglas and Jamie Clapham, the full-back loaned to Leeds by Wolverhampton Wanderers. Of more significance, though, was the simple catch that Westwood was allowed to make by Carole's weak shot at the start of the second half, a close-range chance that the French winger ought to have taken. For the entirety of the contest that preceded Carole's opportunity, Carlisle had depicted themselves as league leaders by default, a side whose entertaining spurt would come to be viewed as nothing more. But Bassett was familiar with Carlisle's manager, John Ward, and his pre-match description of Ward as 'a wily old boy' before kick-off proved astute. Carlisle had been playing possum, or at the very least waiting to feel a rocket fly up a certain orifice, and the jolt was delivered in the form of splendid strike from Simon Hackney in the 61st minute, which arced away from Casper Ankergren and swept at speed inside the goalkeeper's right-hand post. In an instant, United's equilibrium was displaced. Joe Garner flicked a header beyond Ankergren in the absence of any markers to give Carlisle a 2–1 lead with 20 minutes left, and a curling finish from Marc Bridge-Wilkinson in injury time removed the remaining tinge of doubt that United's first league defeat of the season was in the offing. The ease with which Bridge-Wilkinson waltzed into the box after collecting a short corner spoke of exhaustion in the legs of Wise's players and an acceptance that they had, for once, been bettered. Their draws with Gillingham and Leyton Orient had been excusable, results that could conceivably have been more rewarding, but the 3–1 defeat to Carlisle United was an outcome that brought a forthright appraisal from Wise. 'Sometimes you need a wake-up call,' he said. 'We'd not lost in 13, but it's not going to be handed to you on a plate either. It was their day.' That realisation was hard to take after three months of near-flawless results.

By the team coach, Tresor Kandol described the atmosphere inside the dressing room as 'like a funeral', and Andrew Hughes promised that he and his team-mates would go home and 'beat ourselves up'. 'If you don't do that when you lose games then there's something seriously wrong,' he admitted. Hughes is a player who says what he means, and it was easy to imagine the midfielder taking a baseball bat to himself in his back garden until his arms could no long swing, at which point he would ask his next-door neighbour to finish the job. The loss at Brunton Park had hurt. And although an immediate Tuesday night fixture was giving Wise a welcome distraction, the location of their next match – in Bournemouth, 330 miles south of Carlisle – was not ideal.

United's invitation to Dean Court on 6 November was less cordial than it might have been. The most recent visit made by Leeds to the Dorset town had taken place in 1990, but the locals had long enough memories to remember the carnage that had ensued over the course of a fraught and violent bank holiday weekend. Under Howard Wilkinson, United's promotion to the old first division was guaranteed by their 1–0 win in Bournemouth on 5 May 1990, the final day of the Division Two season. In the aftermath of the victory, the club's supporters ran riot, leading to more than 100 arrests, 12 injured police officers and thousands of pounds' worth of damage to property. It is as close as that part of the south coast has come to a war zone since the Nazis threatened the British shores, and Bournemouth – as a club and a town – were relieved to see the back of Leeds. They were also content to have avoided a reunion in the 17 years since. But United's relegation from the Championship, which in turn confirmed that they would once again share a division with Bournemouth, caused immediate concern in the resort. Bournemouth wrote immediately to the Football League to request a midweek game against Leeds, an appeal supported by the local police, who believed an evening kick-off on a Tuesday night would limit the threat of disorder. Stuart Katon, a superintendent with the Dorset constabulary, was quoted as saying: 'Every team in the division is going to be looking at the Leeds fixture and anticipating problems with fans. We have the aggravating factor of what happened here 17 years ago. There are people with long memories, and we have already started monitoring the Internet as part of our intelligence. There was carnage in the town in 1990 and we should be mindful of that, even though time has passed.' So it was that Bournemouth's request met with the approval of the Football League, and United were required to step from Leeds to Carlisle and then back towards the southern-most reaches of England, all in the space of 72 hours.

The schedule was not conducive to cultivating a primed and refreshed squad but Wise was impervious to excuses. Had Leeds beaten Carlisle or taken a point from Brunton Park, he might have enjoyed the opportunity to snap at the Football League and their supposedly random fixture computer, but the defeat in Cumbria relegated that argument to the level of petty squabbles. It mattered less than the reality of a loss which proved to the rest of the division that Leeds were beatable. Wise had long feared what he called 'the kick' – the point at which United's runaway train struck a brick wall – and a long-term loss of momentum would come at a high price. The effect of their defeat at Brunton Park had been to drop Leeds three places down League One, seven points away from the top of the division, and the aftermath of results like that in Carlisle were when United's 15-point penalty was at its most debilitating. 'The defeat at Carlisle hurt all of us,' Wise said. 'I want to get a result as soon as we can, and I don't want this to go for too long. We'll pick ourselves up, dust ourselves down and do what we've been doing for the last 13 games.'

As visibly disheartened as they were by their failure, Wise could see that his players were being hyper-critical of themselves. He was not prepared to join in. Viewed in isolation, Carlisle had accurately identified and exploited the points of weakness in United's squad; but in the grand scheme of the season, it was merely an isolated result. The American author, F. Scott Fitzgerald, once remarked about the danger of confusing a single defeat with a final defeat, and Wise was not about to entertain thoughts of the latter. Bournemouth, after all, had failed to win any of their seven home matches prior to the visit of Leeds.

Ultimately, the gravest fears of all concerned were dispelled in Dorset. Two goals from Tresor Kandol – a tap-in after four minutes and a bouncing header in the 86th – gave Wise a trouble-free evening, while outside Dean Court the ranks of police were spared from the conflict they had expected. The event passed off peacefully, and much as the form book suggested it would. Kandol celebrated his second goal with a familiar back-flip, and the change in his demeanour from the days when negativity and cat-calls stalked him was striking. He was, on that night, the club's leading scorer, with eight goals to his name. 'When you're desperate to prove a point, it can have a negative effect on you,' Kandol said. 'That might have happened with me. But things can turn around any day and when I came into this season I thought: "I want to make this happen." I spoke to the gaffer at the start of the summer and he made it clear that I was in his plans, but I have to admit that I hadn't shown many of the reasons why he brought me here in the first place. I'm in a much better frame of mind now.' In between Kandol's strikes, a curling finish produced by Sebastien Carole put the game beyond the reach of a Bournemouth side who had flirted briefly with a draw after equalising through Jem Karacan in the first half. Karacan's fierce shot from 20 yards was the pick of the goals, but it achieved no more than preventing Casper Ankergren from preserving a clean sheet. To ruin Bournemouth's night further, their experienced striker Lee Bradbury was dismissed in the 62nd minute after swinging an arm with intent towards Matt Heath. Wise saw fit to acknowledge referee Steve Bennett's decision, describing him as 'a fantastic referee' in an unusual display of esteem for officialdom, but he was more concerned with highlighting his team's power of recovery. 'We had a poor result at the weekend, and it was a question of what the players were going to do about it,' he said. The resumption of normal service had been immediate, and it needed to be. The arrival of the FA Cup would see to it that United's next league fixture would not fall for another 11 days, and Wise had been conscious of the possibility that doubts would fester during that interval.

* * *

The FA Cup is arguably the trophy which came to define Wise's playing career. He won the trophy three times – once with Wimbledon and twice with Chelsea – and was a losing finalist twice, most recently while player-manager at Millwall. The east London club had never reached the final before and had not been semi-finalists since 1937, but their progression in 2004 was reason enough to believe that Leeds United could offer more to the competition in 2007 than the token involvement of so many lower-league clubs. Leeds have been drawn away to Hereford United in the first round, and Sky's decision to televise the match at Edgar Street saw the tie staged on Friday, 9 November. It was a draw that Leeds were satisfied with, and though Hereford's form in League Two had been worthy of praise, Wise was weighed down by his order of preference. Leeds were unquestionably good enough to negotiate the first two rounds, but how damaging would it be to supplement their league fixtures with additional cup ties? Would the club welcome a third-round game at the beginning of January and a fourth-round fixture at the end of the same month? And, more crucially, was his squad strong enough to cope? Financially, the FA Cup carried enough incentive but Wise would receive no thanks if the acquisition of pound notes came at the expense of promotion. What he had certainly planned to avoid was a replay with Hereford but a strong Leeds team were held to a goalless draw at Edgar Street, on a night when Wise served the first leg of the three-match touchline ban he had incurred following his verbal scuffle with Danny McDermid at Gillingham. United's line-up would have been virtually full strength had Frazer Richardson and David Prutton not succumbed to illness shortly before kick-off, but the stalemate suggested to Wise that the competition might prove to be a hindrance. Eleven days later, Hereford arrived at Elland Road and took advantage of a weakened Leeds team which failed to perform in every area of the field. Lionel Ainsworth's goal in the third minute was not quite Ronnie Radford reincarnated, but Hereford's victory was highly creditable. Following on from United's 2–1 defeat to Bury in the quarter-finals of the Johnstone's Paint Trophy on 13 November, it ensured that Leeds were absent from every knockout competition they had entered before Christmas. Wise felt justified in prioritising promotion, but could not deny that the club's lack of progression in the FA Cup had reflected poorly on him and his players. 'I can't fault what they've done so far this season,' he said. 'I've changed the team, so maybe it's down to me – it's my fault really. But you think the fringe players will be well capable of getting us through against Hereford. That's partly my blame, I'd say, and partly theirs as well. It's my fault for not putting out a stronger team than I could have done, but a lot of players have played a lot of games. I've been asking a lot of these lads and it's hit us.'

To Wise's relief, and in his defence, his single-minded dedication to United's league matches was justified by a 2–1 victory over his former club Swindon Town, four days after their loss to Bury and three before Hereford's hatchet job at Elland Road. Wise's affinity to Swindon was natural but, on account of his brief spell as the club's manager, it was also slight. He had left behind a team which was conveniently placed in League Two, and for that Swindon's supporters had reason to be grateful. But the credit for the club's subsequent promotion was due largely to his successor, Paul Sturrock, who added 54 points to the 31 accrued by Wise. Sturrock was adept at operating in the lower leagues and, aside from a period at Southampton which had gone south as quickly as Gus Poyet, his track record was excellent. His management allowed Plymouth to thrive, and the Scot was responsible for clearing Sheffield Wednesday's passage from the obscurity of League One. The question of how far Swindon would have travelled under Sturrock was never answered, and 10 days after their match at Elland Road, he walked out of the County Ground to return to Home Park, a stadium which seemed to be something of a spiritual home for him. Financial issues at Swindon, and the drawn-out negotiations surrounding a takeover of the club, made the offer which came to him from Plymouth extremely enticing, but Sturrock's history meant he would inevitably tease a competitive performance from the players available to him during Swindon's game in Leeds. His squad ran United reasonably close but – with utter predictability – found themselves beaten by a head at the finishing line. Jermaine Beckford, United's anointed penalty-taker, tucked away an opportunity from the spot in the first half after a cross from David Prutton struck the arm of Hasney Aljofree, and though Lee Peacock brought the teams level with an easy finish two minutes after half-time, there was nothing surprising about the sight of Tresor Kandol feeding Beckford, who lashed a shot past Peter Brezovan in Swindon's goal. Troubled in patches but victorious nonetheless, it was what the Americans would call a regulation victory. Sturrock saw fit to complain about his squad, which was being stretched to the point where it might snap, but talk of his tribulations did not sit well with Wise. 'Please stop crying, Paul,' he said, with all the compassion that Sturrock would have expected. 'We've been in the same situation ourselves. It's how you deal with it that counts.' Wise also joked about quotes apportioned to Sturrock by a national newspaper, claiming Swindon were a club with more potential than Leeds. Had you been drinking, Wise asked rhetorically. 'I think some national journalist had a bit of journalistic licence,' replied Sturrock. 'I can assure Dennis that I wasn't drinking. It was the journalist that was drinking.' The two men shared a beer nonetheless and then went their separate ways, Sturrock with words of encouragement ringing in his ears. 'He has some decent players who caused us problems,' said Wise. 'I'm sure they'll do well in this league.' The prediction became hypothetical when Sturrock bowed out of Swindon less than a fortnight later.

By now out of the habit of defending himself, the win gave Wise an adequate stick with which to beat back questions over United's FA Cup defeat to Hereford. Leeds were fourth in the league table, with only two points between themselves and Carlisle, who were intent on racing from the front. A place in the second round of the FA Cup was not a prize that Wise would have taken at the expense or sacrifice of what he considered to be his sole aim. On the eve of the season, he and his coaches had predicted that United would reach the play-off positions by March if their strategy went to plan; it was now conceivable that they would reach the top of the division by the first day of December. Even the bookmakers were sold. 'Leeds were a bit of an unknown quantity at the start of the season,' said one. 'You half-suspected that they might do something but it wasn't the biggest of risks to offer them about at a decent price for promotion. It's hardly worth backing them for that now because the odds are so short. We won't take any chances on Leeds.' The players could spot a potential liability when they saw one, and Leeds were threatening to cost them heavily. They certainly expected to pay out to the hordes of punters who were lumping on Wise's players to beat Cheltenham Town at Whaddon Road on the final weekend of November.

The Gloucestershire town of Cheltenham is most famous for its annual National Hunt racing festival, an event of vast popularity which tempts customers to travel in droves from across Great Britain and Ireland. The local police are adept at managing the glut of traffic which floods Cheltenham's network of roads for four days every year, but they were less enamoured by the thought of 1,805 Leeds United supporters descending on their patch en masse. The match at Whaddon Road was originally scheduled for Saturday, 24 November, a date which had also been set aside for the turning on of Cheltenham's Christmas lights. The events appeared unconnected in terms of security, and the request from the police to delay the match until the Sunday afternoon for reasons of safety seemed tenuous as best. It was, however, accepted; as their supporters would come to discover, there is not a police force in England that believes in being too careful when Leeds United are in town. Wise, understandably, was impassive. He would play any time, anywhere against a club whose punches lacked sting. In their 16 previous matches, the results strung together by Cheltenham would have been insufficient to wipe out United's 15-point penalty.

Wise had only one concern – the loss of his goalkeeper, Casper Ankergren. The Dane had suffered a deep cut to his knee during the FA Cup defeat to Hereford, and Ankergren's injury was as galling to Wise as the result itself. Ankergren missed his first league match of the season at Whaddon Road and his replacement, David Lucas, had the misfortune of contributing to the goal which conjured the most unexpected of results. Lucas was an experienced keeper with prior spells at Sheffield Wednesday and Preston North End on his CV, and Wise had recruited him as cover for Ankergren on a short-term contract in September. Before the game in Cheltenham, he had played three times – twice in the Johnstone's Paint Trophy and once as a substitute for Ankergren in United's FA Cup replay. His situation had required patience, and Lucas could have been forgiven for feeling a touch of *schadenfreude* on hearing the news that a more meaningful opportunity was coming his way. Ankergren had been impossible to displace, but he was not invulnerable, as the studs which tore his flesh showed. Wise was happy to turn to Lucas; it was, after all, why the keeper was there. And while the 1–0 defeat which befell United could be blamed in part on the 30-year-old Lancastrian, it was unfair to overlook the reality of a game which seemed destined to reward Cheltenham in some way.

It was, by full-time, the first league match in which Leeds had failed to score, but not for the want of trying. Jermaine Beckford sent one volley careering over the crossbar after a neat piece of skill, and drove another against the frame of the goal shortly before half-time. His third opportunity, from six yards out, sailed into the crowd in the 66th minute, and when his reactive header from Jonathan Douglas's deflected free-kick cushioned the ball into the net 11 minutes later, an offside flag was raised as quickly as his celebration began. A frustrated Wise began to examine Cheltenham tail, fearing that a sharp sting might be hidden beneath their unflattering exterior. His suspicion was realised. With four minutes remaining, a long throw from Lucas fell short of its target, and Dean Sinclair's lobbed pass towards the box dropped into unguarded territory between United's goalkeeper and his defence. Lucas arrived quickly at the edge of his area but scuffed a weak punch towards Steven Gillespie, who chipped his instinctive reply with interest over Lucas' head and into an empty net. Goals at the death had defined and constructed United's season until then, but Wise retched at the taste of his own medicine. It did not help his mood to see Cheltenham scoring with their sole opportunity of note. 'To dominate a game so much and then lose it in the final minutes is so frustrating,' he said. 'They had about two shots – one ended up in the back of the net, the other one went about 200 yards over the stand.' Driven down to fifth in the table, Wise's enmity towards the Football League returned with vigour. 'I don't think I'll ever forget what's happened. We could be 10 points clear at the top and we wouldn't be so down after being beaten by Cheltenham. Unfortunately, we're five points adrift of the top position and that's a big difference. We need a big total.'

November, on reflection, had been a good month to see the back of. A change of assistants and two victories from seven matches provided a warning of possible turbulence ahead. The defeats at Carlisle and Cheltenham summed up a period of partial fatigue; they also denied Wise the opportunity to curry favour by establishing Leeds as League One's leaders when Port Vale made their arrival at Elland Road. Ken Bates had quietly hoped that United's path to the summit would be completed with that particular fixture, providing what he imagined to be the prefect present on 4 December, the night of his 76th birthday.

9

CHAIRMAN

AT THE END OF THE FIRST WEEK IN WHICH HE COULD legitimately call himself Leeds United's chairman – 27 January 2005 – Ken Bates opened his door to the inquisitive wolves on the threshold of Elland Road. A pensioner in years if not in status, Bates agreed to stage a supporters' forum in the stadium's banqueting suite to address the many questions raised by his sudden acquisition of the club at the age of 74. It was estimated that the sale of Leeds United to Bates and the company he represented, The Forward Sports Fund (FSF), by outgoing chairman Gerald Krasner and his board had taken as little as 72 hours to complete, an agreement reached in what Krasner believed was the nick of time. Leeds, it was claimed, were as little as two days from appointing administrators with the expectation that the club would be declared insolvent. The transfer of a majority shareholding to FSF averted that threat, though not indefinitely as it would later transpire. But the club's supporters were unsure whether this particular package constituted the rescue of Leeds United or another step towards the gallows. Images of the most distinctive beard in football next to United's crest created an uneasy feeling and some pressing doubts. The city of Leeds was not so backwards as to insist on Yorkshire people for a Yorkshire club, but Bates appeared so far removed from the county's ethos as to be Lancastrian. Above all, few could understand why a man pushing 75 had any interested in unpicking the tangled web that was Leeds United.

The forum was called for 7 p.m., and Bates arrived early. Bedecked in a plain blue suit when body armour might have been more appropriate, he jousted enthusiastically with the crowd present in a way that, with hindsight, outlined the eccentric and incomparable stewardship which would follow. With his wife Suzannah to his right and Krasner to his left – in the days when the two men saw eye-to-eye – Bates ran the show with confidence and efficiency, unflustered by the situation he was in. His opening gambit came with the order of 'mobile phones off, thank you', followed later by the chiding of a skinhead whose musical ringtone interrupted proceedings. 'Are you going to give us a cabaret?' he asked. 'Oh, and get your hair cut.' It was classic Bates – a joke in one hand, a hammer in the other, and a single mind thrust in between. The average owner would have approached the forum with the intention of feathering his nest among those who seemed to matter most; Bates, in contrast, was the wolf in sheep's clothing who took control of the lion's den. He tangled readily with the fans whose questions were ponderous and talked over those unwilling to accept his points. But the devil was in the detail, as it always tends to be. Leeds United were projecting an annual loss of £6 million, the equivalent of £120,000 per week; season ticket prices were therefore bound to rise. 'We won't tell you what we want to do,' said Bates with brutal honesty. 'We'll do it and then tell you what we've done.' The standing ovation he received could not drown out the reverberations of that final, telling comment.

Bates' performance in the unremarkable surroundings of Elland Road's banqueting suite was a full-frontal display of his personality. Some of the audience were convinced by his positive outlook, while others were amused by the realisation that he was truly as dogmatic as his legend suggested. If nothing else, he had avoided the accusation that the image portrayed to his new footballing family was in any way fraudulent. This was Bates as he understood himself, and how Leeds United's supporters would come to know him in the weeks, months and years that followed. It was and is a fascinating relationship which defies description and, on occasions, sense. As the old proverb says, marrying is easy. It's the housework that's hard.

Whether by design or default – default being the monopoly of attention that Leeds United's league results were commanding – Bates kept an unusually low profile through the first half of the 2007–08 season. As a resident of Monaco, the tax haven which had become home to him and his wife, his freedom to roam in Leeds was automatically restricted by income tax laws which allowed Bates to be classed as a non-resident on the understanding that he spent no more than 90 days annually in the United Kingdom. The convoluted and prolonged process of United's administration – extended further by the time taken to secure the Football League's co-operation – had swallowed up a large portion of his allowance, and Bates was present at fewer home matches during the initial months of the season than might otherwise have been the case. His newspaper appearances were likewise relatively minimal, and his unreserved opinions were sought less frequently than they had been during an epic and destructive summer. The matchday programme at Elland Road continued to speak his mind in the boldest possible terms, but United's agenda no longer centred around Bates. His management team and the club's players had become the focus of attention, deservedly so and not before time. Even Bates would have conceded that his dealings – the club's off-field dealings – were a topic of conversation which ignored too easily Leeds United's primary purpose as a professional sporting entity. Wise had fought his fight with the supporters and apparently settled their differences. A more uneasy truce existed with Bates, who had tried the patience of many either directly or indirectly for the duration of a painfully long close-season. However intentional his period of quiet was, it seemed perfectly judged. Leeds United as a club were breeding optimism. Debates involving their chairman tended to cloud the issue.

The question so prevalent before the supporters' forum – the 'why' of Bates' desire for frontline duty at Elland Road – was every bit as pertinent while the club's insolvency crisis was at its height. Arriving with a clean slate in 2005 was a challenge in itself, but stretching his tenure beyond the stage where his relationship with the supporters seemed to be broken, and fighting so hard to ensure that extension, was less understandable. During a pre-season friendly at Burnley in July 2007, the occupied terraces at Turf Moor echoed to the refrain of 'shoes off, if you hate Ken Bates', a song of slightly bizarre lyrics which made its point nonetheless. The mood was militant and uncompromising. What motive persuaded Bates against walking away? Some said money, a claim Bates rejected utterly. His boast from the start of his tenure was that he had 'never taken a penny out of Leeds' and had never demanded a salary for the hours he worked. 'It's taken time,' he told the *Yorkshire Evening Post*, immediately after United's defeat in the 2006 Championship play-off final, 'but we've finally got rid of all the hangers-on, the free-loaders and the time-wasters. This place was full of them.' His wife Suzannah – unquestionably Bates' most loyal supporter – had a different explanation. 'The thing about Ken,' she once said, 'is that he won't let something go until it succeeds. That's why he's still here.'

Bates, in any case, was not remotely scared of confrontation and was no slave to popularity. That, he claimed, was Peter Ridsdale's game. A perfect demonstration of his faith in his own judgement came on the day that Wise was presented to the media in his new capacity as United's manager. Wise's arrival at Elland Road was as surprising as Bates' own introduction had been, and created even more suspicion. 'If you don't like it,' Bates said, grabbing the ears of grumbling fans, 'you can go and support someone else.' Bullish his comments may have been, but tactful they were not. Among their supporters, Leeds possess followers of seriously long service, men and women whose knowledge of United and relationship with the club is more detailed and far-reaching than that of Bates. If some of their number disliked the idea of Wise as manager, that was their prerogative, and they paid in spades for the right to express it. Yet Bates had a valid point, obscured slightly by the brash terms he employed. Football clubs rarely sought the advice or permission of their fanbase before naming a new manager (Luton Town, unusually, had done exactly that in the lead-up to their selection of Mike Newell in 2003, asking supporters to take part in a telephone vote) and, as Gordon Strachan once put it when asked whether his team selection at Celtic should reflect the opinions of the club's fans, 'it's not a popularity poll; it's not like *The X-Factor*'. If by ordering certain individuals to go forth and multiply Bates was suggesting that Wise deserved a fair and reasonable chance to make his job work, United's chairman was unquestionably right. It was simply not his style to say so in such bland and unimaginative terms.

The first meaningful test of Bates' relationship with the city of Leeds came little more than two months into his tenure, after a honeymoon which had progressed reasonably peacefully. On April Fools' Day of 2005, details of season-ticket prices for United's second year in the Championship began dropping through letterboxes in the city and the country. The date was coincidental, and Bates made that point in his own authoritative style to a radio interviewer who asked him subsequently whether the prices were a well-timed joke. The cost of season tickets had not remained static; on the contrary, it had careered through the roof. Individual mark-ups were as high as 100 per cent, and passes for the East Stand and the John Charles West Stand, the terraces which ran along the length of the Elland Road pitch, started at £640 for adult renewals and £680 for new applicants. In no area of Elland Road was it possible to buy an adult season ticket for cheaper than £450. In Premier League terms – and in comparison to several Premier League clubs – the prices appeared incredibly hefty. In the Championship, they were virtually impossible to justify beyond the explanation that Leeds United's past excesses had made the increases necessary. It was not a line the public were prepared to swallow. Punished once by a financial strategy which wrecked a club of Champions League standard with outrageous ease, the supporters believed they were bearing the cost of that damage for a second time. Bates was unrepentant. 'If people want a team that is good enough to reach the Premiership, it has to be paid for,' he argued. 'We're losing £120,000 a week and that has to stop. The prices have been carefully worked out and I think most supporters will understand what we're doing. The alternative is to have a second-division team at Elland Road.' By the spring of 2007, United's fans would have the worst of both worlds – prices befitting of the Premier League and a football club heading for England's third tier – but the skirmish over season-ticket charges and Bates' resilience to criticism was an ample demonstration of his determination not to rule by committee, or at least not by one which took excessive heed of the voice of the fans. United relented slightly and revised their payment scheme by allowing staggered and interest-free instalments to help with the challenge of funding their tickets, but it was not a major concession. Bates' financial strategy had been laid out with those elevated charges in mind and was non-negotiable. Matchday tickets also increased in price, to as much as £36 for Category A fixtures during the season when Leeds were relegated from the Championship. How financially successful the changes were is for Bates to say, but the revelation of the club's £35 million debt suggested their accounts were already in a dire state when the rises were announced. What cannot be denied is that the increased prices coincided with a noticeable drop in crowds, a decrease which seemed too great to be coincidental. Some 671,769 spectators passed through the turnstiles of Elland Road during United's 23 home matches between August 2004 and May 2005, an average gate of 29,207. Over the same period 12 months later, those figures had dropped to 514,159 and 22,354 respectively. The statistics were, in truth, commendable for the Championship but worrying nonetheless, and in real terms around 10,000 fewer spectators attended each fixture during the 2006–07 season than had done so in the months before the revision of ticket prices. Sunderland, whose season-ticket charges had been frozen for several years running, were more in tune with the thoughts of United's supporters. A spokesman for the Wearside club told the *Yorkshire Evening Post*: 'We have a financial plan like everyone else but we also have to be mindful of the economic circumstances of the surrounding area. Sunderland isn't the richest place in England and the bottom line is that supporters have to be able to afford season tickets.' Bates might have countered by pointing out that Leeds United weren't the richest club in England, and that the end would justify his means. It took relegation to League One for the upward trend of season-ticket prices at Elland Road to finally reverse.

Sunderland, meanwhile, recently announced their own increases of as much as 12 per cent, no longer impervious to financial pressure.

How much the prospect of League One worried or unnerved Bates is difficult to gauge. As a rule of business, he never flinches. I met him in his office at Elland Road two days after United's fateful 1–1 draw with Ipswich Town to discuss what relegation could mean, both immediately and hypothetically – the material issues being financial, and the long-term doubts more concerned with the possibility of Leeds being lost in the wilderness. A short while later, the walls around his desk were knocked down during a project of redevelopment of the administrative area of the stadium's East Stand, a suitable metaphor for a club where the walls threatened to cave in repeatedly during the summer. Over a cup of what looked like herbal tea, he dealt readily and ruthlessly with the idea that United's league position was a questionable reflection of his stewardship, or that it might represent the end of his particular line. He was not enamoured either with the insinuation that the nine months behind Leeds had irreparably damaged the club. 'Actually, I'm very bullish,' he said. 'In football, the game's full of ups and downs. Here's food for thought. Look at some of the clubs in the Premiership – Middlesbrough, Bolton, Wigan, Sheffield United, Manchester City, Aston Villa, Portsmouth, Fulham. They've all been in the third and fourth divisions. Let me tell you this much. We've been overwhelmed by faxes and emails, all saying 100 per cent that they want me, Wise and Gus (Poyet) to stay next season. They're saying: "You're the right people and you're going to get us back where we should be."' I did not doubt that Bates was receiving messages of support – a large pile of printed emails sat in front of him as he spoke, a hard copy of indisputable evidence – but it was equally clear that sections of United's support were losing faith in his regime. Those who had doubted Bates from the outset felt vindicated; those who had trusted him felt somewhat betrayed. All had an idea of where they felt the buck should stop. 'Ridsdale is trying to distance himself from this again,' said Bates in defence of himself. 'But the fact is that he got the club in the mess that it's in. Trevor Birch [United's former chief executive] didn't do a great deal and didn't tackle the underlying problems. Nor did Gerald Krasner's mob. They pushed things around and did deals, but they didn't tackle the fact we were spending too much money. We've done that and it will be the most important chapter in all this.' Unfortunately for Bates, financial promises emanating from Elland Road created a sense of *déjà vu*. Heard it all before, people would say.

A feeling existed in Leeds that Bates would not survive relegation, that the intolerance of a despondent city would force the issue of his continuing reign at Elland Road. The debate was never opened, at least not by Bates. He stood firm and he stood fast. In fairness to him, that rigid stance was his prerogative. For more than two years, he had taken responsibility for the day-to-day operations of Leeds United, assisted by his selected team of directors and staff. There were no exact or accessible figures detailing how much money he or the investors behind him had provided the club with during that period of time, but it was unfair, and no doubt inaccurate, to suggest that Bates had added nothing of value in terms of finance. When KPMG's bidding process for the ownership of the club reached its height in July, I found one club chairman privately but robustly defending Bates' tight grip on Elland Road. 'Do you honestly expect him to just walk away?' he asked. 'I can't say precisely how much money Bates has put into Leeds, but the answer is some. No one would ever suggest that a man who has invested in a more conventional business should cut his losses without a second thought, but people think it's fair to argue that Bates should piss off and leave the club for somebody else to pick up on the cheap. It's absolutely ridiculous. There's potentially a lot of money to be made out of Leeds in the future and the other bidders are in line for a bargain. But they haven't been running the club for the last two years – Bates has. He's sacrificed the time and the money.' Simon Morris, one of Bates' most prominent and bitter rivals for possession of Leeds United, accused United's chairman of 'hanging on for dear life', but Bates rarely gave that impression. It was highly unusual for him to sound despondent or defeatist, even though the intensity of the schedule he maintained through the summer was exhausting. He routinely described Morris and other would-be owners as 'chancers', dismissing them as counterfeit models of a genuine football club chairman.

Though thoroughly satisfied with his tenure, Bates was not deaf to criticism and was not afraid to address it as often as was necessary. After United's 4–0 defeat to Stoke City on 14 October 2006 – a result and a performance which reeked of a rotten dressing room – a small crowd of supporters approached Bates as he headed for his car outside Elland Road. All made the same demand: tell us what the hell is going on. Bates could not have been more transparent, describing the squad as 'the shit we've got' in a conversation recorded quietly on the mobile phone of a nearby fan. The subsequent sale of the video to a Sunday newspaper was something of a cheap shot – Bates later described the supporter responsible as 'Judas' – but it did make the point that he was aware of the troubling extent of the club's problems. At the start of the season, he had pushed the idea that the squad in Kevin Blackwell's possession had the makings of a 'strong team'. Three months later, he was turning to Wise and crossing his fingers that United had the legs to stay clear of relegation. But there were times when he grew tired of the sniping from the terraces. In a set of his ever-gripping matchday programme notes later that season, his abrasive tendencies emerged once more. 'Nobody has been more open and honest with the fans than me,' he wrote. 'You may not like what you read but it is the truth. When I hear the moans and groans, at the age of 75, it would be easy to say f-off to the lot of you and take the advice of some so-called fan to return to Monte Carlo. Believe me, if I did that you would have no club – there are no rich investors – just chancers. However, I will complete the task I took on and we will succeed in due course.' A timescale for that success was sensibly omitted. United by then were three-quarters of the way down the slope to League One.

Bates knew well enough that criticism en masse was a football chairman's penance. As the former owner of Chelsea, and Wigan Athletic and Oldham Athletic before them, he had learned quickly that the heroes of supporters reside in the dressing room. Targets of their frustrations are more likely to sit in the boardroom. There were few bedroom walls in England plastered with posters of football club chairmen. It seemed to me that his verbal exchanges with United's fanbase were not necessarily driven by a belief that supporters are not worth an opinion. It is perhaps truer to say that Bates made a point of giving as good as he got. At the supporters' forum in the first week of his chairmanship, Bates began proceedings by openly inviting searching comments towards himself. 'Just make sure you can take them in return,' he added, with a twinkle in his eye. It represented the drawing of battle lines which have remained in place ever since. How far they would have shifted had Bates lived in Leeds and mixed with the populace on a daily basis is less certain but he is not backwards in the coming forwards. When supporters wrote to him complaining about the contentious rise in season-ticket prices, he would reply by phoning them directly to discuss the situation at length. It was not the case that the apartment Bates owned in Monaco provided him with a hiding place; it was simply where United's chairman chose to live. He attended few away fixtures – which is to say virtually none – but would only miss home matches when circumstances demanded it. More often than not, he would be present at the front of Elland Road's directors' box, his arms perched on the blue iron bar in front of him and his white hair blowing in the breeze. In his absence, his programme notes spoke for him.

His personal two-page spread is the highlight of Leeds United's matchday publication. Comical at times, curious at others and – when necessary – deadly serious, they are surely the only chairman's column in England to have touched on the issue of Beijing hosting the 2008 Olympics (the connection was made in relation to the cost of ferrying the Olympic flame through London and managing pro-Tibetan protests in the capital. Bates takes a dislike to those who argue that football clubs should bear the cost of policing the streets around their stadiums when matches are in progress. Patrolling the Queen's Highway, as Bates puts it, is currently the financial responsibility of the taxpayer, a situation which certain politicians would seek to alter, though not if Bates has anything to do with it). What can seem like a scattergun is actually more akin to a carefully aimed rifle, with shots fired in the direction he intended. On more than one occasion, Leeds City Council bore the brunt of his dissatisfaction for refusing to assist his plans to develop a complex at Elland Road in a similar vein to Chelsea Village, built in his time as chairman at Stamford Bridge (Bates also liked the idea of Elland Road being renovated to a high enough standard to allow it to be chosen as a host venue should England stage the FIFA World Cup in 2018). The Council argued that, for as long as the owners of Elland Road – Teak Corporation Limited – remained anonymous, public funds would not be committed to enhancing the ground. The impasse appears to have been gradually resolved. Also the subject of Bates' musing were previous owners and directors of Elland Road, and politicians based in Yorkshire who had involved themselves in the various arguments surrounding administration. Prominent in those debates, and consistently the source of outspoken views against Bates, were three Members of Parliament: Phil Willis, George Mudie and Colin Burgon. Bates resented their intrusion and accused them of 'despicable behaviour'. He also questioned whether any of the trio were bona fide Leeds United fans. I had no dealings with Willis or Mudie, but Burgon was and is a genuine supporter of the club, and attended games as often as his job allowed. The likeable Labour representative for the constituency of Elmet was vocal with his view that United would be better served by a different leadership, which is not to say that he was definitely right but merely that he was entitled to an opinion. From the perspective of his constituents, he was arguably paid to express it. At the time of Bates' re-purchase of Leeds in 2007 he was not alone with those thoughts, though it goes without saying that Bates did not share them. 'Those MPs don't represent Leeds,' he was quoted as saying in an interview with the *Sunday Mirror* on 29 July 2007. 'They probably got 35 per cent of the votes. Just fucking ignore them. That's what really frustrates them.' It became a never-ending battle, and when Leeds announce in March of 2008 that the rights to live radio coverage of their league matches would be held exclusively by Yorkshire Radio – a digital station founded by Bates in 2006 – from the start of the 2008–09 season, the unofficial ceasefire between Leeds and Parliament was broken. The present incumbents, BBC Radio Leeds, had bid for the rights but were adjudged by Leeds United to have undervalued them, and their offer was unsuccessful. Given the chance to increase their bid, the Corporation declined, insisting their valuation was both accurate and final. The allocation of rights provoked an angry response from a number of supporters who realised that live FM coverage of the club's matches would no longer be available. Yorkshire Radio itself endured much of the heat, most of which was unjust. Their staff were professional and capable workers who did a good job with integrity, and the negotiations with the BBC had been nothing to do with them. They were, however, the victims of the belief that a station founded by Bates was the beneficiary of a decision which many fans believed would affect them adversely. Burgon subsequently tabled an Early Day Motion in the House of Commons expressing regret at the decision and asking Bates to reconsider. With the speed of a man who knows his way around the jungle of politics, Bates responded with pointed questions over the transparency of MPs' expenses, which had, by coincidence, jumped to the top of the national media agenda around the same time. All his reaction lacked was the cry of 'touché'.

Yorkshire's Members of Parliament were generally adept at rolling with the punches, but there was less of a pantomime feel about the breakdown of the relationship between Bates and the Leeds United Supporters' Club (LUSC), for years the largest organised affiliation of United's fans. Historically, the Supporters' Club made a habit of forging solid links with Leeds United, as a group of their size and importance should, but they mixed with Bates like water mixes with oil. I found the members of the Supporters' Club committee agreeable and courteous, and it seemed to me that their hearts were in the appropriate place – the starting point of their *raison d'etre* was a commitment to following as many of Leeds United's footsteps as possible. I bumped into Phil Beeton, their vice chairman, in the foyer of Slovan Liberec's stadium midway through United's summer sabbatical on the continent. He was pursuing his hobby of collecting official teamsheets distributed to the media for every game that Leeds play, though with some difficulty. The official at reception spoke basic German and not a word of English.

His fluent Czech did not threaten to solve the deadlock. It was hardly a surprise to see him abroad, but I had not expected to cross his path. 'We go everywhere us,' he said. And so they do. Not everyone in Leeds is a member of the Supporters' Club and not everybody would want to be, but the organisation were Ronseal in human form – they did exactly what they said on the tin. The acrimonious atmosphere between them and Bates was therefore unexpected, and difficult to understand. The most basic issue was perhaps the fact that United's chairman appeared to see no special or meaningful role for the Supporters' Club within Elland Road, and if he could, it was never established. In the months after his takeover, Bates established the official Leeds United Members' Club, which would be organised and managed from inside the walls of his stadium. At the time of its launch, the Members' Club was never promoted as an alternative or rival to the independent Supporters' Club, and the two groups were in fact intended to operate side-by-side. It has never truly been thus, and though never at open war, Bates and the Supporters' Club have long been at odds. The distribution of away tickets – once the responsibility of LUSC – was taken in-house by United's chairman, and premises at Elland Road used exclusively by the Supporters' Club were opened up to the general public. LUSC eventually acquired new premises by purchasing the Old Peacock pub directly behind Elland Road's South Stand. Season-ticket holders were automatically enrolled in the Members' Club, and fans with membership were generally among those given priority amid the chaotic scramble for tickets before particularly attractive fixtures, none more likely to see demand outstrip supply than play-off games. The Members' Club was actually a useful database of the supporters who attended United's games most regularly, and it was also a minor revenue stream. Annual membership for adults living in the UK was charged at £30. As the lines of healthy communication between Bates and LUSC deteriorated, Bates became increasingly partial to counting heads. At the last tally, affiliation of his organisation had cleared 25,000, a figure well in excess of LUSC's membership, though many season-ticket holders were enrolled in both. The Supporters' Club saw the comparison as meaningless and maintained that they had no desire to fight with the club. The public perception of the dispute was unhelpful, however, and it prompted Eddie Gray, United's former player, manager and coach, to stand down as LUSC's president, citing 'the in-fighting that's going on between the Supporters' Club and the club itself'. The mantle of president passed to United's recently retired defender Gary Kelly, who seemed genuinely touched to have been offered the position when he attended LUSC's annual dinner at the Royal Armouries in Leeds at the end of March 2008. Attempts to iron out the issues dividing Bates and the Supporters' Club have moved with the speed of the Hundred Years War, but it is to be hoped that a solution can be found. Football clubs on the scale of Leeds United need organised and coherent representation of their fans. The supporters require a voice. That argument has persisted for as long as the professional game itself but, in football's present climate, it is arguably more imperative than ever that views of those who are so often placed towards the rear of the queue of importance are given oxygen and attention.

But for all his unconventional mannerisms and all of his idiosyncrasies, Bates had a tenacious capacity for fighting off attacks from anyone he believed to be victimising or exploiting Leeds United. Liberties taken at the expense of Elland Road were never taken freely. When Chelsea plundered the club's academy to sign two of United's younger prospects, Michael Woods and Tom Taiwo, they soon felt the metaphorically iron grip of Bates around their throat. He had good cause to be angry. The academy at Leeds had been built and maintained at great expense – its quality made it a model for other professional clubs in England – and the point of that investment was not to allow Premier League clubs to go fishing on the cheap. Woods and Taiwo were well regarded by United's youth team staff and Bates was unimpressed by what he considered to be an illegal approach. At a press conference staged at Elland Road on 2 August 2006, his wrath was made public in a way that caught Chelsea by surprise. The board employed by Roman Abramovich at Stamford Bridge took offence at Bates' use of the phrase 'Siberian shysters' and accused him of anti-Semitic undertones. It was a ludicrous accusation that was never likely to stand up to scrutiny, and the Football Association took no interest in Chelsea's complaint. It seemed to Bates that the London club might be muddying the waters. 'I haven't laughed so much since Ma caught her tits in the mangle,' said Bates with spontaneous wit. 'Racism is the last card of a desperate man.' He preferred to concentrate on the grievance he had raised, and on that particular front United's interests were protected to the tune of compensation which administrators KPMG revealed to be 'circa £4 million'. Chelsea had initially offered a tenth of that sum.

The image of Bates as a dog with a bone, sinking his teeth into matters of controversy, was more pronounced by the issue of United's 15-point deduction, a contest of principle with the Football League which United's chairman prolonged until the bitter end over a duration of nine months. Bates was in tune with much of the city of Leeds in challenging a penalty which this book will address later. The deduction created a sense of baffled fury and was routinely condemned as victimisation, both by United's owner and his flock. There was no love lost between the terraces and the Football League; the problem for the average supporter was that the Football League were essentially beyond the reach of their dissent. Bates took their fight and his to the Football League's front door with gnashing teeth and a clunking fist. That his action ultimately failed denied United's chairman the chance to be cast as the warrior poet, but it was a conquest that garnered strong support. Throughout that period, there were perilously few individuals willing to fight Leeds' corner. Bates eventually turned on a string of newspapers whose reporting of the 15-point deduction failed to match his own understanding of the facts. Of particular concern were comments alleging that Leeds had broken Football League rules during their insolvency. To this day, that claim has not been conclusively proved and Bates does not accept it as fact. A series of apologies followed, and with them came several compensation payments. Bates, who estimated the total raised by litigation to be around £12,000, handed it all to the club's academy. In those instances, his defence of the club was ferocious to a degree that few other chairmen could match. One supporter whose opinion I valued found Bates to be a confusing character. 'At times I really don't get the guy,' he said. 'Some of what he does and says seems totally bizarre. But the one thing he does do is stand up for the club, and there aren't many people who do that for Leeds these days.

That assessment of Bates was fair but simplistic. There was more to him than the sole ability to engage in battle whenever his club were cornered. On purchasing Leeds in 2005, he had taken on a precarious business which was only just a going concern. Two days from administration, Bates would claim, which cannot have been so far from the truth. It is fashionable, or perhaps natural, to forget the position that Leeds were in two and a half years ago, but administration was being mentioned as a possibility at Elland Road long before the name of Ken Bates was ever uttered. At the end of the club's insolvency in 2007, I wondered whether any other chairman in the history of English football could possibly have emerged unscathed from the summer that Bates survived. It may be equally pertinent to ask whether any other individual would have possessed the bloody-mindedness to keep Leeds afloat for the time that Bates has, through a period which has been as unsteady as any the club is likely to experience. It can be argued with justification that Bates, as chairman, is accountable for his share of that turbulence, but it is difficult to imagine an alternative timeline since 2005 – without, that is, the instant solution provided by the obscene riches of a Roman Abramovich. United were always destined for serious problems once the misjudgements of Peter Ridsdale's board came to dominate the club's agenda. During administration, hundreds of people lost money they were owed by Leeds, a situation which was inexcusable and horribly regrettable. But professional football itself has been responsible for creating a culture where – in a financial sense – sport comes before society. Bates was a man with skin thick enough to allow him to tackle the club's debts in a way that football accepts. How he will be remembered when his tenure ends is for United's supporters to decide. But among the more relevant footnotes beneath his name may well be that which records how a club on its deathbed with debts of £35 million on 4 May 2007 was reaching for the top of League One as Christmas approached.

10

CHRISTMAS COMETH

LEEDS UNITED'S PREMATURE ELIMINATION FROM THE FA CUP left a vacant weekend at the beginning of December which, from Dennis Wise's point of view, was not without its uses. A charity match arranged by the Professional Footballers' Association (PFA) had been scheduled for 1 December as part of the union's centenary celebrations, and Wise was intent on digging his boots from the back of the cupboard and playing. The pulling power of the PFA was such that the exhibition at the City of Manchester Stadium – a Rest of the World XI versus an England Legends line-up – had generated serious interest, and not solely among potential spectators. Retired players who were at a loose end on that particular weekend offered their participation in droves. Paul Gascoigne put his name forward, as did Alan Shearer. Roberto Di Matteo and Gianfranco Zola, two of Wise's former team-mates at Chelsea, asked to be included in the Rest of the World team. Wise welcomed the opportunity of a reunion, and also found his competitive juices stirring. The likelihood was that of all the players involved, few would have kept in better shape than him, and once it was clear that Leeds United would not be involved in the second round of FA Cup fixtures on the same weekend, he made sure his name was added to the relevant list. A charity match it might be, but the players involved found the concept of a meaningless fixture difficult to grasp. 'Do I want to win?' asked Di Matteo. 'Take a guess. Will Dennis want to win? Stupid question. He's a great character off the pitch but a nutcase on it. I can tell you now that there's going to be a competitive edge. Dennis will be doing what he does best.' The Italian knew his enemy. Wise returned to his old berth in the centre of midfield for 45 minutes, and scored with a curling finish which would have thrilled him in his prime. It did not prevent the Rest of the World XI from winning the match, but the real victory was that of the new Manchester Children's Hospital, which received around £100,000 towards a rehabilitation and physiotherapy unit as a result of the charity event.

Ken Bates' experience of the friendly was rather less satisfactory. United's chairman had contributed to the fundraising exercise by booking a dinner table in one of the City of Manchester Stadium's hospitality suites. The cost of the reservation was not at all cheap, but Bates was happy to add his money to the pot in return for a day's entertainment. On his arrival at the ground, he changed the number on his designated table to 15 in a deliberate and well-humoured jibe at the Football League, and he enjoyed the charity game immensely. But his agreeable mood was darkened by a charge unexpectedly levied for bottles of water – an additional cost demanded on top of the attendance fee already paid by him, a fee which had stretched well into four figures. Unimpressed by what he felt was an unreasonable demand, Bates and his party vacated their table and exited the stadium early. They are said to have concluded their evening in a popular Italian restaurant in Leeds instead.

As early birthday parties go, it had not been perfect, but Bates staged an official gathering at Elland Road on the eve of his 77th year, 24 hours before United's home game against Port Vale. There was much to reflect on. In the 12 months since his last birthday Leeds had been relegated and become insolvent, a combination which must rank among a chairman's most vivid nightmares. Administration helped to sweep aside debts that Leeds would otherwise have been incapable of clearing, but the most relevant fact about the club's insolvency was the punishment it had incurred from the Football League. Bates had not forgotten about his club's 15-point sanction, and nor had he let go of the issue. On the contrary, a team of legal experts had been instructed by him to examine the decision in minute detail, and Bates was badgering the Football Association to review the penalty and rule on whether the Football League had the power or the justification to enforce the deduction. In September, an appeal for assistance from Elland Road was considered by the FA's Director of Governance, Jonathan Hall, who replied by stating there was nothing to suggest the Football League had acted improperly. Leeds reacted to the knock-back by requesting that the governing body open a Commission of Inquiry to investigate the matter fully, a demand which was passed to the Football Regulatory Authority (FRA) for consideration. The FRA is a regulatory division of the FA which operates semi-autonomously, but the answer was identical. In the FRA's opinion, the Football League had no case to answer. Bates was not happy. He saw both replies as a whitewash, and though the FA confirmed that he was entitled to seek independent arbitration against the governing body over their refusal to launch a Commission of Inquiry, United's chairman was beginning to give serious thought to the possibility of taking his fight against the Football League to the High Court. It was not an idle threat; the matter, in truth, had seemed destined to fall into the hands of the judiciary from the moment the 15-point deduction was upheld. There was one obvious problem, though, created by the waiver signed by Leeds in August in return for their 'golden share', agreeing that they would not mount legal action against the Football League over the terms of the share transfer. A judicial review would require that deal to be broken and the document declared void. The FA were not enthusiastic about the opportunity to embroil themselves in that. 'The decision on whether to refer the matter to the High Court is a matter for Leeds and not the FA,' said the governing body in a terse statement.

The effect of United's league form, however, had been to relegate the argument from view. Of all the considerations to be made on his birthday, perhaps the most satisfactory for Bates was the possibility that Leeds might be promoted regardless, and possibly as League

One's champions. It was certainly true to say that the club would take more pleasure from decimating a penalty which was designed to cripple them than they would from regaining their 15 points, and their results prior to the start of December had disregarded the deduction completely. Wise, by now, was asking his players to aim for the top of League One on New Year's Day, but the immediate priority was to ensure that Bates' birthday passed off peacefully, and without the upset caused by expensive bottled water. United's chairman had flown in from his residence in Monaco to attend his birthday party and the match against Port Vale; it would not do to disappoint.

The nine days between the club's defeat at Cheltenham Town and their next league game at home to Port Vale had allowed the importance of the opportunity missed at Whaddon Road to stew. Fortune was guilty of abandoning Leeds on that afternoon, but it was wrong to apportion blame entirely to a shortage of luck. United's finishing was unusually charitable, showing mercy to a team who should have been ready-made victims. Port Vale, the league's bottom club, were derived from the same category, and Wise was adamant that Leeds would not be found wanting twice in the space of a fortnight. Port Vale had a multitude of problems which were pointing them towards League Two even before Christmas. Their manager, Lee Sinnott, had been recruited from Farsley Celtic – the non-league club within spitting distance of Elland Road – at the start of November, but the meagre squad available to him made the task of lifting Port Vale from the bottom of the league arduous to the point of impossible. Like Wise, it seemed that Sinnott would have to stomach relegation before his work could begin in earnest, and with positive effect. Dave Bassett felt genuine sympathy for Sinnott, who he managed at Watford in the 1980s. 'The team might take time to take on his ideas and his methods,' said United's assistant manager. 'Some of the Port Vale players may not be good enough for what he requires. It might be that Vale have to go backwards before they go forwards. The fact that he's been a success in non-league shows he has some powers, man-management, coaching ability and a personality. He's a studious, honest type and I'm sure he will do it. It might just take time.' Patience, though, was wearing thin at Vale

Park. The club had succeeded where Leeds had failed by reaching the second round of the FA Cup, but their involvement was not a cause of celebration. Two days before travelling to Elland Road, Port Vale were held to a 1–1 draw by Chasetown, a club whose week-to-week concerns involved the obscure British Gas Business Southern League Midland Division. The gap between the teams in the English football pyramid was some 101 places, and Port Vale were primed for the upset which befell them on 11 December when they lost the second-round replay 1–0. In between, their contest with Leeds offered few straws for Sinnott to clutch.

David Prutton opened the scoring after 18 minutes at Elland Road with a header from Andrew Hughes' searching cross, and the match from there was a procession. Port Vale's contribution was dogged and committed, but the sagging belief in Sinnott's players was undisguised. Luke Rodgers slashed their clearest chance wide of the post, and David McGoldrick stabbed a tame chip into the arms of Casper Ankergren, having found himself face-to-face with United's goalkeeper. At the opposite end of the field, a shot from Jermaine Beckford which crashed against the post suggested the threat to Vale was more severe, and his turn and finish inside the box settled the match with 55 minutes gone. Vale did not merit further punishment but it came regardless via a sweet volley from Tore Andre Flo, which dipped over their keeper, Joe Anyon, from the edge of the box. It was the promise of that type of finish which persuaded Wise to invest United's money in an aging Flo, though four days into December the goal was only his second of the season. The Norwegian striker had undergone surgery in October on an injured foot which had caused him problems on and off for the whole of his short career at Elland Road. Flo broke a bone in his foot after his first league appearance in January 2007, and broke it again before the end of the 2006–07 season. An initial operation to pin the bone was unsuccessful, and when the start of October brought about another session of surgery, Wise found himself combating suggestions that Flo's foot was symptomatic of a man whose days as a player were numbered. Was it the knackers' yard for a one-time thoroughbred? 'He's going to be very important towards the end of the season – an important person to us,' said Wise. It was wishful thinking. Like his manager, Flo would not see the end of United's season, and on 11 March 2008 he announced his retirement from professional football.

On the night of their victory over Port Vale, however, Flo's goal was a worthy talking point which hinted – perhaps inaccurately – at the strong range of strikers available to Wise. Flo had appeared as a substitute in the 67th minute, and scored with virtually his first chance. He was a potential match-winner who, on account of the other players available to Wise, did not warrant a place in United's starting team. Managers call it strength in depth; Sinnott might have called it a bloody luxury. By full time at Elland Road, Port Vale were seven points from a safe position and in the first throes of relegation. Backwards before forwards, as Bassett had warned.

Vale were not alone in their disarray. With a game at Elland Road looming in five days' time, Huddersfield Town had problems. The club were making hard work of the first half of the season, and their turbulent tendencies were summed up by their visit to Southend United on the evening of Port Vale's defeat in Leeds. Huddersfield were beaten 4–1 at Roots Hall, and at great expense. Their goalkeeper, Matt Glennon, had been sent off in the 75th minute, and an appeal against his dismissal was rejected by the Football Association. It mattered not, apparently, that Leon Clarke – the player who Glennon was penalised for fouling – had written to the governing body to support the keeper by confirming that no contact had been made during the challenge. To compound the situation, a red card shown to Frank Sinclair in injury time rendered both he and Glennon ineligible for the Yorkshire derby with Leeds.

Sinclair's experience was expansive, among it a long spell as a teammate of Wise's at Chelsea, but his vacancy was easy enough to fill. The void left by Glennon was complicated in comparison. Huddersfield's manager, Andy Ritchie, had neither the time nor the freedom to recruit an additional keeper on loan, and the only option available to him was Alex Smithies, a player with much potential but one who had not yet reached his 18th birthday. His first and only senior appearance had been made at Roots Hall during the 15 minutes that remained at the point of Glennon's dismissal. It was already anticipated that Elland Road would hold a capacity crowd for Huddersfield's arrival on 8 December, a cauldron in which Smithies would either sink or swim. 'I'm sure he'll do well,' said Ritchie supportively.

The attendance was perfectly estimated by Leeds, and the crowd peaked at 32,501. It would represent the highest attendance of the season until 3 May at a stadium where the average crowd cleared 25,000. In modern times, that figure for a League One club was almost unheard of, and the scale of crowds elsewhere were a measure of United's magnetism. On the afternoon of 8 December – and over the course of the entire weekend – only six clubs pulled in attendances in excess of that recorded at Elland Road. They were Aston Villa, Chelsea, Everton, Manchester United, Newcastle United and Tottenham Hotspur. It is on the basis of such statistics that Leeds United can describe themselves as a Premier League club locked in League One without the need for a sense of irony. But swathes of supporters bring their own problems, and the concern within West Yorkshire Police about the potential for violence on the outskirts of Elland Road brought the kick-off forward to 12.15 p.m. It was a sensible decision justified further when word of the vandalism caused to Billy Bremner's statue outside United's stadium began to spread through Leeds and across the relevant Internet message boards. The boys in blue were anxious to prevent trouble, but the lines of spray paint on the base of Bremner's memorial suggested a small section of Huddersfield's supporters were asking for it. Worried though the police were, the tense situation was swiftly washed out by a sustained and torrential downpour which even the most hardened of scrappers saw sense in sheltering from. If West Yorkshire's finest had prayed for rain, their plea had been answered at speed. The only massacre during that afternoon would take place on the pitch of Elland Road.

United's hospitality towards their visitors had not been entirely to Huddersfield's liking. Their supporters were granted a ticket allocation of just 1,710, a figure which fell below the stipulated requirements set down by the Football League. Clubs are required to set aside either 2,000 tickets or 10 per cent of their total capacity for away fans, whichever is lower, but Leeds defended their decision on the grounds that it facilitated effective segregation between the two sets of supporters. The Football League agreed with United's assertion and, tucked into a cheese wedge of yellow seats in Elland Road's south-east corner, Huddersfield's travelling contingent were a small break in a thick sea of white. Their club captain, Jon Worthington, was unconcerned about the atmosphere. In previous seasons, a play-off final in Cardiff and an FA Cup tie at Chelsea had taught him to deal with larger crowds. 'Those were big events which came with a lot of pressure,' Worthington said. 'We handled them fine. There's a bit of a misconception that we're a very young set of players, and quite inexperienced.' His words were convincing but, from his withdrawn position, they were also akin to Field Marshall Haig shouting the odds over the Somme. Beset by a hernia for several months, Worthington was only able to experience the derby as an unused substitute.

For 20 minutes, the absence of his presence or that of anyone else was of no consequence to Ritchie. His side adapted to their surroundings quickly, and with more conviction than Leeds. Ronnie Wallwork should have opened the scoring with a side-footed shot in the second minute but it drifted wide of the post. Far from sending the adrenalin rushing, a minute's applause to mark the 10th anniversary of Bremner's passing appeared to have tranquillised Wise's players, who were awoken when a sweeping volley from Jonathan Douglas evaded Smithies' desperate dive in the 24th minute. Douglas's finish – a low strike from 25 yards with the outside of his boot – was sublime, though against the run of play seemed a more accurate description for Ritchie. It was, in fact, United's first shot on goal, and the lack of invention infuriated Wise. His players had been made aware of Smithies' age and reminded repeatedly of his inexperience. The obvious plan had been to test his nerve. But as composed as the 17-year-old looked, Elland Road became an unforgiving stage for his full debut. A lovely cross from David Prutton invited Jermaine Beckford to slide the ball into the net by an unguarded near post in the 49th minute, and Huddersfield's afternoon quickly got out of hand. Stood alone in front of Elland Road's Kop, the unfortunate Smithies was introduced to football's wicked sense of humour and lack of charity as chants of 'two-nil, it's your keeper's fault' circled around the stadium. It was not, of course, Smithies' fault. Over the course of 90 minutes, he was virtually blameless. Twice in the second half, the young keeper made exceptional saves from Prutton and Ian Westlake, only to see the rebounds bundled into his net by Beckford and Tore Andre Flo. It was that sort of day. 'Bless him,' said Wise afterwards with genuine sympathy, but as natural as it was to feel sorry for Smithies, his performance had been more creditable than those produced by several of Huddersfield's other players.

The crushing 4–0 win left Wise purring and, in a rare moment of ambitious projection, he declared Leeds safe from relegation. United had moved on to 32 points and, after 19 games, stood in fifth position, 17 points above the bottom four clubs. 'I'm expecting to survive,' said Wise. 'We're looking beyond that now. We're in this group of six and our aim is to keep well away from the seventh team. We also intend to catch the top two. Many things can happen over the next 27 games, but we're doing well and we're up amongst them. We need to stay there and put other teams under pressure.' The week behind him had successfully negated the damage caused to Leeds by Cheltenham. Two games won, seven goals scored and none conceded; their defeat at Whaddon Road had been the exception to the rule. People should have known better than to question the fortitude of his players, said Wise. The driving rain soaked him through as he walked alone along the touchline at Elland Road an hour and a half after full time, illuminated by the stadium's glaring floodlights. Wise exited the deserted stadium and climbed into his car with damp clothes but shielded by a confident warmth. United's season had been baptised once more.

Moreover, he suggests, the pressure building in League One was being brought to bear elsewhere. 'I don't want my players to feel any pressure and they don't need to,' Wise claimed. 'We're doing very well and the players know they are. They're confident. They had a bit of a bad spell in November but they still didn't show it. You have to remember the pressure that was on them at the start of the season – the pressure on us was whether we were going to stay up. It's off us slightly now. It could all go pear-shaped and it could all go wrong.

If we lose the next 15 games, I'd be out of a job. But we have to feel confident because we've done very well so far.'

The idea that other clubs were toiling in the heat did not really figure. On the contrary, the leading 11 teams in League One were divided by a total of seven points, and most would retain an interest in the play-offs for several weeks after Christmas. Among them were Walsall, a club who had been promoted as League Two's champions at the end of the previous season and were performing with spirit again. It was simplistic to assume that Walsall were punching above their natural weight, and insulting to their manager, Richard Money, to suggest so. Dickie Dosh, as he was affectionately known by their supporters, did not like to hear it said that the appearance of Leeds at the Bescot Stadium was his club's most prestigious game of the season. He was even less enamoured by the insinuation that Walsall were an inferior team to that owned by Wise. His players had completed 10 matches without defeat in the build up to United's descent to the West Midlands on 15 December, and Money felt expectant. His quiet confidence was well-placed.

Wise was required to omit the suspended Tresor Kandol from his starting line-up after an act of dissent during United's victory over Huddersfield prompted the striker's fifth booking of the season. Kandol was fined for his lack of discipline, and his loss was Leon Constantine's gain. A broken ankle had prevented Constantine from starting a single league game before the match at Walsall, but his recovery gave Wise an automatic replacement for Kandol. It seemed like a straightforward swap, and United's manager did not imagine that any number of changes would see his team endure the battering they sustained throughout the first half at the Bescot. Mark Bradley smashed a volley against Casper Ankergren's crossbar in the seventh minute, and a strike from Tommy Mooney was disallowed by an offside flag. Bradley and Scott Dann missed further chances, and Mooney's shot in the closing seconds of the half brought an excellent one-handed save from Ankergren. United's fans occupied around a third of the stadium, and the first 45 minutes had forced them to stand passively amid Walsall's onslaught. The half-time whistle brought welcome relief, and the chance for the travelling supporters to involve themselves. They broke immediately into a rendition of 'We are the champions, champions of Europe', their unique and distinctive terrace song which might baffle listeners. According to official records, United never won the European Cup, but the club's fans maintain that their absence from the roll of previous winners is a travesty. In 1975, Leeds qualified for the final of the competition at the end of Jimmy Armfield's first season as manager but were beaten 2–0 by Bayern Munich in Paris. To this day, the defeat is still blamed on the performance and ineptitude of the match officials involved at the Parc de Princes. Michel Kitabdjian, the French referee, overlooked two claims made by Leeds for a penalty, and Peter Lorimer was denied a goal by an offside decision against Billy Bremner. At the final whistle, United's supporters ripped seats from the terraces at the Parisian venue and protested in the riotous style that they knew best. A ban from European football was imposed on the club, but Leeds felt the moral victory was theirs. For the entirety of the 2007–08 season, United's matchday programme – on the insistence of Ken Bates – carried the 'real' League One table, published without the club's 15-point deduction. The supporters who witnessed the defeat in Paris felt a 'real' list of European Cup winners was also in order. Leeds United's name should be included. It is with a sense of injustice and defiance, then, that their fanbase openly declare the club champions of Europe. The repetitive song is sung with scarves and shirts twirling in the air, a well-rehearsed flurry of arms and fabric which tours the country over the course of each season. Newcastle United believe they have the monopoly on bare chests but Leeds possess an adequate share of that market, whatever the weather. On a freezing day in Walsall 10 days before Christmas, the clamour rang out from the first minute of the interval to the last, when the reappearance of the players saw the chant dissipate. It was eminently more entertaining than what had gone before.

The second half did not take long to warm up, and Walsall scored in the 76th minute when a corner from Daniel Fox spilled to the feet of Mooney, who thrashed the ball into the net from no more than a yard out. The goal had been coming, and all afternoon. With 14 minutes remaining, Money could visualise the win that would vindicate his optimism before kick-off. United did not look like scoring. But in injury time, a free-kick from Alan Thompson struck the head of Ian Westlake, who did his best to evade the flight of the ball, and a sizeable deflection carried beyond Clayton Ince in Walsall's goal. Thompson and Westlake both laid claim to the goal, but it was a classic example of a situation where the scorer's identity was irrelevant. United had skipped jail with another display of their immense talent for damage limitation. Money still maintained his point had been made. 'That wasn't our cup final,' he said pointedly. 'We've played like this for months. Three points against Leeds is the same as three points against any team, whatever anyone says. We deserved to win, and anybody in the stadium who says differently was at a different game.' Wise did not have the energy for an argument. 'It wasn't a fantastic game,' he said simply, distracted as he was by an injury to Jonathan Douglas, who had been carried from the field on a stretcher after blocking a shot on the edge of his own box. The fall appeared to have damaged knee ligaments, and Douglas left the Bescot Stadium on crutches. Wise had already resigned him to an inactive Christmas; it soon transpired that United's vice-captain and Republic of Ireland international would miss the bulk of the club's remaining league games.

Wise's uninspired assessment of the 1–1 draw did not provide a full account of what he had seen at the Bescot Stadium. One thing at least had held his attention, and within days of the fixture an offer of around £250,000 was faxed from Leeds to Walsall. The target of their interest was Daniel Fox, Money's young and talented left-back who Wise hoped to acquire in the first few days of the January transfer window. However critical the injury to Douglas would prove to be, the consolation for Leeds was the imminent freedom to begin improving their squad again. Wise had money to work with, which was something of a novelty for managers at Elland Road, and him especially. Six months earlier, he would have struggled to find enough pennies in United's accounts to fund a pot to piss in. His preparation for the transfer window was completed silently in the background, assisted by the club's chief executive Shaun Harvey and their technical director

Gwyn Williams. Wise had three more games to worry about before English football opened for business.

Leeds were preparing to arrive at Christmas after their match against Bristol Rovers at Elland Road on 22 December, and by Boxing Day they would be standing one game short of the half-way stage of the season. The portents were good, even if United's performances were beginning to speak of excessive wear and tear. A fortuitous deflection had reeled in Walsall, and it took an own goal six minutes from time to master Bristol Rovers. Steve Elliott was responsible for the mistake, shouldering a header from Sebastien Carole into the net as Rovers' goalkeeper Steve Phillips came to collect the ball. It was the only goal produced by either team, and despite hitting the crossbar in the fourth minute, Leeds lacked panache. But players past and present were sold on their chances of promotion, Eddie Gray among them. His attitude was philosophical. 'I wouldn't say that Leeds have played particularly well this season,' he remarked in the *Yorkshire Evening Post*. 'But there's no team like them at grinding out results and producing late goals. That's the second time in the last two games that Leeds have got more than they deserved, and I came out of Elland Road thinking sometimes your name's on the title. It'll take a very consistent side to stop Leeds winning the league.'

A team with the necessary consistency were beginning to flex their muscles, however, and Swansea City spent Christmas Day as League One's joint leaders. When they hosted Leeds in Wales on 29 December, it was painfully apparent that the title was more likely to rest on Welsh soil than in God's Own County come May. At that moment, Wise would realise that winning half the battle was halfway short of winning the war. But as Christmas approached, the spirit of the club's supporters was indomitable, blind to the possibility that their satisfaction might be threatened. It was, after all, the season to be jolly.

WE'RE GOING TO STAY WITH YOU FOR EVER . . .

PHYSICALLY AND METAPHORICALLY, ELLAND ROAD IS A dominant feature of Leeds. The stadium floods the skyline as travellers enter the city along the M621, its hulk of an East Stand dwarfing the surrounding area of Beeston. Time has left its mark, and three sides of Elland Road have the dilapidated look of a venue which has remained unadulterated year after year. In an age when uniform arenas dot the sporting landscape from Southampton to Hull, Leeds United's home is a throwback to the days before football was sanitised in the name of customer service. Like the club itself, the stadium is rough, ready and wonderfully intimidating. Where once United's training ground stood on Fullerton Park, adjacent to Elland Road itself, a wide expanse of pot-holed wasteland is now employed as a car park. The design of Wembley Stadium in London has been criticised for its obsessive attention to corporate facilities; Elland Road still caters for football as the sport was meant to be. Kevin Blackwell, the club's former manager, offered an apt description when he called the stadium 'a cathedral'. Since the turn of the century, Elland Road has been the site of many an anxious prayer.

Blackwell understood the social importance of Leeds United, both to the city's population and its reputation. In the months after his sacking by Ken Bates, he travelled abroad to take up short-term coaching opportunities in Europe and South America, filling the gap between his departure from Leeds and the managerial opportunity which would present itself at Luton Town six months later. He would not have claimed to be immediately recognisable on foreign soil, but something on his CV was. 'Whichever country you go to, when you say "Leeds" they say "Leeds United",' said Blackwell. 'People don't necessarily know the city, but they're guaranteed to know the football club.' An example of the club's stature is its sprawling fanbase, which has outposts across the world. The Leeds United Supporters' Club consists of almost 80 branches stretching from Adelaide to Scandinavia. So great is the interest in Norway and Sweden that pre-season tours to both countries became habitual for several years. During the second half of the 2007–08 season, the club embarked on an international census in an attempt to discover how far and wide their name had spread, and confirmation was received of Leeds United supporters residing in 168 of the world's 193 recognised countries. Rwanda, Somalia and the Ivory Coast were among the nations unaccounted for, but even the rigid borders of North Korea had not prevented United's name from slipping through. It is on the basis of such support that Leeds consider themselves a global brand, and why their descent from the Premier League was such a blatant contradiction of their popularity and reputation. 'It does break my heart to see the club where it is now, but it will be back,' said Blackwell as United's relegation from the Championship loomed. 'It's too big and too well-respected not to be.' The idea that Leeds United looked out of place in League One was not unfounded but, on the basis of their results alone, League One was precisely where the club deserved to be. It was not in the city's interests for United to remain there.

Leeds, to a degree, is defined by its football club, and its inhabitants take pride in rallying behind the banner at Elland Road, however torn or ragged it may be. If you arrive in Leeds inadvertently, your location is easily revealed by the obligatory stickers which adorn the windows of every second vehicle on the roads. Car stickers exist in cities across England, but they are something of a fashion accessory in Leeds. Most display the club's current badge – the design of a shield drawn up while Peter Ridsdale was chairman – and they are everywhere. When you buy a car in Leeds, you buy a car sticker. Then you worry about insurance and breakdown cover. There are perhaps more drivers in the city with stickers on their back windscreens than there are with tax discs on the front. It is that type of club and that type of institution. Of all the things lacking at Elland Road last summer, loyalty among their fanbase was not one.

It has never been in the nature of United's supporters to desert the club en masse, however demoralising life might be. In the summer of 2004, after Leeds were relegated from the Premier League, around 17,000 season tickets were sold, close to half of Elland Road's capacity. Increased prices imposed by Bates – the most contentious issue of his eventful stewardship – were followed by a noticeable drop in renewals, but by the start of United's first year in League One, season-ticket sales had reached 10,800 in spite of the fact that for most of the close-season the money was being paid to a club who were financially stricken. Both United and their administrators, KPMG, promised that the cash paid for season tickets had been ring-fenced and safe-guarded to allow for the slight possibility that the club might fold completely, but renewals and new purchases were made with a considerable leap of faith. Each supporter was paying out in anticipation of a season which, at the end of July, was not certain to start; moreover, the season did not seem to hold any realistic promise. Better bargains existed for £500, but 10,000 applications came forth regardless. It was income that United could not have done without.

The attitude of through-hell-or-high-water was always commendable and often amusing, and never more so than during the club's summer tour of Germany and the Czech Republic. The cancellation of a planned friendly between Leeds and Dynamo Dresden occurred in part because of the sheer weight of numbers expected to fly from England to Germany in time for the Saturday afternoon kick-off.

The police in Dresden did not relish the task of marshalling more than 1,000 Englanders from dawn until dusk, and had not anticipated such a high turnout for a game of absolutely no consequence. Why the interest, asked one bemused journalist from Berlin? It was a fair point, though not as pertinent as the question of how so many fans succeeded in relocating to the Czech Republic at 24 hours' notice for United's rapidly-arranged friendly against Slovan Liberec. In the car park outside Liberec's stadium, a dark blue people carrier pulled up bearing five supporters with slightly bleary eyes. How did you get here, I asked. 'We flew into Berlin this morning and drove down to Liberec in one go,' said one. Got a hotel booked? 'No, we're camping.' Where? 'In the first field we can find.' I never discovered if they made it home alive but their safety was apparently less of a concern than their attendance. Within minutes they were lost in the beer tents, their priorities in order.

Liberec welcomed Leeds with outstretched arms, but the members of League One were less enamoured by the thought of United on their doorsteps. Large crowds were certain to travel away from Elland Road, providing every other club with revenue and attendances in excess of the average League One fixture, but chairmen and directors feared what else might come with the package. So did the police. Years had passed since the height of hooliganism and the heyday of the Leeds Service Crew, and fighting on the terraces was not the thriving culture it had been. Number one when it mattered, they say of the Service Crew, which explains the extent to which hooliganism has faded from the radar, even in the minds of those who were once in the thick of it. If anything, football violence had become a subculture which showed its head infrequently in the face of more sophisticated policing. But it was naïve to assume that the threat was non-existent, and though United's appetite for destruction was generally over-exaggerated, their season did not pass off peacefully. There were battles in Northampton and scuffles before their match at home to Millwall. The return fixture at the New Den required the attention of 375 Metropolitan Police officers and a security plan that was eight weeks in the making, while a collection of pubs were trashed in Carlisle hours before a ball was kicked at Brunton Park on 3 November 2007. Yet the brushes of the law also tarred those who were divorced from the violence but bore the relevant crest on their chests. One group of United supporters told how they were expelled by police from a bar in Penrith for no reason other than the fact that the carnage underway in nearby Carlisle had given the local constabulary itchy trigger fingers. Until their eviction, they had exchanged a flurry of banknotes with a very happy landlord who knew how to treat a gift horse. Football allegiance was not his concern. And though publicans in Carlisle had just cause to feel differently, Carlisle United were pleased with their lot. The attendance of 16,668 generated by their game against Leeds was their highest crowd since 1976, a gap of some 31 years, and their gate receipts are said to have exceeded £200,000. On a typical match day, Carlisle's crowd tended to dip beneath 7,000. Those clubs who, for the purposes of tranquillity and security, would have rather avoided a visit from Leeds United were by no means blind to the trappings of the cash cow. Any hassle was most likely worth the money.

The sense that United were not entirely welcome in their division was nevertheless apparent. Bournemouth's idea of hospitality was hinted at by their immediate request to the Football League for a midweek match against Leeds, the club whose supporters had done so much damage to the Dorset coastal town on their last visit in 1990. Bournemouth, understandably, had not forgiven the violence, but the concerns of the club and the local police seemed to be founded as much on their historical impression of Leeds as they were on the realistic possibility of chaos. Very few of the supporters known in Leeds for their violent tendencies bothered to make that trip; many other fans did. United sold their full allocation of 2,116 tickets, and helped to provide Bournemouth's biggest and most lucrative crowd of the season – a record attendance for Dean Court. 'We want this to be a positive experience for everybody,' said their chief executive, Laurence Jones, before the game. The sight of police lining attack dogs across the field as the fans from Leeds were held inside the ground at full time begged the question of whether everybody included Bournemouth's visitors. As if to demonstrate their placid mood, United's contingent treated the police and their pets to a rendition of 'what a waste of money'. The Alsatians, it should be said, went home hungry.

Phil Woodhouse was among the throng who emerged from Dean Court *sans* bite marks. A financial advisor from Yorkshire, Woodhouse is what you might call a veteran of Leeds United-related travel. Addict would be an equally appropriate description. His first season ticket was bought for him at the age of 14, 27 years ago, and five after he first watched Leeds United in the flesh. Trailing the club's path has taken him to the continent on 15 occasions, and in 20 seasons he has missed around 50 of United's fixtures. At times his support is a labour of love, but following Leeds United is what he does as a matter of course and a matter of habit. In that, he is by no means alone. 'The division we're in makes no real difference to us,' Woodhouse said. 'If it was Rose and Crown away in the Leeds Sunday League, we'd still take a coach. Just as long as it's Leeds United.'

Woodhouse is a founder member of the Maverick Whites, one of countless organised groups of supporters who follow Leeds wherever and however they can. The Mavericks pride themselves on being the earliest bus-load to depart Leeds on a Saturday morning, and theirs is typically the first coach of United fans you pass on the motorway home. Either their driver likes the slow lane or their post-match watering holes keep them a little too occupied. The experience of League One promised to be a stark change of scene for fans who, in recent memory, had traipsed alongside United through UEFA Cup and Champions League campaigns. The Mavericks' giant flag flew in the Estadio Mestalla on the night Valencia hosted Leeds in the semi-finals of the Champions League in 2001, and – like the club their standard honoured – it is unaccustomed to the backwaters of English football. But United's supporters are not especially precious. Some, says Woodhouse, still consider the 1989–90 season – the year in which Leeds won promotion from Division Two under Howard Wilkinson – to be a more memorable experience than the campaign which brought the club the Division One title in 1992, their first since 1974. 'It's a disappointment to be going to the likes of Yeovil less than seven years after gracing the likes of the San Siro,' Woodhouse said. 'We had a team that looked like it was going to be at the top in Europe for a long time. But many of us have been here before, or very nearly anyway. The 1980s were not happy watching and we were regular visitors to places like Gay Meadow and Boundary Park during some inglorious years. League One wasn't a total culture shock. Many of us actually gained more satisfaction from the promotion year of 1989–90 than the Championship triumph in 1991–2, and I think with all the money, the over-the-top BSkyB coverage, the new brand of supporter and annual trips to the same stadia, there was a slight sense of excitement about "going back" to the smaller clubs.' At times, they wondered whether their excitement was shared by the clubs they were associating with in League One. Apprehension seemed to be the order of the day where Leeds were concerned. Over the course of the entire 2007–08 term, the dates and kick-off times of eight matches were revised on police advice, all related to issues of crowd control. No alteration caused more dissatisfaction than that which moved United's penultimate game at Yeovil Town – coincidently their second-longest trip of the season – to a Friday night when a Saturday fixture had originally been planned. Three further matches were repositioned to suit the broadcasting schedule of BSkyB, and two more were postponed. Including their meetings with Southend United and Huddersfield Town, both of which were rearranged twice, Leeds were subjected to a total of 15 changes to their fixture list, affecting more than a quarter of their games and regularly sending travel expenses up in smoke. The assumption that three o'clock football is the domain of the lower leagues was a fallacy but despite the fluid and unpredictable schedule, as a club's official response was sensibly diplomatic. 'It's inevitable that there will be a bit of nervousness about the scale of our travelling support,' said Shaun Harvey, United's chief executive. 'Clubs have decisions to make and you'd expect that these decisions are taken for the right reasons.' But if the erratic nature of the club's season risked reducing the strength of their travelling support, the threat was an idle one. 'Our away support is legendary,' said Woodhouse. 'It always has been and always will be, whether we're successful or not. The same faithful crowd will always be there at Plymouth on a Tuesday night. I would say the majority of clubs were fairly welcoming towards us; it's their respective police forces who weren't too happy to see us. Away supporters are very thick-skinned, and we became accustomed to rearranged kick-offs at short notice, most of which were ridiculous and needless. In League One, you have smaller towns and police who aren't used to larger crowds. I think their memories are very clear of the behaviour of United's supporters in the 1970s and early '80s, and they don't realise that times have changed. At Bournemouth, our treatment was scandalous. Memories in Dorset are still very vivid of what happened 18 years ago, and we were treated like a set of criminals. Every police officer was aged over 40 and most seemed still to be bitter about what happened in May 1990. They were keen to tell us that they hadn't forgotten. We were held in a compound for about an hour before kick-off for absolutely no reason, and in some respects I think that Leeds United – as a club, not a team – are too big for League One. You almost got the impression that everyone would get on better without us.' That impression was compensated by the undeniable reality that, for one season at least, Leeds were a draw of unrivalled attraction. During the 2006–07 term, Nottingham Forest were statistically the most high-profile opposition in League One, and nine clubs drew in their biggest crowds of the season when Forest were on display. United eclipsed their magnetism instantly, and by the end of the 2007–08 season, Forest were one of only two clubs whose highest league attendance had been produced by a game involving opposition other than Leeds. Forest's match against Yeovil Town on 3 May pulled in 28,520 spectators to the City Ground, 2,300 more than watched United win 2–1 at the same ground during the final weekend of August. Crewe Alexandra's largest turnout came at home to Oldham Athletic, also on the last day of the season. But elsewhere, the pulling power of the Elland Road club was unrivalled. Of the 17 clubs present in the league during both seasons, 14 saw their highest attendance increase year-on-year, all bar Forest's delivered by matches against Leeds. Most filled their stadia to capacity. The crowds seen at Doncaster Rovers' Keepmoat Stadium and Swansea City's

Liberty Stadium – two of England's newest venues – set new records for both grounds, and United's biggest away following travelled to Oldham's Boundary Park in October, when 3,732 supporters stepped over the Pennines on a Tuesday evening. Amazingly, it was also the only occasion before Christmas when Leeds failed to sell their entire allocation of tickets for an away fixture. There were, allegedly, free seats in Oldham, though not to the naked eye. The flood of interest in United's season provided an extended harvest time for the accountants charged with balancing the finances of League One's clubs. 'Clubs like the fact that their attendances are swelled by 3,000 Leeds United fans, and by an extra 3,000 home fans,' Woodhouse said. 'They can't be so keen on the policing bills, but there we are.' At certain stadiums, United's supporters took to singing 'we filled your ground for you', and League One's average attendance for the 2007–8 season – marginally less than 8,000 – was the largest it had been for 36 years, showing an annual increase of 6.7 per cent. The Championship, which dispensed with Leeds at the end of the 2006–07 term, suffered a striking drop in crowds of 6.6 per cent. United's presence in League One was helping the majority of clubs around them to pay the mortgage.

A mortgage was something that Leeds United themselves did not possess. Since 2004, both Elland Road and their training facility at Thorp Arch had belonged to third parties – initially to Jacob Adler, a property developer from Manchester, and latterly to Teak Commercial Limited (TCL), an off-shore firm based in the British Virgin Islands. Little was know about TCL, its directors or its purpose, save that the money paid annually to the company was a painful drain on United's finances. The cost of the lease on Elland Road and Thorp Arch had risen gradually between 2004 and 2007, and by the start of the club's first season in League One it was costing around £2 million a year to rent both properties. To put the figure in context, a contract agreed by Ken Bates with Italian shirt manufacturers Macron – allowing the company to provide United's kit from the summer 2008 onwards – was worth half as much, meaning a deal which Bates claimed was the most lucrative of its kind outside the Premier

League served only to fund 50 per cent of the club's rental costs. It was that sort of liability which had bled the club white. Bates drew up financial figures at the start of the season and decided to budget on the assumption that Leeds would average attendances at Elland Road of around 22,000. The target was achievable with almost 11,000 season-ticket holders on the books, but the reliability of supporters who purchased stubs match-by-match was more difficult to predict. Relegation and administration had damaged much of the goodwill in the city, and ticket prices were a bone of irate contention. In the two years since Bates first took the decision to substantially raise season-ticket costs, the statistics showed that around 10,000 fans per game had turned their back on the club, and crowds that recently nudged 30,000 were now more likely to fall below 20,000. Howard Wilkinson, United's title-winning manager, predicted pessimistically that Elland Road would become 'a graveyard' in League One, and in moments of doubt, Bates might have concurred. But the presumption could not have been further from the truth.

Bates' forecast of 22,000 was revealed as an under-estimate when 24,005 fans appeared for the first home match of the season against Southend United, hundreds queuing across the tarmac behind Elland Road's West Stand. Rats desert a sinking ship, it is said, but football supporters go down with their vessel. There was, at that time, an element of masochism about the willingness of the crowd to cling to their club. Perhaps on a Saturday afternoon they had nowhere else to go, but many would have argued instead that there was nowhere else they should be. Three o'clock meant Elland Road, and Elland Road meant Leeds United. To some, the sight of the Rose and Crown XI lining up across the halfway line would not change that. 'Home crowds are a different kettle of fish to our away support,' said Woodhouse. 'Recent pricing structures turned some fans away, whilst others maybe used that as an excuse not to bother. But fans will always watch winning teams, and before Christmas, when our results were excellent, the crowds got bigger and bigger. It came as no surprise. I got the feeling that some of the fans who enjoyed the lean times in the 1980s had come back, and that the siege mentality created by minus 15 points also drew people in. Our crowds are the envy of at least a third of the Premier League clubs, but I expect nothing else.'

The attendance produced by Southend's visit on 18 August created a rolling stone, but one which gathered a huge amount of moss. More than 26,000 fans attended United's next home match against Luton Town, and the figure rose further when Hartlepool United came to Elland Road on 8 September, the day when Leeds shook off their negative points tally. The final days of September saw the first attendance over 29,000, and a similar number saw Dennis Wise's players draw 1–1 with Leyton Orient midway through October. There was no limit to the growth until the available capacity of Elland Road was reached during the West Yorkshire derby against Huddersfield Town 17 days before Christmas. United's stadium was capable of holding more than the 32,501 who squeezed into the ground, but Leeds had opted to close the upper tier of their imposing East Stand. It required a cosmetic upgrade, but the closure also spared the club from annual business rates of around £90,000. During their summer of insolvency, it had been inconceivable that Leeds would be required to open the upper tier, but before 2007 was out, supporters began to ask if and when the decision would be taken to increase the capacity of Elland Road to its maximum. The figures were impressive enough, though, and only one Championship attendance eclipsed the turnout against Huddersfield. Leeds, however, ensured that they laid claim to the highest Football League crowd of the season by opening the upper level of the East Stand for their final League One fixture against Gillingham on 3 May.

League One offered novelty value, and a break from the routine; the chance to 'knock a few different grounds off the list', as Woodhouse puts it. A lower division did not alter the demands of home-and-away travel, and nor did it remove the element of adventure. On the journey home from Gillingham at the end of September, the Maverick Whites' coach ground to halt with engine problems on the M25, a few miles away from Romford. The passengers exited their vehicle and walked over the nearest embankment, intent on finding civilisation. In the streets nearby, they stopped a car to seek directions, and the wound-down window revealed the face of Graeme Le Saux, the retired England international. 'Where's the nearest pub?' they asked. 'That way,' said Le Saux, pointing helpfully. The Mavericks declined to inform him that he was listed on their official website as their second 'most hated footballer' – beaten to first prize by Robbie Savage – though Le Saux might have had an inkling. His choice of pub was a West Ham United stronghold. Fortunately, the Leeds supporters were well-received to the extent that their bleary-eyed coach driver was jeered and booed by the crowd of drinkers when he rolled into town with a new bus. The journey home to Leeds was completed in the early hours of the morning, proving that the experience of following football is as good as you make it. 'The Premiership is our ultimate target,' said Woodhouse, 'but we're missed by the division as much as we miss it. Who would Manchester United rather be playing? Reading? Wigan? Or Leeds United?'

The argument was valid, but it was also hypothetical, and the disparity between clubs was clearly displayed on Boxing Day. Manchester United found Sunderland in charitable and festive spirit on 26 December and routed the Wearside club 4–0 at the Stadium of Light, reaching the top of the Premier League in the process. Some 22 miles south, Leeds United's supporters were holed up in Hartlepool, where their club scrambled towards the summit of their respective division with a 1–1 draw at Victoria Park. With a firm prod from police advisers, kick-off against Hartlepool United was agreed for 12 noon, and with Manchester United in the vicinity, the match was lucky to kick-off at all. Leeds were unusually lethargic, and having conceded a goal to Michael Nelson's far-post header in the 21st minute, they fell back on Jermaine Beckford to conjure an equaliser with the most route-one of goals in injury time. That Beckford could have won the match seconds later with a side-footed finish from six yards was immaterial: Leeds had been comprehensively outplayed, and were scarcely worth their point. But the point was crucial and, helped by their early kick-off at Victoria Park, Leeds were League One's leaders for two hours on

Boxing Day. Mediocre they may have been, but the achievement of climbing the full length of their divisional ladder in the space of 137 days was beyond special. On that particular afternoon, their statistics showed sixteen wins, four draws and two defeats from twenty-two games. Wise, in his wisdom, had cautiously forecast United's arrival in the play-off zone towards the end of March; that honest estimate, he admitted, was ill-conceived. 'I could never have predicted this, but I'd like to be top on 4 May and not now,' he said. 'It's nice to put our toe on there and dip it in, but there's a long way to go. It's nothing.' He did not hold back on questioning the attitude of his players at Victoria Park. 'Too many Christmas puddings or Christmas dinners?' Wise asked. 'I don't know. But we weren't at the races.' By 4 p.m., they were no longer at the summit of League One either. With a 4–1 victory over Cheltenham Town, Swansea City had invaded the penthouse and thrown Leeds United back onto the street. Boxing Day, in effect, had been an afternoon of posturing, of dominant peacocks strutting aggressively. It was the perfect preamble to the tussle that would ensue between Swansea and Leeds in the south of Wales on 29 December.

Swansea's recent history is as chequered as United's, and their transformation into a forward-thinking club had not been achieved without the outlay of blood and tears. The tenure of former chairman Tony Petty, an Australian businessman who had become involved with Swansea as part of a low-key takeover in October 2001, left particularly harrowing memories. Petty possessed a footballing background insofar as he had worked within Australia's soccer scene, and his intentions sounded fairly astute, but the inhabitants of Swansea were sceptical from the outset about a man who apparently lacked a natural connection to the club. On Christmas Eve 2001, City's players were sent home with the news that there was insufficient money to fund their wages for December. By 28 December, a transfer embargo had been placed on Vetch Field on the orders of the Football League, and the following month Petty sold Swansea to a consortium of bidders, granting the wishes of the supporters who had fought relentlessly to rid him from the club. Swansea City, in January 2002, was a shell of a professional outfit, but the years since then had been kind. A move from Vetch Field to the Liberty Stadium, an under-stated but sparkling ground which is also home to the Ospreys rugby union club, increased their financial potential and was completed in time for City's promotion from League Two in 2005. The Championship was starting to beckon, and their manager, Roberto Martinez, liked the look of the League One title. Wise had eyes for the same prize, and was unimpressed by the strength of public feeling that said Swansea would win the division. Over his flayed body, if at all.

The crowd at the Liberty Stadium passed 19,000 for United's visit, the largest attendance seen inside the ground to date. Among that number were 2,456 travelling fans, crammed into one end of the arena. At the end of a very long journey they were treated to an epic fixture, but one which asked difficult questions – questions of Wise, and questions of his squad. Leeds had looked slightly weary at Hartlepool; on the south coast of Wales, they were positively jaded. Andy Robinson and Jermaine Beckford traded early goals, the latter's a sublime chip from a tight angle inside the box, but Garry Monk and Jason Scotland scored before half-time to give Wise a serious problem and Swansea a 3–1 lead. In between their goals, Ferrie Bodde – Swansea's Dutch midfielder – was sent off for a callous stamp on Jonathan Howson, but the numerical disparity gave Leeds no apparent advantage. Darren Pratley produced a rampaging performance in the centre of midfield, which compensated for Bodde's self-inflicted absence, and though Alan Thompson scored with a free-kick at the start of the second half, and drove another set-piece against a post 60 seconds later, Swansea's 3–2 victory was a fair reflection of their superiority. On the touchline afterwards, Wise picked through the debris. He raged at Bodde for what he described as a 'disgraceful tackle', and tangled verbally with a journalist who asked whether United's players had been right to surround referee Andre Marriner to insist on the midfielder's dismissal. Though not seriously injured, Howson had needed a stretcher to remove him from the field. Wise also chided Matt Heath and Rui Marques for the mistake which presented Scotland with Swansea's third goal at the end of the first half, but it was not the time for excuses. 'That's why they're sitting where they are, said Wise, conceding that Swansea's credentials at that moment were stronger than those of his own club. The strain in his voice had been noticeable at Hartlepool and was present again in Swansea. Wise looked exhausted. 'We've had 23 games and we've got 52 points,' he said, in a legitimate defence of his team. 'The players have been fantastic so far.' The whitewash of positivity covered cracks in United's façade, but it failed to prevent the conclusion that all was not well in paradise.

12

JANUARY SALES

ONE OF THE MOST DEPRESSING ASPECTS OF PETER RIDSDALE'S legacy at Elland Road was the extent to which the financial mismanagement of his plc board exposed Leeds United to hawkers and traders. Where the transfer market is concerned, English clubs divide themselves into two categories – those who buy and those who sell. Every club is required to do both, but the differentiation is all to do with necessity. Manchester United are filthy rich, so their incoming signings matter more than the players they release. Generally speaking, the individuals who leave Old Trafford have served their purpose and become expendable. Budgets in the lower leagues are extremely modest in comparison, so talented players are more likely to be auctioned for the good of a club's long-term health. Crewe Alexandra, for example, have profited financially on a regular basis from the list of established professionals produced by their academy, but have also borne the cost of sacrificing their better players. Crewe never were a Premier League club, and probably never will be. Their *modus operandi* makes that target almost unreachable. But they are run effectively and managed with sense, alive to their limitations. Theirs is the way of a large part of football's world, and a productive transfer market requires sellers as readily as it needs buyers. Every player has his price.

Leeds United do not think of themselves a selling club historically but, in the wake of their financial collapse, it was what they became. The most troubling sign of the club's weakening position had been the sale of Jonathan Woodgate to Newcastle United on the final day of the January transfer window in 2003. Woodgate was a supremely talented centre-back who, in spite of his well-documented conviction for affray, had become part of the furniture at Elland Road. The supporters warmed to him and saw the defender as indipensable; they believed the club shared their attitude, but United's monetary state said otherwise. Woodgate was traded to Newcastle for £9 million in a deal which Ridsdale said gave Leeds 'peace of mind' but which was actually the pre-cursor to an endless string of crises. In a conversation with Freddy Shepherd, then Newcastle's chairman, Ridsdale is said to have remarked that the transfer would cost him his job at Elland Road. Two months later it did, but the club he left behind were entrenched in a mindset where valuable squad members were seen as a key source of income. Paul Robinson was sold to Tottenham Hotspur in 2004, and Alan Smith left Leeds to join Manchester United for £7 million 12 days later. The list of other players who upped sticks in the months and years since the end of Ridsdale's reign as chairman includes James Milner, Aaron Lennon and Scott Carson, some of whom were arguably sold for what they could raise, rather than what they were worth. The long fingers of the Premier League were even reaching into United's academy, far beyond the confines of the first team. At the start of the 2006–07 season, Ken Bates reported Chelsea to the Football Association after the Stamford Bridge club recruited two of United's younger prospects, Michael Woods and Tom Taiwo. The argument over the allegation that Chelsea's approaches had been made illegally was settled by way of financial compensation, but Taiwo and Woods moved on to Stamford Bridge nonetheless. At the same time, another of Leeds' youngsters, Danny Rose, was persuaded to ignore Chelsea's interest and remain at Elland Road, but it was a short-term reprieve. The following summer, a matter of days after United completed their process of administration, Rose signed for Tottenham. Leeds were not alone in seeing their resources ravaged by Premier League clubs, but Elland Road was an obvious place for vultures to scavenge.

January was therefore traditionally a time for United's supporters to hold their breath, and the transfer window at the start of 2007 was no exception. Eight days into the month, Matthew Kilgallon was allowed to join Sheffield United for a fee of £1.75 million, another player with roots in Leeds' academy who had become expendable for financial reasons. That particular window saw Wise deal predominantly in free transfers – the limit of United's ready cash – but 12 months later the landscape had changed. Leeds were no longer besieged by creditors owed £35 million; for the first time in years, the club was essentially free of long-term debt. They had reached the turn for home after 23 matches of the season, with 52 points and a place inside League One's top six, progress made despite the hasty manner in which their squad had been constructed in August. Wise accepted the complications of the summer with good grace, but it was not an experience he wanted to repeat. By 1 January 2008, he was ready to spend. And unlike previous seasons, Leeds United were prepared to line his pockets.

The club's transfer budget was discussed at the beginning of December, giving Wise the freedom to make tentative enquiries about the players who interested him. Certain areas of his squad needed addressing, not least the position of left-back, which had been occupied for three months by loanee Jamie Clapham but was now available. A bid was made swiftly for Walsall's Daniel Fox, a 21-year-old defender whose younger years were spent at Everton. Walsall wasted no time in turning down United's offer of £250,000, and though Leeds suspected the club were simply driving a hard bargain, the impasse was never broken. Fox made it known that he wanted to leave Bescot Stadium, but United were unable to meet Walsall's asking price, and the full-back eventually joined Coventry City for an undisclosed fee. It proved to be a rare failure in a month of regular success and Wise's defence was already suitably rigid. His midfield, on the other hand, was giving him sleepless nights.

* * *

Sifting through his squad after the 3–2 defeat in Swansea, Wise realised that a problem was brewing. Oldham Athletic were due to first-foot Elland Road on New Year's Day, and a head-count at Elland Road produced a worryingly low figure. Jonathan Howson was unavailable due to the bruised shin caused by Ferrie Bodde's studs, and Jonathan Douglas's rehabilitation from a knee injury was in its infancy. Alan Thompson and Bulgarian Radostin Kishishev – the latter on loan at Leeds from Leicester City – were also lacking perfect fitness. The holes in Wise's midfield were gaping, and it was a sign of his desperation that he extended an olive branch to a player who, until then, had been estranged from United's season. There was no doubt in the minds of United's supporters that Shaun Derry was an able midfielder with capabilities above those required in League One – he was to many the one Leeds player who had gained credit for his performance in the Championship play-off final in 2006 – but his position at Leeds was unclear and confusing. Named as Wise's vice-captain and deputy to Kevin Nicholls in October 2006, the relationship between Derry and his manager appeared to have deteriorated quickly. Neither man spoke ill of the other, but it did not take much imagination to read between the lines. Derry missed the start of the 2007–08 season after developing a nasty cyst on his ankle, but Wise's reaction to his recovery in November was to send him on loan to Crystal Palace, the club who sold Derry to Leeds in 2005. The fans were mystified, especially by Wise's insistence that Derry needed to improve his physical condition before he could be considered for selection at Elland Road. The credibility of that explanation was stretched by Derry's first nine appearances for Palace, which coinciding with seven victories and two draws. In that time, Palace had progressed from a position near the relegation places in the Championship to the fringes of the division's top six. The suggestion that Leeds had no use for Derry was ridiculous. But as 2007 entered its closing hours, Wise needed him and needed him badly. He swallowed his pride and picked up his phone.

United anticipated that, when offered the chance to play against Oldham – his first start in a Leeds shirt for some 367 days – Derry would be on the motorway from London to Yorkshire immediately. But after a sequence of phone calls involving Wise, Derry and Crystal Palace manager Neil Warnock, it became patently clear that the midfielder intended to see out the remainder of his loan at Selhurst Park, which was due to expire on 19 January. Against their better judgement, Leeds had failed to include a recall clause in his deal and they had no contractual right to cut short the loan. Wise was livid, but Derry was unyielding – Warnock had given him an opportunity at a time when Wise refused to do the same, and Palace deserved his loyalty. He was also aware of the possibility that his former club would attempt to sign him permanently before the transfer window was out, and Wise's attitude had not projected a long and happy future for him at Elland Road. A transfer to Palace might actually be in the best interests of everyone. Warnock attempted to water down a controversial story by claiming that he had been responsible for rejecting United's request personally, but the decision was ultimately Derry's. It was confirmed through a voicemail left on Wise's mobile phone. He did not return to Leeds to greet Oldham, and he would not set foot inside Elland Road as a United player again.

For Wise, his experience of 1 January 2008 was far from the essence of a happy new year. In the early hours of the morning, he was driving home from a dinner in the centre of Leeds when his Range Rover was attacked with stones by a group of teenagers. It is doubtful whether the mob knew the identity of the driver, but it was soon revealed when Wise leapt from his car and chased them down the street. He had good reason to be upset; his two children, Amber and Henry, were in the car, the latter preparing to be Leeds United's mascot for the game against Oldham later that day. Wise's pregnant wife and his mother-in-law had also been travelling with him. He was later accused of 'racially aggravated threatening behaviour' and, rather bizarrely, of kidnap and assault, but no charges were brought against him. He denied the claims from the outset, and the police accepted unequivocally that the allegations were inconsistent and implausible. Wise himself declined to take any legal action over the damage caused to his car, and the matter was left to lie. But if he had the feeling that 1 January might be one of those days, he was right. Elland Road was gripped by fog as he arrived at the stadium, and in the harsh glare of the yellow floodlights, the misty ground possessed an eerie aura. The atmosphere at Elland Road had suffered badly during the season which dragged Leeds beneath the Championship, a season epitomised by the meagre crowd of 16,268 that appeared for United's game against Wolverhampton Wanderers in September 2006. Temporarily, the venue was stripped of its raucous ambience by climbing ticket prices and rapidly declining performances, as poisonous a combination as exists in the minds of supporters. But the club's appearance in League One had, ironically, flushed that toxin from their system, and redressed the apathy that held Leeds in its grip for a short time. Elland Road had learned to bounce again, encouraged by consistently inspiring results. The sterile atmosphere on New Year's Day was therefore a direct reflection of the manner in which Leeds United were murdered on the field of play.

The suspicion that Leeds had stumbled onto rocky ground, if not entirely lost their way, was conceived at Walsall on 15 December and strengthened by Bristol Rovers seven days later. Their performances against Hartlepool United and Swansea City followed a similar, unconvincing theme. Oldham's manager, John Sheridan, had great affinity with Leeds and, on the back of a seven-year playing career at Elland Road, was highly regarded among United's fans. There were many supporters who would rather have seen Sheridan in the home dug-out than Wise. But business was business, and in his capacity as Oldham's boss, Sheridan might have seen New Year's Day as a convenient time to grace his former home. The tiger which had savaged League One for five rampant months appeared to be flagging, and Oldham took their chance to poach the beast with some style. Though Leeds had been well beaten in Swansea three days earlier, the consolation for Wise was that his players had at least made a contest of their battle at the Liberty Stadium. Oldham provided no such mitigation.

United's fourth defeat of the season was ensured before half-time at Elland Road. Reuben Hazell's searing volley from the edge of the box opened the scoring in the 28th minute, and a free header from Neil Trotman doubled Oldham's lead nine minutes before the interval. As half-time approached, a cross from Craig Davies struck the unfortunate Andrew Hughes, who was unable to prevent the ball from deflecting into his own net. Unlucky the third goal may have been, but the crowd of 25,906 saw no reason to show compassion. Wise's players were booed from the field, chased down the tunnel by unified cries of 'what the fuck is going on?' It was a query that Wise himself wanted answered, and the sight of his squad rushing back onto the field five minutes before the start of the second half gave some indication of the raging monologue which had taken place in their dressing room. The situation improved momentarily as substitute Leon Constantine scored with his first touch, but his goal was a minor and expensive highlight of a dire afternoon. It later transpired that Constantine had badly broken his arm while diving to head home his chance. The post-match huddle which United's players and staff had previously maintained in victory or defeat was abandoned as Wise disappeared from view at full-time, and he took the decision to bypass the scheduled press conference afterwards. In saying nothing, Wise spoke volumes. His assistant, Dave Bassett, did appear, and gave a fierce critique of the way in which Leeds had welcomed in 2008. 'We've got to look at the last five games,' he said. 'We haven't played well in those five games and we've been warning the players that if they weren't careful, a performance like this would happen. This is a questionable time for this set of players because people will ask: "Have Leeds cracked?" They have to show us that they're up to it now. Those who don't will find themselves out of the team.' Bassett suggested that certain players were showing signs of burn-out, a claim which tallied with the tired performance he was picking apart in full gaze of the press. The saving grace was that United had run short of steam at the very start of the January transfer window, and from that point of view, the defeat to Oldham had not been completely useless.

Wise and Neil Kilkenny, Oldham's Australian midfielder, had met for the first time the previous summer when their paths crossed in Dubai. Wise's purpose was a well-earned holiday; Kilkenny was involved in an international tournament with Australia's Under-23 squad. United's manager liked what he saw of the diminutive midfielder, who strangely believed his performance had been an 'absolute stinker', and the two spoke briefly about nothing in particular, chewing the fat as football men do. The fact that Leeds were constrained by a transfer embargo rendered any thought of a permanent move to Elland Road redundant, and Birmingham City were not open to the idea of selling Kilkenny. He left St Andrews to join Oldham on a half-season loan in July. But their meeting planted a seed in Wise's mind, and when Kilkenny's instrumental performance in the centre of midfield cut Leeds to shreds on New Year's Day, an offer was scrambled in the direction of Birmingham. Oldham were anxious to retain Kilkenny, and Doncaster Rovers were also seriously interested; Kilkenny took the time to look around Doncaster's facilities as he considered his options at the start of January. But he liked the sound of Wise's proposal and chose to leave Birmingham for West Yorkshire. His time at St Andrews had not been especially happy, and he had cutting words for the club's former manager Steve Bruce and their managing director Karren Brady following his departure. Bruce had refused to sell him, the 22-year-old claimed, despite never playing him. Brady, meanwhile, was 'a very awkward lady, and not very nice'. It had taken Bruce's switch to Wigan Athletic and the arrival of Alex McLeish as Birmingham's new manager to finally free Kilkenny. The fee paid by Leeds was in the region of £150,000, and the deal gave United their first major signing of the transfer window. Wise had already recruited Sebastian Sorsa, a young Finnish winger, from HJK Helsinki, but Sorsa was seen as a raw prospect. Kilkenny was a player around whom Wise intended to build his midfield.

Kilkenny made his debut against Northampton Town on 5 January and ran the show with all the authority he had given Oldham on New Year's Day. It looked immediately like an astute signing. United's limp performance against Sheridan's team was replaced by a purposeful swagger, and though it took until the 43rd minute for Leeds to open the scoring with a wonderful finish from Frazer Richardson, Northampton's negative approach meant a single goal was ample protection. Nevertheless, Rui Marques guided home an improvised header early in the second half, and Curtis Weston completed a 3–0 victory with a vicious volley in front of the Kop in the final seconds of injury time. That, said Wise, was more like it. 'We needed a lift,' he admitted, 'and sometimes you need to bring personnel in to do that.' Leeds had signed Kilkenny on an emergency loan to allow him to be registered in time to play against Northampton, and a three-and-a-half-year contract was on the table, ready for his signature. 'If the club still want me, I'd love to sign,' he said. The journalists who heard him tried not to laugh. After such a convincing debut, United would renege on the agreement over Wise's dead body.

Before kick-off, Leeds had announced another signing, that of left winger Peter Sweeney from Stoke City, and a fee had also been agreed for Bradley Johnson, Northampton's young midfielder. Johnson sat out of the fixture in Leeds on 5 January and took the weekend to consider United's offer. By the following Tuesday, £200,000 had changed hands between Elland Road and Sixfields and the transfer was complete. Other approaches had come to nothing – Leeds were unwilling to match Barnet's valuation of Jason Puncheon, and the club were unimpressed by the financial demands of Luton Town's Dean Morgan. A bid submitted for Morgan was withdrawn just as swiftly. But four new players signed inside nine days of the transfer window was precisely what Wise had ordered, and it was not difficult to spot the strategy that United's manager had adopted; between them, Kilkenny, Sweeney, Sorsa and Johnson had an average age of 22. Only Darren Kenton – signed on loan from Leicester City on 10 January – was anywhere near the wrong side of 30.

It was one of his elder statesmen, however, that Wise was most concerned about. For the bulk of his tenure, Wise's defence had been constructed around the rugged frame of Rui Marques, a centre-back of Angolan descent and a member of United's squad who had come to define himself as virtually indispensable. It had not always been so. The story of his career at Elland Road could be split into two distinct halves – a period of stagnation under Kevin Blackwell and one of growth under Wise. Signed by Blackwell in 2005, Marques' position was best described as peripheral. In his first season with Leeds, he made one appearance in a League Cup fixture and finished the term on loan with Hull City. At the point where Wise replaced Blackwell as United's manager, Leeds were beginning discussions aimed at terminating Marques' contract, a move which seemed to suit everybody. Sebastien Carole was also being offered the chance to terminate his deal. 'There is no point in keeping players who have no part in the manager's future plans, and it is unfair to just keep them in the reserves, wrote Ken Bates in his programme column before Leeds' game against Southampton at Elland Road on 18 November 2006. 'It also saves on laundry, tea bags and toilet paper!' Before striking him from the list, Wise wanted to be sure that Marques was ready to leave. He sat down with the defender, and listened intently to a player whose simple wish was to be given a chance. 'I asked him what the situation was because I understood that he was just going, and that was it,' said Wise. 'He was mentally gone – fed up. But I had a chat with him and I said I'd give him a chance. If he wanted to go, he could go, but if he wanted a chance then he could have one.' His chance came on 1 January 2007, when he was unexpectedly included at centre-back against Coventry City at Elland Road. His performance was convincing and the point of no return. But his resurgence came at a price, and Wise was not entirely surprised when Marques was named in Angola's squad for the 2008 African Cup of Nations tournament in Ghana. The competition was due to begin towards the end of January, but Angola had insisted on his release at the start of the month. Twenty-four hours after United's 3–0 win over Northampton, Marques boarded a plane and departed England, resigned to missing five League One matches. Wise did not begrudge him the opportunity of international exposure, but he was less than delighted by the loss of a pivotal player. Marques gave a modest assessment of his impending absence, claiming Wise's squad were good enough to thrive without him. Wise had little desire to find out.

Predictably, there was no sudden subsidence. United travelled to Crewe Alexandra on 14 January for a game televised by Sky Sports, and collected a 1–0 victory, with a clean sheet which was as convincing as any other to date. Jermaine Beckford scored the only goal with a header from Sweeney's cross in the 36th minute, satisfying United's players and manager alike. 'I've played here many times before,' said Sweeney. 'It's a hard place to come to. If we're going to get out of this league we have to be winning at grounds like this. It can be the difference between going up and not.' Seated in the crowd that night was Paul Jewell, Derby County's manager, who was thought to have arrived at Gresty Road with an eye directly on Beckford. Derby had been strongly linked with the striker, and though the speculation never prompted a bid, Wise was unequivocal about talk of Jewell's interest. 'I've got no intentions of selling Becks,' Wise said. 'People are talking about Derby but we're a bigger club than Derby. If you were talking about the big four or five then it's a bit different. But I'm not prepared to let him go.' The goal at Gresty Road was Beckford's 16th of the season, every one scored in league fixtures. Wise's defence of the striker struck a chord; Leeds could scarcely afford to lose him.

The victory over Crewe, in Wise's opinion, reaffirmed United's standing as one of the most competitive teams in the division. It had certainly been a conclusive performance at a stadium where Leeds had never won before. But it was not an acid test on the scale of United's visit to Swansea City in December, and it was not comparable with the examination that Leeds would undergo at the hands of Doncaster Rovers the following weekend. To Wise's disgruntlement, United failed both. Doncaster's start to the season had been slightly ponderous, but it did not take long for the South Yorkshire club to climb League One with the speed and conviction that so many expected of them. The wage bill at the Keepmoat Stadium was sizeable and their squad was extremely well balanced, a collection of reputable players who were not necessarily big names. Under the management of Sean O'Driscoll, their approach to football was one the game's purists could not fail to appreciate. The game at Elland Road on 19 January was the first meeting between the clubs for 52 years, and their rivalry was less intense than it might have been given their close proximity. Before kick-off, supporters of Doncaster laid a wreath on the statue of Billy Bremner, a man who had played for and managed both clubs. John Ryan, Rovers' chairman, was keen to promote a feeling of mutual respect, but not to the point of submission. Doncaster had never won at Elland Road before, and Ryan fancied their chances. 'It's quite amazing to think that we're playing there at all,' he said. 'A few years ago we were stuck in the Conference and a long way below Leeds. But a successful period for Doncaster Rovers has been an unmitigated disaster for Leeds United. As a team we're going to Elland Road as equals, and we won't have an inferiority complex.'

As if to demonstrate Ryan's confidence, Doncaster's performance was serene. They scored in the 21st minute with a free-kick from Brian Stock which crept through United's porous wall and left Casper Ankergren flat-footed on his goalline, and the outcome from there was a formality. Mark McCammon – a towering striker who Wise had worked with a Millwall – ran Leeds' defence ragged with his rampaging style, and Doncaster's chances flowed freely. Jason Price drove a volley into the side-netting and headed another chance wide, and Ankergren's feet prevented McCammon from scoring at the start of the second half. The away crowd's taunt of 'we're just too good for you' was close to the bone and painfully accurate, a fair assessment of a one-goal lead which was going on six. Leeds had been outplayed before, but not to the extent where a 1–0 defeat represented a lucky escape. The scale of the disparity must have hurt Wise, and he retired to lick his wounds, leaving Bassett to carry out another post-mortem. 'We had too many players who were below par whereas most of the Doncaster players were on top of their game,' he said. Below par was an adjective that had dogged Leeds for more than a month.

In weeks to come it was pertinent to ask whether Wise had uncovered a hidden message between the lines of the defeat to Doncaster. Had he seen a team who, in spite of their early impetus, were grinding to a halt? Had Leeds United progressed as far as they could with Wise as their manager? It was clear that the club were no longer ticking with the force and reliability that they had before Christmas. Something at Elland Road was out of sync. Wise was still consumed by the January transfer market, and within 72 hours of Doncaster's victory, he released Alan Thompson on loan to Hartlepool – virtually the end of Thompson's competitive career with Leeds, though largely because of injury rather than a lack of favour – and sold Shaun Derry to Crystal Palace. Thompson's transfer was something of a surprise, ridding Leeds temporarily of their club captain. After long standing hamstring and calf strains, Wise insisted that the midfielder needed to address his match fitness elsewhere. Derry's sale, meanwhile, was the worst kept secret of the month. His move to Palace on loan appeared to be the prequel to a permanent transfer, and his refusal to assist Wise against Oldham on New Year's Day served to burn that particular bridge. Many supporters sympathised with his estranged position at Leeds, and few resented his decision to leave. 'Signing for Leeds United was such a proud day for me,' Derry said in an interview with the *Yorkshire Evening Post*. 'There can't be a single player who wasn't sad to leave the club. If I'm being honest with people then I'd say that Dennis Wise is not someone I got on with personally. That's often the case in football. You can't see eye-to-eye with everyone and I don't wish ill-will on any individual at Leeds. In fact, I wish them all the luck in the world. But there wasn't much left for me as things stood.' Derry also took the opportunity to confirm that he had not been responsible for leaking Wise's line-up to one of Crystal Palace's players before the Championship game at Elland Road 12 months earlier, a controversial incident which cast suspicion on Wise's entire squad and left United's manager vowing that the individual concerned 'will not be playing for this club again'. Derry's link to Palace made him an easy target of innuendo, especially since Palace's defender, Danny Butterfield, had been best man at his wedding. But the fingers pointed at the midfielder were misguided. 'I can look every fan and every one of my team-mates in the eye and say I wasn't responsible,' he said. 'I don't want to be looked upon as the guy who gave the team away. It wasn't me.' Wise, meanwhile, conceded that Derry's departure had been set in stone on 31 December, when the voicemail message left on his phone by the midfielder announced that he had no intention of abandoning his post at Palace. 'Shaun made it clear that he wanted to leave after the message he left me,' Wise said. 'He's gone now.'

Derry was the only player sold by Leeds during the transfer window, though his transfer perhaps maintained the recent tradition of United selling their better players. Wise, however, had planned for his departure and was more intent on completing his recruitment drive before the end of the month. He wanted to sign another striker, and Leeds bid successfully for Bristol City's Enoch Showunmi, but the Nigerian international was not interested in United's offer. He declined to discuss terms. The rumour in Bristol was that Showunmi's head had been turned by an offer from a club higher up the English pyramid of leagues. Though few in Leeds were aware of the fact, the same was true of Wise.

United's manager took his players to Kenilworth Road on 26 January to play a club in the midst of critical emergency. Luton Town had been declared insolvent in November, incurring a 10-point penalty by entering administration, and their prospects were grim on every front. Nick Owen, the one-time *TV-am* presenter, was fronting a consortium bidding to buy the club from their administrators, but the conclusion of that deal was far from completion. In the interim, it was taken as read that Luton would be relegated. Kevin Blackwell, their previous manager, had been sacked midway through January – inadvertently tackling the risk of another touchline confrontation between him and Wise – and the reins passed to Mick Harford, a popular character with the supporters at Kenilworth Road. Wise claimed publicly that Harford would guide Luton away from relegation, but his prediction sounded more like support for an old friend than a realistic presumption. Still, Leeds could not avoid doing their bit for charity.

Leading for 63 minutes through a header from Paul Huntington, United were caught at the death by a glancing finish from Sam Parkin, seconds before referee Mike Dean sounded the final whistle. A point was of limited value to Luton, but the loss of two was unacceptably damaging for Leeds. In the build-up to the game, Wise had specifically warned about the cost of failing to take advantage of a club who were hanging by a thread. He was entitled to be furious at full-time, and the waiting media expected his well-worn fuse to blow; surprisingly, the anger in his voice was heavily tinged by detached resignation. He bemoaned a 'poxy goal' and described his players as 'naïve'. When asked about Showunmi's rejection, Wise smiled and shrugged his shoulders. That's the transfer window for you, he said. Some you win and some you lose. Until that point, the market had treated Leeds fairly. But the club had one more major deal to complete, and within 24 hours of the defeat at Kenilworth Road it became clear that managers, like players, have their price.

GARY MAC

R EADERS OF THE *MAIL ON SUNDAY* AWOKE TO A PECULIAR
story in the publication's sports pull-out on the morning of 20
January. Hidden at the bottom of page three was a short article entitled
'Wise in the frame to be Kevin's Newcastle No 2', which detailed
the management strategy of Newcastle United owner Mike Ashley.
Newcastle were in the middle of momentous transition after sacking
Sam Allardyce and recalling Kevin Keegan to St James's Park to take
up the manager's job for a second time. With the Messiah in place,
the *Mail on Sunday* claimed the next stage of Ashley's recruitment
process would see Dennis Wise, Leeds United's manager, employed by
Newcastle in a role equivalent to what the Europeans call a director of
football. Wise, the report said, would take responsibility for scouting
and the acquisition of new players, and would enjoy 'authority over
every aspect of the football side of the club except the first team'.
It sounded utterly laughable, for a several reasons. First, Wise – at
the age of 41 – did not fit the stereotype of a director of football,
a position for which a man with the experience and background of
Gerard Houllier would have seemed more appropriate. There was also
the question of how comfortable and workable Keegan's position would
be with an ambitious and spiky character like Wise immediately behind

him. It would not do to upset Keegan; his appointment had received unanimous approval in the North East, as it was always likely to do. But more puzzling still was the idea that Wise would vacate a frontline position at a club like Leeds United for a job behind the scenes on the banks of the Tyne. A League One entity Leeds may have been, but there were some in Yorkshire who honestly believed that the club's potential was greater than Newcastle's. The immediate temptation was to dismiss the story as unfounded speculation; at the same time, it sounded ridiculous enough to be true.

Wise was asked about the report later that week, before United's game against Luton Town at Kenilworth Road. Bizarre story of the week, or a claim with firm foundations? 'I don't know anything about it, chaps,' he said. 'Honestly, I don't.' Wise smiled as he spoke, though not in a way that appeared disingenuous. His tone was dismissive. But at that late stage, on 24 January, he must have been aware that Newcastle's interest was more than the figment of a journalist's imagination. Football's grapevine moves with great haste when it needs to, and the jungle drums were sounding from St James's Park. The suggestion that Wise was deaf to them was implausible, considering that Ashley's background in business did not mark him out as a man who left anything to chance or took no for an answer. But it is fair to assume that, however much Wise knew about the opportunity being offered by Newcastle, his resignation was not in the post when he stifled the speculation two days before the League One game at Kenilworth Road. His mind might still have been open. What seems utterly certain is that the 1–1 draw at Luton – conspired by Sam Parkin's goal in the depths of injury time – closed the deal with Ashley.

Until then, Newcastle's interest was news to Leeds United and something the Elland Road club were happy to leave without comment. It had always been possible that a manager whose club had won 18 of their 28 league matches would be susceptible to outside interest but it was not a threat that have ever concerned Ken Bates unduly. He and Wise had been close friends for years, and the former was godfather to the latter's children. 'Dennis didn't come to Leeds on a whim,' Bates told the *Yorkshire Evening Post* on New

Year's Day. 'He wanted the job from the day I took over. We've got the best manager in the division in my opinion, and I'm not worried if other clubs start taking notice. Dennis is an honourable man and, in any case, he wouldn't want me to stop giving presents to my godchildren.' It sounded conclusive enough, as did Wise's previous comment that his position at Elland Road could be his 'last job'. But while the challenge of reviving Leeds United brought with it all the romance that a character like Wise could have asked for, a move to Newcastle promised to fulfil certain practicalities that the regime at Elland Road could not meet. As a lucrative kick-off, the Premier League club were naturally offering him a substantial wage increase. Even more appealing must have been the flexibility afforded to a director of football, something a manager could never ask for or expect. Despite receiving his wages from a club based in Tyne and Wear, Wise would be able to spend much of his working week in London, closer to his wife, his children and their family home. In all his time as United's manager, Wise had never been tempted to relocate to Yorkshire, preferring instead to undertake a regular and arduous commute from the capital. Combined with United's national tour which, over the course of six months, had taken him from Carlisle to Bournemouth and every conceivable area of England in between, the travelling requirements seriously restricted the meaningful hours he was able to devote to his family. At specific junctures, it was difficult to imagine that Wise was seeing them at all. Football managers expect their lives to revolve around their jobs because the nature of their employment demands that they must, but most are as human as the rest of us. It was surprising that Wise believed he could manage a club on the scale of Leeds United while living inside the M25, and his reluctance to move north did not depict someone whose commitment to the job came at all costs. Still, it is easy to insist on complete dedication when the demand is made of someone else, and if protecting his private life provided Wise's motivation for taking what many observers considered to be a backwards step – from the trenches of management to the padded seats that directors of football prefer to occupy – it was harsh to criticise him for that.

Twenty-four hours before United's draw at Luton, it was apparent to Bates and his administrative staff that Wise might be preparing to tender his resignation. Contact from Newcastle had been received, confirming that the *Mail on Sunday*'s analysis of their intentions five days earlier was perfectly accurate. There was no angle or argument with which to dissuade Wise from leaving Elland Road, and discussions over compensation began swiftly. Unlike the sustained bartering that was played out between Leeds and Tottenham Hotspur over the valuation of Gustavo Poyet, the price for Wise was easier to agree, and Newcastle possessed the funds to meet any reasonable demand from Elland Road. In the end, Wise's signature is believed to have cost the Tyneside club in excess of £1 million – a sizeable sum for a man who would be peripheral to Newcastle's first team. Fifteen months after his controversial appointment, Wise's reign as the 24th permanent manager of Leeds United was over. He left without a word to the media or the supporters.

The timing of Wise's exit was complicated, and deeply inconvenient. Leeds had a league fixture arranged at Southend United's Roots Hall stadium on Tuesday, 29 January, three days after their stalemate with Luton. Rather than make a wasted journey back to Yorkshire, Wise and his players stayed in a hotel in London over the weekend in anticipation of their midweek game. Leeds were granted the use of Tottenham's training ground – an offer which may well have been extended to Wise by his former assistant Gus Poyet – and they prepared as usual. But in the back of his mind, Wise will have realised that the likelihood of his manning the dug-out at Roots Hall was minimal at best. If, as seemed probable, Newcastle and Leeds could agree compensation before then, his presence would be a distraction that the squad he was leaving behind could do without. On Monday morning, the day before the game against Southend, news of Wise's imminent departure began to break, filtering its way down to the players in London. Most were caught by surprise and were understandably shocked. Wise gathered them together to confirm that the rumours were true and that his exit would be ratified within a matter of hours; he was ready to place his letter of resignation on the desk of Shaun Harvey, United's chief executive, and a figure of compensation was successfully negotiated on the Monday afternoon, providing Wise with closure. He started work at Newcastle immediately.

According to the man who would ultimately succeed him, he left behind a 'sombre' dressing room where uncertainty was rife. A large majority of the players had been with Wise since the start of the season and rightly expected that a campaign derived from such resilience and unity – the essence of siege mentality – would be completed with the 41-year-old at the helm. As with Poyet, that belief was unfounded. In another corner of the dressing room were players signed by Wise that very month and who had been sold a transfer to Elland Road on the basis of the vision presented to them by their outgoing manager. It is highly unlikely that negotiations during the January window included an admission from Wise that he himself might not see the end of it. His exit was made silently, and without public explanation. Family issues were clearly prominent in his mind, but the manner of his departure – midway through a season which still held plenty of promise – left other puzzles unanswered. Did Wise believe he had taken Leeds as far as he was able? Did he fear that the squad at his disposal had already maximised their potential and might fall away before May? Even by his standards, the frustration he displayed at Luton was excessive, perhaps that of a man who was at a loss to explain why his team were failing in situations where they had consistently excelled at the start of the season. David Prutton, one of the players who stood by Leeds without a contract during their summer of insolvency, attempted to rationalise the sudden change which, for better or worse, had come at a time when United's results were not as reliable as they had been. 'I'm sad in a way because the last six months have given us a little bit of success,' he said. 'You think about how enjoyable it's been and about the feeling that's been generated within the group of players. But things don't always last, and it's another chapter for Dennis and for the club. It's not something you take too personally. I don't know how the other lads feel, but as you play more and play for more managers you come to realise that this is what happens. Players come and go, and managers do as well.'

If Prutton's comments were intended to suggest that a period spent pining for Wise would come at a high cost to Leeds, the hierarchy at Elland Road wholeheartedly agreed. Far from allowing a vacant chair to catch them off balance, the wheels of recruitment were in motion before Wise could say Toon.

In the minutes after Newcastle presented an official request for Wise's services to Elland Road, Ken Bates' first response was to establish whether or not his manager planned to leave. His second was to begin pulling together a list of possible replacements at a time when few managers were immediately available and fewer still would be allowed to leave their current employers without the persuasive hook of substantial reimbursement. One candidate stood out immediately. Leeds had discussed the possibility of appointing Gary McAllister as their boss in October 2006, while the caretaker reign of John Carver was arriving at an unfortunate and unseemly end. At that time, McAllister had been a leading contender for the job but was overlooked by Bates' decision to allow Wise and Poyet to try their hand at managing the club. One newspaper went as far as announcing that McAllister and Eric Black, his former assistant at Coventry City, had been offered the job in 2006, much to his surprise and that of Leeds. 'If they'd come and asked me about the job then I'd have been interested and I'd have listened,' McAllister said, some three months before Bates finally came knocking. 'There was a lot of talk that I was going to get the job and that I'd already got it, but the fact is we never spoke. When you're talking about going back to a club where you played and where you won the league, you'd find it difficult to go past. But it never came to that.' With Wise on the road to Newcastle, Bates had no doubt that a free and available McAllister was now the most suitable replacement. The only issue was whether McAllister was ready and willing to resume his managerial career.

The Scotsman was an immensely popular character whose career as a professional football was riddled with stellar achievements. He was capped 57 times by Scotland and deserved to be listed among the most dedicated and talented midfielders to carry the tartan flag.

Among Leeds United's supporters he was remembered more vividly for his six-year contribution to the club, and most significantly his performances during the 1991–92 season when he and the rest of Howard Wilkinson's squad won the Division One title. It was United's first top-level championship for 18 years and also their most recent, and to describe McAllister as central to that triumph would be like describing a car's wheels as fairly important. The midfield constructed by Wilkinson – containing McAllister, Gordon Strachan, Gary Speed and David Batty – was as skilled and effective a collection of players as United had seen for two decades. McAllister's transfer from Elland Road to Coventry City in 1996 created a few murmurs accusing him of chasing the pound, but the insinuation seemed to do him a disservice. The reality, said McAllister, was that Leeds were set on selling him. In general, McAllister was eminently respected and the thought of a Leeds man at the head of the city's professional club was refreshing, especially after the connections possessed by his predecessor. The most startling aspect of Wise's departure was the rank indifference with which the development was greeted by United's fanbase. Some accused him of a lack of loyalty but most gave a casual shrug of the shoulders when asked for their reaction. It was a strong indication that, for all the undeniable progress made in their relationship, the attitude of the fans towards Wise had never quite stretched to acceptance. If anything, they learned to tolerate him. During the second half of his tenure, Wise might have felt he deserved more affection, but he could never establish the natural connection to Elland Road that McAllister possessed. Wise had been the outsider hampered by scepticism; his successor was a former hero, returning home.

McAllister's only previous role as a Football League boss had been carried out at Coventry between April 2002 and January 2004, but the four years which elapsed between that job and his appointment at Leeds were in no way a reflection of how employable or capable a manager he was. McAllister resigned as Coventry's player-manager in 2004 to spend time with his family and to care for his wife Denise, who had been diagnosed with breast cancer around the turn of the century. His decision was selfless and what he felt was 'the natural thing to do'. In March 2006, six years after being diagnosed with cancer, McAllister's wife passed away. It is a period of his life that he treats extremely privately, and one which football journalists do not expect to hear him discuss. Frankly, McAllister's experience is none of our business. It always seemed likely, however, that he would return to football – the profession he had pursued from the ranks of Motherwell Boys' Club – at a moment of his choosing, and when the time felt right. As much as McAllister would be answering a missive from Leeds by agreeing to replace Wise, it seemed like the opportunity he himself had been waiting for.

United made contact with McAllister through Gwyn Williams, their technical director, on Sunday, 27 January, two days after Newcastle's approach for Wise was received. When asked if he wanted the job, McAllister's affirmative answer is said to have been instantaneous. It was as much assurance as Bates needed and plans were drawn up to fly the 43-year-old Scot to his apartment in Monaco, where a contract was produced and signed. That it ran until the end of the season – little more than three months away – did not seem to bother McAllister. 'The job brief is promotion,' he said. 'I'm here until June and quite simply my job is to come here and kick-start it. When a new manager is appointed late in January it's usually to pick up the pieces of failure, but this is different. The boys are in a fantastic position and I'm joining a winning club.' Bates was no less content. Though not the sole reason for his choice, it was satisfying to see a positive reaction to McAllister's appointment. 'I'm not backward in making unpopular decisions but on this occasion I hope it's popular because it's both constructive and logical,' Bates said. As for who else might have been interested in the job, United's chairman could not resist having his fun. 'Quite a number of chairmen would be dismayed if they knew their manager had applied for the job,' he said. 'But their secrets are safe with me. I'd like to wish them all well in their existing jobs.'

The deal with McAllister was officially announced around 5 p.m. on Tuesday, 29 January, less than three hours before Leeds were due to kick-off against Southend. Earlier in the day, Wise's assistant Dave Bassett and his first-team coach John Gannon had been relieved of their positions after a discussion with Williams. With McAllister residing with Bates on the coast of the Mediterranean, and few other coaching staff available, Williams was asked to take charge of the first team at Roots Hall, a thankless assignment if ever he'd seen one. Preparation for individual fixtures did not get any more turbulent or chaotic; so short of numbers were Leeds that Andrew Hughes was required to take the pre-match warm-up. In those circumstances, it was no shock to see a collection of players whose heads must have been swimming beaten 1–0 by a first-half goal from Southend striker Lee Barnard. United's performance was disjointed, but there was no justice in aiming criticism at anyone concerned.

United's tired squad were called to a meeting with McAllister at their training ground near Wetherby the following day, where they listened to him outline his perception of their season so far, and his strategy for the 17 fixtures that remained. McAllister saw considerable promise in the results prior to his appointment and seemed happy with the range and ability of players he was he inheriting. The only slight concern, he admitted, was that the fitness of the squad was slightly below the standard he expected. But with 24 hours of the January transfer window remaining, he took the opportunity to make four signings before the deadline passed. Lubomir Michalik, a centre-back who Wise had coveted for months, completed an expensive transfer from Bolton Wanderers, and Darren Kenton's loan from Leicester City was converted into a permanent deal until the end of the season. Kenton's Leicester team-mate, Alan Sheehan, soon followed, joining Leeds on a temporary basis for the remainder of their campaign. United considered re-signing Wolverhampton Wanderers' left-back Jamie Clapham, who had completed three months on loan with Leeds earlier in the season, but the experienced defender went instead to the Walkers Stadium, allowing Leeds to move for Sheehan. McAllister suspected that, in a roundabout way, he had landed the better player. To complete his business, Anthony Elding – a striker with 15 goals to his name – moved east from Stockport County. Elding's arrival was the end of a steady influx which had seen eight senior players land at Elland Road and only Shaun Derry leave. Whether McAllister would have sanctioned

Derry's departure had the decision been his to make was impossible to say. But with a modified squad and a matter of hours to adapt to his role, McAllister's prospects of producing a win on his debut on 2 February were as slim as those faced by Williams in Southend. United's pool of players were in his possession, but it was not yet fair to describe Leeds United as McAllister's team. He needed a full view of the unit he had taken on and a complete understanding of their strengths and weaknesses. The areas requiring the application of tender loving care were laid bare by Tranmere Rovers on 2 February, the date of McAllister's managerial bow.

Six changes were made to United's starting line-up, and Leeds performed accordingly. Ronnie Moore, Tranmere's manager, suggested beforehand that his club's visit to Elland Road could not have come at less opportune moment, but by full-time he was forced to admit that the timing of the game had been ideal for him. Very soon, Moore claimed, McAllister's influence would take hold, but the day of his debut had belonged to Tranmere. Jennison Myrie-Williams broke the deadlock in the 61st minute with a shot which zipped off the outside of his boot and past goalkeeper David Lucas, and Ian Moore's header eight minutes later put the game beyond United's reach. The fervent reaction which greeted McAllister as he walked from the tunnel before kick-off dipped to a subdued grumble by the final whistle, a far cry from the conclusion to United's game at Prenton Park on the first day of the season. 'A Dick Turpin job' Moore had called his side's last-minute defeat on the Wirral on 11 August, but there were no accusations of robbery at Elland Road. McAllister's own assessment was refreshing. 'It's obvious that there's work to be done,' he said. 'We've got to do better than that.'

On the evening of his appointment, McAllister had remarked on how unusual it was to be asked to take charge of a club who were already within touching distance of promotion and the play-offs. But in a sense, he was understating the job he had taken on. The 2–0 defeat to Tranmere was United's third loss in four games, during which time they had taken one point from a possible twelve. Their most recent victory had come at Crewe Alexandra on 14 January, and it was pushing the boundaries of truth to describe United as a team in form. Stale was a more appropriate word. McAllister promised an alternative style of football to that seen under Wise, with more finesse and greater attention given to patient passing, but that intention was only as important as his plan to stem the flow of blood from United's season before it began to damage their position. 'We don't want to be sitting after games saying we've played well and not won,' he said. 'That's the crux of it. We've got to enjoy playing but we've got to be winning. We're under no illusions – it's a results business and we need results from now until the end of the season.'

It was down to the quality of the first half of the club's season that their league position still offered encouragement. United sat in eighth place but much closer to the coalface than their ranking indicated. Doncaster Rovers – in second – were six points ahead with a total of 50, and sixth-placed Tranmere were only two points better off than Leeds. The one frustration was that Swansea City had disappeared at the top of the division, 16 points clear of McAllister's players. While United's manager was not exactly clinging to automatic promotion – a prize that Leeds could easily reach – the title had become a fanciful possibility, unless Swansea planned to capitulate with improbable speed. Until that point, the Welsh club had shown few signs of nerves, and the championship would be theirs before the end of April. McAllister was happy to leave Swansea to their own devices and turn his attention to massaging the optimism of his training ground. 'The confidence has been affected because we've had a bad run of results,' he admitted. 'I recognise that I've arrived at a time when there's been a downturn. It's very clear. The changes have shocked them. But we've got to snap out of it, and losing yourself in hard work is the way I did it over the years as a player. You keep working away, and it will come back.' Jermaine Beckford, the club's top scorer, later confirmed that the temporary absence of stability between Wise leaving and McAllister settling in had impacted upon the dressing room, if only temporarily. 'Change always effects people, no matter whether they show it or mask it up,' he told BBC Radio Five Live. 'Unfortunately for us it showed in a few of the results.'

Among the immediate priorities of United's manager was his search for generals to join him at the war table. With Bassett and Gannon gone, the club's coaching staff had been trimmed to the skin. Andy Beasley remained in place as goalkeeping coach, and Neil Thompson, the club's popular and diligent academy manager, provided another pair of hands, but McAllister had two key appointments to finalise. He made an immediate approach to Sammy Lee – the former Bolton Wanderers manager and first-team coach at Liverpool while McAllister was a member of the playing squad at Anfield – but Lee was tied up in financial negotiations over the termination of his contract at the Reebok Stadium, and was unable to take up the post of McAllister's assistant. In the blink of an eye, McAllister turned to his former Liverpool team-mate Steve Staunton, who had been absent from the public gaze since the end of a gruelling spell as the Republic of Ireland's manager. Staunton fell on his sword after the Republic's failure to qualify for Euro 2008 but McAllister liked his style and his background. Within seven days of McAllister's arrival, Staunton was installed as his second-in-command. 'What I like about Steve is that he's been brought up in the Liverpool way,' McAllister said. 'We'll benefit from that influence because I want the players here to approach the game in the right way, with a certain type of performance.' Shortly after, Staunton's selection was followed by the announcement that Neil McDonald had agreed to leave the assistant manager's job at Lincoln City to become McAllister's first-team coach. McDonald was blessed with his own managerial experience, and had reigned at Carlisle United for 14 months before he was inexplicably sacked after one game of the 2007–08 season. His dismissal was never adequately explained, and nor did it seem at all fair. That Carlisle were almost promoted to the Championship at the end of the same season made their decision more difficult to question, but it did not necessarily justify it. McDonald was mystified. But since leaving Brunton Park, he had worked in Sweden with Ostersunds FK before coming to Elland Road by way of Sincil Bank. As a trio of coaching staff, a League One club could not have asked for a stronger combination than McAllister, Staunton and McDonald.

* * *

Their first match together was away to Northampton Town on 9 February, at a ground Leeds had never visited before and were given few incentives to visit again. Jonathan Howson converted Bradley Johnson's cross with a fierce volley which flew off his foot to give Leeds a 1–0 advantage after 38 minutes, but Northampton equalised with 15 minutes remaining, just as it seemed that McAllister's first victory was in the offing. Ade Akinfenwa's goal was a touch fortuitous, bobbling into the net after Casper Ankergren had attempted to smother the ball at the striker's feet, and though Leeds were no less lucky to see out the final 15 minutes without a second concession, the sight of Jermaine Beckford's header being nodded of the line by Brett Johnson represented the clearest opportunity for either team. McAllister had reason to feel aggrieved, as did the travelling support. A crowd of them failed to make it to their seats for kick-off, having been rounded up in Northampton town centre and marched to Sixfields in time for the start of the second half. Fortunately, Sixfields is one of the few stadiums in England where it is possible to watch league matches for free (Leyton Orient's Brisbane Road is another, though admittedly a clear view requires the purchase or rental of one of the apartments that have been built in all four corners of the ground) and the exiled fans huddled together on top of the hill behind the North Stand, just in time to see Akinfenwa strike. As days out go, it did not represent an example of money well spent.

Financial prudence was high on the agenda the following Monday when United announced a four-year shirt deal with Italian kit manufacturers Macron, worth in the region of £1 million a year to the club. 'The biggest deal outside the Premiership,' Bates said with satisfaction. McAllister was present at the press conference called to announce the agreement, but his thoughts were elsewhere. Nottingham Forest were due at Elland Road 24 hours later, along with a crowd which would fall narrowly short of 30,000. He had already watched his players drop five points against two of League One's less fancied clubs; the challenge of hacking down Forest – the perennial favourites for promotion – was a more serious appraisal of those who planned to retain places in a settled starting line-up. 'This game's got the butterflies going,'

McAllister said. His opposite number, Colin Calderwood, doubtless felt the same. Forest do not accept failure, even though their supporters have been forced to grow accustomed to it, and Calderwood's head was on the block. Having seen the club lose in the play-off semi-finals at the end of the previous season – his first as manager – the common belief was that McAllister's ex-international team-mate would be sacked if Forest failed to establish themselves as a Championship club by May. It was not beyond the bounds of possibility that he might be sacked regardless, despite a managerial record which was largely beyond reproach. But a victory at Leeds would help to keep the wolf from the door.

A cold night looked likely to run in Forest's favour when Julian Bennett rose unmarked at the back post to crash home a header from Kris Commons' cross late in the second half, but McAllister had spoken about the ability of Elland Road's Kop to 'suck the ball in', and the magnetic drag of the North Stand was irresistible. With seven minutes remaining, Wes Morgan pulled at the shirt on Tresor Kandol's back inside Forest's box, and Jermaine Beckford fought off the pressure with a fierce penalty which flew past Paul Smith before Forest's goalkeeper hit the ground. United's 1–1 came four weeks and a day after their last league win, but Beckford's goal was worth clinging on to. In those moments when Forest were threatening to run away with the result, Leeds had shown steel in their eyes and fire in their stomachs. 'I feel that there's a nice honesty about the place,' McAllister said, a statement which summed up the evening perfectly.

The reality, though, was that Leeds were pleased to reach the end of February. Their game against Doncaster Rovers, scheduled for 19 February, was postponed as a result of a frozen pitch at the Keepmoat Stadium, though not before McAllister and his players had arrived at the ground in their team coach. The squad had, by coincidence, shared a hotel in Wakefield the night before with match referee Andre Marriner and his assistants, and the suspicion that something was amiss was fostered by the sight of the officials hurrying from the lobby while breakfast was being served on Saturday morning. But it was not until United's bus pulled up at the doors of the Keepmoat Stadium that the postponement was confirmed. The ground staff had failed to cover the entire pitch with frost sheets, and the freezing overnight temperatures had done their worst. 'We've been left looking like idiots,' said Doncaster's chairman, John Ryan ruefully, angered further by a wasted journey he had taken from Cape Town to England to attend the match. The claim that United had been fortunate to avoid an in-form club at a time when their own results were questionable did not wash with McAllister, who wore the unimpressed look of a man being told his wedding had been double-booked. When Crewe held out for a 1–1 draw at Elland Road a week later – a result which relied on an 86th-minute goal from Tresor Kandol – the feeling that fate was dealing him a raw hand was unavoidable. But February was almost out, and McAllister took a positive view. The half-empty glass valued three successive 1–1 draws as eight points lost. 'The three draws have been frustrating, but if we get two or three victories on the bounce then those draws might turn out to be not bad results,' said McAllister. A top-up of optimism left his glass half-full; now for that maiden win.

EASTER RISING

TO THE SOUTH OF SWINDON TOWN'S COUNTY GROUND LIES A marvel of infrastructure and eccentricity known colloquially as the Magic Roundabout. Built over a section of the old Wiltshire and Berkshire Canal, the giant circular is an odd collection of five mini-roundabouts designed to assist the merging of five different roads near Swindon's town centre. The architect responsible evidently applied the chaos theory to his design and must have seen sense in the idea, right up until the day when he was committed to the asylum. Named in 2007 by a British magazine as one of the world's worst junctions, it is possible on the wrong day, at the wrong time, to become trapped on the Magic Roundabout for what feels like eternity. Rather like a football manager whose first victory is refusing to yield.

Winless streaks vary in length and severity. Four matches without a victory – and seven in total, including the games preceding his appointment – was not Gary McAllister's idea of a crisis, but its effect was relative. In August, football pundits would have described United's sequence of form as an early-season malaise. With two months of the season remaining, it had the potential to inflict untold damage on their league position. There is a time and a place for temporarily losing your way, and the League One run-in at the beginning of March was not it. February had been an expensive month, consisting of a defeat to Tranmere Rovers and stalemates against Crewe Alexandra, Northampton Town and Nottingham Forest; McAllister might reasonably have expected to win three, if not all, of those fixtures. As it was, goals in the final 10 minutes had been necessary to prevent further defeats to Crewe and Forest, and the division showed Leeds in ninth place, cut adrift of both second and sixth. But McAllister would gouge out his eyes before he allowed negativity to sweep through his dressing room and write off the club's season. His players had come too far for that. 'When you go through a spell like we're going through, you sometimes have a little doubt,' he said. 'We have to banish that and get rid of all the negativity. There's still only one team who have won more games than us, and we've still got the leading goalscorer in the league. It's there in black and white.' It was a good argument. Aside from Swansea City, no other club in League One could out-do Leeds in a straight comparison of statistics, and only Swansea's Jason Scotland was seriously threatening to out-run Jermaine Beckford as the division's premier marksman. On 3 March, and due largely to the 16 goals he had scored that season, Beckford was named as League One's player of the year, an award which also took into account the pivotal role he had played in Scunthorpe United's promotion from the division while on loan at Glanford Park towards the end of the 2006–07 term. The achievement was both deserved and remarkable – remarkable for the fact that three years previously Beckford had made a living by replacing car windscreens. The story, as Beckford tells it, is that in order to take up the offer of trials with professional football clubs, he was forced to dodge shifts with his employers. His boss eventually cottoned on when *The Sun* revealed that Crystal Palace were in the process of assessing the striker's potential. But it was Leeds who had invested in Beckford's talent in 2005, and Leeds who were banking on his ability to see them safely through the final two months of the League One season. The best striker in the division, and the second-best team. They were sizeable straws that McAllister had every right to be grasping. Privately, he suspected that one victory would revive United at a stroke.

* * *

United's team coach fought its way over the Magic Roundabout and landed at the County Ground on 1 March. Inside the stadium, McAllister was greeted by Swindon manager Maurice Malpas, a man he knew well from their days as Scotland players. Malpas made his international debut in 1984, the first of 55 individual caps he received; McAllister won 57 in total, his first coming in 1990 against East Germany. Of more interest to McAllister was his former colleague's club background, which consisted of a career devoted exclusively to Dundee United. Malpas was an uncompromising full-back whose schooling was carried out by Jim McLean, a manager of strict and disciplined repute but a coach whose imaginative style had produced one of the most respected teams ever seen at Tannadice. Dundee United had reached the 1987 UEFA Cup final, eliminating Barcelona en route, and it seemed probable that parts of McLean's style had rubbed off on Malpas. Swindon were certainly in need of inspiration after losing their previous manager, Paul Sturrock, to Plymouth Argyle in November. Sturrock's position had verged on the impossible due to financial complications which threw up the real possibility that Swindon would cease to exist. The positive news for Malpas was that new owners had acquired the club in January, allowing him to work without the fear that he might step out of bed one morning to find Swindon Town in ruins. Leeds United understood implicitly how important that security was.

The afternoon in Wiltshire did not begin as McAllister had planned. His players were approaching the end of their warm-up when Stephen O'Halloran – a young left-back signed on loan from Aston Villa 48 hours earlier – fell to the ground with pain in his knee. United's medical staff made a rapid assessment of his injury and realised that something was seriously wrong. By Monday morning, he was returning to Villa Park with severely damaged cruciate ligaments and without a single appearance for Leeds on his record. McAllister was philosophical, but the loss of O'Halloran was typical of the way that football treats managers in need of all the assistance they can get. United's boss was happy to take responsibility for his club's results; it did not help when fate was kicking him where it hurt. But the timing of the injury so close to kick-off prevented McAllister from dwelling on his luck, and Frazer Richardson was promoted from the substitutes' bench without a second thought. O'Halloran, in the end, was scarcely missed.

The match was 25 minutes old and finely balanced when a flat cross from David Prutton picked out Tresor Kandol at the far post. The striker had not scored for 18 matches before his goal against Crewe on 23 February, but the arrival of one bus was, as usual, followed by another in its slipstream. Kandol sized-up the cross and planted a delicious header into the corner of Swindon's net, far beyond the reach of their goalkeeper Phil Smith. Leeds pushed their luck from there on and though O'Halloran's injury was an apparent sign of trouble to come, the free header that Simon Cox flicked wastefully over Casper Ankergren's crossbar hinted that this might be McAllister's day. Only once in his previous four games had United held the lead, and unlike Sixfields, where Northampton Town replied 15 minutes from time, McAllister's defence was ironclad at the County Ground. Ankergren's brilliant low parry repelled a goalbound shot from the enigmatic Christian Roberts with 17 minutes remaining, and with the chance went Swindon's hope. Ankergren's concentration was commendable since his second half had been played out to the sound of abuse from the stand behind him, and the occasional hail of missiles. The Dane reacted at full-time by lobbing a cigarette lighter back into the crowd, an offence which earned him a charge of improper conduct from the Football Association. Ankergren pleaded guilty to the charge and, two games before the end of the season, received a £750 fine. McAllister had accepted the probability that Ankergren would incur a suspension which, in the final throes of April, would have prevented the keeper from taking part in some or all of League One's play-offs. The FA spared him that punishment, citing 'the provocation of objects being thrown onto the pitch during the second half of the game'. Their leniency saw to it that McAllister's first victory as manager arrived with full value.

United's boss had treaded cautiously around the topic of his winless run, attempting to prevent the issue from dominating the agenda and morphing into a fixation, but his reaction at full-time was a mixture of elation and relief. He punched the air, applauded the Leeds fans present in the County Ground and allowed a broad smile to spread on his face. With a satisfied shout of 'Hallelujah', he grabbed Gwyn Williams in a friendly embrace on the touchline, a sight which underlined his feeling of release. 'When you come back into football having been out for a while, there's nothing like winning a match,' he said. 'There's an old adage that I've used all the way through my career, which is that the harder you work, the luckier you get. These guys have been working really hard and they deserved a break.' It was Gary Player, the renowned South African golfer, who had first used the saying uttered by McAllister in Swindon, and the correlation between graft and fortune was undeniable. The repeated late goals produced by Leeds during the first half of the season were routinely described as lucky. Dennis Wise would respond by saying that creating the chances in the first place relied entirely on hard work. The one accusation McAllister would never allow to be thrown at his squad was that their commitment was lacking. 'I'd have liked the results to be better, but the response from the players has made it all worthwhile,' he said. When asked about the result, Malpas tore a page from Ronnie Moore's phrasebook by saying 'Dick Turpin springs to mind', but the result mattered more to Leeds than it did to Swindon, who were safe from relegation but realistically removed from the issue of promotion.

The momentum that McAllister was desperate to establish began to grow with a 2–0 victory over Bournemouth at Elland Road seven days later. Bournemouth's season had been trashed by insolvency and while their players were never easily subdued, their prospects in Yorkshire looked grim. The club's position in the relegation zone was beginning to take on an ominous hue, and Bournemouth's utmost concern was to ensure that they would be in business to start the following season, whichever league they were part of. The newspapers on the south coast were flooded by talk of Bournemouth's administration, and their game at Elland Road was a secondary issue compared to the anxiety over the club's long-term health. But the intriguing connection between the clubs was that of Gerald Krasner, the insolvency practitioner tasked with finding a suitable buyer for Bournemouth. Krasner had been United's chairman for almost a year between March 2004 and January 2005, and despite agreeing the sale of Leeds to Ken Bates, he vehemently opposed the buy-back deal reached between Bates and KPMG in the summer of 2007. Krasner offered his advice and expertise to United's local creditors, who stood to lose thousands of pounds, and he and Bates became verbal adversaries for the duration of the club's administration. Given their chequered history, Bournemouth's visit to Elland Road was an occasion that Krasner might have been inclined to miss, but he made the journey as a representative of the Dorset club. There was no invite to the boardroom and no seat for him in the directors' box. Krasner instead took his place among United's supporters and watched Bournemouth concede goals in either half to Bradley Johnson and Neil Kilkenny. Johnson's effort was humiliating, a gentle tap-in laid on by a collision between Bournemouth goalkeeper David Forde and one of his centre-backs. Kilkenny's finish, on the other hand, was special, and his disguised strike from the edge of the box ignited Elland Road with a ferocity which McAllister, as the club's manager, had not seen before. Johnson, whose goal was his first for Leeds, admitted he could feel the confidence in United's dressing room oozing. 'We've looked at the fixtures we've got left and to us they're all winnable games,' he said. 'We all believe that we can go up automatically. Our bad run's behind us.'

An interesting sub-plot to the result at the Elland Road was the appearance on 69 minutes of Dougie Freedman, one of McAllister's five substitutes. Freedman had been signed on loan from Crystal Palace the previous Thursday, but the negotiations that concluded the deal were unconventional to say the least. Freedman, who was 33, had strong ties to Crystal Palace, a club he had served for almost 10 years during two different periods at Selhurst Park, and an initial approach from Leeds was met with reluctance. His family were based in London and Freedman had taken on the responsibility of coaching Palace's reserve team; on top of that, his contract with the club ran for another season. There was plenty of duties to keep him occupied in the capital, but first-team football was not one of them. The three league starts he had been granted by Neil Warnock during the previous five months fell far below his expectations, and McAllister hoped to exploit his inactivity by selling him the idea of contributing to United's promotion to the Championship. Freedman pondered the offer at length, but declined. 'I just feel that I have something to offer Crystal Palace,' he said. 'I want to play here. Any other team is a dead duck.' The admission was McAllister's cue to accept defeat but his determination to sign Freedman was intense, and phone conversations between the pair continue regularly. Come to Leeds for a challenge, McAllister told him, and get this great club out of League One. 'Gary McAllister kept perstering me to come and sign,' Freedman said after the victory over Bournemouth. 'When you get two or three phone calls a day, from nine o'clock in the morning to nine at night, telling you what the club's all about and putting the challenge in front of you, it's difficult to say no. It sunk in and I thought let's give it a go.' Freedman was clear about his reasoning – Palace were in his blood, and he was not coming to Leeds to kiss the badge and depict himself as McAllister's white knight. 'If I said I'd jumped through the door at Palace the moment Leeds came in for me then it would be a lie,' he said. 'The supporters deserve better than that. It was a difficult decision from the point of view that I felt a strong bond to a club I'd played with for 10 years. But I'm here and I want to be here, there's no question about that.' What he could promise was the sacrifice of every ounce of his energy and every sliver of experience collected in his 16 years as a professional player. Actions, in short, would talk louder than meaningless words. The persistence of McAllister and the signing of Freedman was to prove a defining moment in United's season, of more significance than any supporter could possibly have imagined. It explained why United's manager was loath to take no for an answer.

Freedman was a substitute again on the evening of Tuesday, 11 March when Leeds were unexpectedly beaten by Cheltenham Town at Elland Road. The record-keepers registered a narrow 2–1 defeat, but everyone present in the slanting rain saw McAllister's team manhandled by a supremely confident Cheltenham side. Leeds had been mugged at Whaddon Road in November but Cheltenham's victory in Yorkshire was far less deceptive. It was a 2–1 thrashing on a night when McAllister's thoughts must have strayed from quiet optimism to perplexed contemplation. There was no obvious reason for United's inept performance – something they had rarely been guilty of – and no explanation for their inability to master a team four places off the bottom of the division. The finger could hardly be pointed at McAllister; his team was as close to full-strength as it was possible to be, and the victory at Swindon had been a catalyst of sorts. 'It was a night of frustration,' he said. 'In the final third we lacked touch, guile and assurance. We were sloppy at that end of the park, and that was our downfall. We've got to take more pride and care in the final third.' Anthony Elding claimed United's goal with a close-range header five minutes from time but the damage had been done by then, and a late equaliser would have distorted the true nature of the contest. David Bird drew first blood with a shot from the edge of the box seven minutes before half-time, and Alex Russell's blistering finish in the 63rd minute from the very corner of Casper Ankergren's box put Cheltenham within touching distance of victory on their first appearance at Elland Road. For a club who had waited three-quarters of a century to play Leeds in a professional and competitive fixture, Cheltenham had quickly gained the measure of their high-profile opponents. No other club had succeeded in beating United at home and away.

Keith Downing's side were intended to be the second leg of a triathlon of games which McAllister hoped would elevate Leeds to the play-off positions and, more significantly, place additional pressure on the clubs squabbling over the second automatic promotion place behind Swansea City. Bournemouth were in disarray and had been dealt with comprehensively, and the plan was to dispatch Cheltenham as efficiently as possible. With Port Vale, the team bringing up the rear of League One's field, to come, the crop that Leeds hoped to harvest was rich and ripe for the picking. But the loss to Cheltenham was a stick between the spokes at the time when McAllister needed it least, and the trip to Vale Park on 15 March would be a stage for hardened nerves and strong stomachs. 'The manager has come here with the express intention of winning promotion,' said David Prutton. 'Losing to Cheltenham doesn't really help that. If we're going to do anything then it's time to perform and get results.'

* * *

The angst created by Cheltenham's win was greater than the harm it had done to Leeds. Bruised pride was naturally galling but the blemishes on their league position were more difficult to spot. Two points separated United from Southend United in sixth, and other clubs were wallowing in deeper inconsistency than Leeds. Tranmere Rovers had failed to win their previous three matches, and Leyton Orient were fading gradually, a decline which would continue unchecked until the end of the season. Brighton and Oldham Athletic were potentially dangerous but Leeds believed they had the legs to win a straight race to the death against any of the teams around them. A victory over Port Vale, whose own constitution was highly questionable, would be a good start.

Lee Sinnott had worked gamely to hoist Port Vale away from relegation during his four months in the job, but his task was doomed to failure. The squad he had agreed to manage in November were denounced as 'gutless and spineless' by Mark Grew, Port Vale's former assistant manager, and though Sinnott did not necessarily concur with Grew's scathing analysis, it was clear that his pool of players fell beneath the requirements of League One. By the time Leeds United came calling at Vale Park, the game was almost up. 'There's a limit to how quickly you can turn an oil tanker around,' Sinnott said. 'It's some test for us [against Leeds] but a good one. It's like another step in my crash-course of Football League management.' It was fitting, then, that an enthralling game of intense drama treated United with all the subtlety and compassion of a multi-vehicle pile-up.

United's first-half performance was not, by some distance, their most coherent of the season, but the 2–0 lead they constructed before the interval was all McAllister was interested in. A flying volley from Rui Marques (which a talented striker would have been proud of) and an instinctive strike from Freedman turned the game in Leeds' favour in the space of two minutes, just as the half was meandering towards a goalless finish. A 0–0 scoreline would have suited Port Vale; two goals adrift after 45 minutes, Sinnott's players looked shot. But news of their execution was dispatched prematurely, and with the aid of a dubious penalty in the 65th minute, a foregone conclusion became an open game once more. The match referee, Clive Penton, was tempted into waving his arm towards the penalty spot after a flick off the head of Marc Richards struck Andrew Hughes inside the box. The award ignored the short distance between the players – a case of ball played man – and Penton's misjudgement became indefensible when replays showed the ball had hit Hughes in the face. 'I couldn't see out of my eyes at first because it smashed against my nose,' the full-back said. 'I tried to tell [the referee] what had happened but he wouldn't listen to me. He said he had to stick with his linesman, and to me that's not good enough.' A crestfallen Hughes was booted in the proverbials for a second time as an unwarranted yellow card issued by Penton took him over the threshold of 10 cautions for the season and incurred a two-match suspension. To complete a hat-trick of misfortune, Paul Harsley steered a vicious finish into the roof of the net, a textbook penalty if ever Leeds had seen one.

The change of mood was sudden, and within two minutes Danny Whitaker's close-range volley created a problem where McAllister had believed there to be none. A two-goal lead squandered, Sebastien Carole was launched into the fray from the bench, and the substitution took effect four minutes from the end when his cross was nodded into the net by Freedman, apparently too late for Port Vale to respond. Freedman led a ferocious celebration at one end of the field, but the explosion in the terrace behind Joe Anyon's net – filled to the nth degree with yellow and white shirts and a complete contrast to the thin scattering of Port Vale supporters at the opposite end of the pitch – spoke of a winning goal as vividly as the deathly silence which gripped the away stand in injury time spoke of their disbelief. It was with the final kick of the ball that Luke Rodgers, Vale's bald and stocky striker, stroked the ball past Casper Ankergren with the goalkeeper's defence marking shadows. United's players did not need to reach their dressing room to appreciate the extent of their failure and McAllister, who was not prone to spin at the best of times, made no effort to talk up the result. 'To lose a goal with the last kick of the ball is not good enough,' he said. 'The fact is that if you come away from home and score three goals, you should be going home with the points.' Hughes' feelings were no less transparent. 'Time's running out and it's running out fast,' he said, conscious of the fact that for the next two games he would be banned from duty.

The points surrendered in the 3–3 draw were again under-played by United's position in League One, which never fell to an unmanageable level, but the road ahead of Leeds was a mass of potholes and landmines. Walsall were scheduled to arrive at Elland Road a week later, closely followed by Brighton. In the weeks beyond those two home fixtures, Doncaster Rovers, Leyton Orient and Carlisle United would have the opportunity to take a bite out of Leeds, an animal that was limping if not yet seriously wounded. All five clubs had designs on the top six, some more realistic than others. But as he had after United's draw with Crewe – one of three successive stalemates – McAllister preached positivity to all who would listen. Big games suit big-game players, said a man who had fitted that description himself. 'We've got a few games against teams in and around us now. That might be a good thing,' McAllister predicted. 'People will be looking at us and saying our push is fading a little, but we're not going to roll up and hide in a corner. We've got to be there for the final run-in.'

The chance to assess the condition of United's equilibrium was presented to the entire nation on 22 March, courtesy of the only league fixture televised live from Elland Road by Sky Sports all season. The broadcasting schedule for their game against Walsall required a 5.20 p.m. kick-off, a time which encouraged traditional supporters to vomit, and the presence of television cameras placed Leeds in a daunting position. Sink, and the scorn of the English nation would follow them to the seabed. Swim, and the talk of a busted flush would cease instantly. McAllister is not adverse to a flutter, and he liked the look of the cards dealt to him. Jonathan Douglas had finally recovered from his knee ligament injury and, against the expectations of the club's physiotherapists, was able to sit amongst the substitutes during a game when United's poker hand struck gold without the need to gamble on the turn or the river.

Walsall's ambitions of qualifying for the play-offs were credible, but their five-man midfield took the risk of allowing Leeds to dictate the flow of the match. It was a costly misjudgement. In the 29th minute, Jermaine Beckford anticipated a through-ball from Neil Kilkenny, danced around Clayton Ince and flicked a shot over the line with the assistance of Anthony Gerrard's legs. It took 51 minutes for Beckford to strike again, but his second goal was almost a mirror image of his first. Kilkenny picked out his run with another lovely pass from midfield, and though Beckford's first touch was overly heavy, his pace allowed him to meet the ball early enough to flick a deft chip over Ince's body as Walsall's goalkeeper attempted in vain to sweep up for his unreliable defence. In between, United had treated Sky's viewers to a display of professionalism, always in control and rarely in danger. It was a rout without the flurry of goals, though it helped that Tommy Mooney had contrived to miss a sitter moments before Beckford's second goal concluded a 2–0 win. Richard Money, Walsall's manager, gave ample credit to Beckford while conceding that a place in the Championship had moved beyond his realistic expectations. 'At the end of the day, the centre forward was the difference between the teams,' said Money. 'We couldn't handle a very good player, who's obviously too good for this division. I would think he'll go into the Championship with Leeds next year, and possibly into the Premiership with Leeds the following year. The reality is that we're going to be a League One club next year.' Walsall were not mathematically finished, but with his closing comment Money indicated that one of United's key competitors was close to accepting elimination from a contest where the fittest survived at the ruthless expense of the rest. Money was justified in pointing out that respective budgets of the two clubs was an influential issue.

At the time, McAllister could not have realised the wider importance of the 2–0 victory over Walsall. It was clearly a valuable result but, in his head, it would come to represent the stage at which the frosty garden he agreed to tend for Bates had thawed at last. 'At the time I was reluctant to say it was must-win,' McAllister later admitted. 'But I think the players knew it was a game they had to get three points from. To get three points under the eye of a big crowd and the TV cameras, but also with a good performance . . . from there I started to have a better feeling. That was the push-on point.'

The strength of impetus was not so great that Leeds were able to avoid a goalless draw with Brighton at Elland Road the subsequent Saturday, a draw that was ably assisted by a linesman whose reading of the offside rule appeared to have been done in Braille. His wayward performance left Dean Wilkins, Brighton's manager, unimpressed, conscious as he was that Albion were only a small step ahead of Leeds in sixth position. McAllister reserved his criticism for his players, though the chastisement was deservedly mild. The clearest chance had fallen to Dougie Freedman, who was thwarted by a two-handed save from Michel Kuipers as he ran clear towards Brighton's goal, and Leeds in all had fashioned 16 shots on goal. 'It's absolutely two [points] dropped,' he said. 'I can't fault anybody for effort and workrate but we huffed and puffed rather than being smooth.'

A fluctuating month arrived at a low-key conclusion, but McAllister was satisfied – satisfied that his players had the guts for the fight he was asking them to win. The same cast-iron stomachs had rendered the club's 15-point penalty impotent, and their manager suspected he had re-discovered that hardened interior. The subject of the 15 points, meanwhile, was once again the focus of intense debate, and a grievance which Ken Bates had neither forgiven nor forgotten.

15

FIFTEEN POINTS, WHO GIVES A F**K?

A S FAR AS LORD BRIAN MAWHINNEY, THE FOOTBALL LEAGUE'S chairman, was concerned, Leeds United's protest against their 15-point sanction started and finished with the ill-fated appeal to the League's member clubs on 9 August. The appeal hearing had been expedited – organised and concluded within the space of six days – with the specific aim of reaching a resolution before the first weekend of the 2007–08 season, and Mawhinney considered the unanimous vote in support of the Football League to be the end of the matter. His organisation had been vindicated, and Leeds had signed a legal waiver which precluded the club from any further appeals. Case closed. It was standard practice for the League to insist on such an agreement with any club returning to a solvent position after a period in administration. Shortly after discharging the appeal hearing, Mawhinney appeared on the steps of the Churchill Hotel in London for an impromptu television interview. 'We had a vote which overwhelmingly endorsed the decision that there should be a sanction,' he said. 'Leeds are starting the new season in League One as a valued member of the League's football family but with a penalty of 15 points.' A former Member of Parliament and Shadow Home Secretary for the Conservative Party, Mawhinney's use of spin was skilful. Leeds United did not feel valued; on the contrary, they felt horribly oppressed. And if Mawhinney believed the club would take a beating without punching back, he was woefully under-estimating the tenacity of the man with whom he was sharing a ring.

With hindsight, Bates' intentions had been made clear by the letter he sent to the Football League's club chairmen two days before his unsuccessful appeal in London. The language in the document was powerful and emotive: Leeds had broken no rules, he argued, and their administrators, KPMG, had complied with the 'law of the land'. The challenge against his Company Voluntary Arrangement (CVA) by Her Majesty's Revenue and Customs was 'a sham'. But the most revealing phrase came in the letter's final paragraph, where Bates described the sanction as 'wholly unfair and a breach of natural justice'. In effect, it was a veiled warning to anyone who expected Leeds to roll over and submit simply because the majority of the other 71 Football League clubs had told them to do so. Within days of United's failed appeal, Bates set his legal representatives the complicated but urgent task of picking through the Football League's rules and regulations to establish how legitimate the 15-point penalty was, and whether or not the organisation had the power to impose it. Leeds thought not, and a statement from the club – humorously entitled 'Leeds United 0 Taxman 1 (og Football League)' – denounced the outcome of the appeal hearing as 'perverse'.

United's first port of call was the Football Association, who were asked in a written letter sent to Soho Square in September to review the penalty and the Football League's decision-making progress. The letter was passed to Jonathan Hall, the FA's Director of Governance, who ruled that there was nothing to suggest to him that the Football League had ignored their own rules. Like a tennis ball, the correspondence sent to Elland Road outlining Hall's opinion was returned to Soho Square with a probing forehand from Bates, who in turn requested that the FA open a Commission of Inquiry to investigate the deduction. The governing body passed the request to the chairman of the Football Regulatory Authority (FRA), who sought external legal advice but still agreed with Hall that the Football League should be absolved of any presumed guilt. The season by that stage had reached November and, on that particular avenue, Leeds had reached an blockade. The FA were clearly unwilling to fight United's corner. Bates was furious and accused the governing body of 'evasive behaviour and delaying tactics' and 'shambolic administration'. The FA informed Leeds that the club had the right to challenge the FRA's refusal to open a Commission of Inquiry through independent arbitration under FA rules, but the argument was threatening to become hopelessly convoluted. Bates suspected the authorities were purposely complicating the dispute, and when the FA's agreement to independent arbitration was followed by the warning that they had, in Bates' words, 'reserved the right to apply to the courts to strike out the arbitration', United's chairman decided to go the whole hog. On 19 January, in his programme notes before Leeds' 1–0 defeat to Doncaster Rovers at Elland Road, he announced that the club had resolved to sue the Football League directly.

The realisation that the dispute might reach the High Court was of no surprise to anybody who knew Bates and had followed the case closely. United's 15-point deduction was as contentious and confusing as the disagreement between Sheffield United and West Ham United at the end of the 2006–07 season, which concerned West Ham's registration of two Argentinian players, Carlos Tevez and Javier Mascherano. That particular argument was eventually placed in the hands of the judiciary and seemed incapable of reaching a definite conclusion. Leeds' gripe with the Football League bore the same legal hallmarks; to most onlookers, it had the High Court written all over it. On 4 February, United served a writ on the Football League, confirming their intention to sue for the return of their 15 points. Eight days later, a claim form was lodged in the High Court of Justice's Chancery Division. Claim number HC08C00384 requested a 'declaration that the defendants [the Football League] acted unlawfully in imposing a 15-point deduction on the . . . claimant in respect of the 2007–08 League One football season'.

The most surprising aspect of the writ was the inclusion of Barnsley Football Club 2002 Limited as a second claimant alongside Leeds. The Football League were shocked to discover that Barnsley had agreed to stand side-by-side with United, but not as surprised as Barnsley themselves. Gordon Shepherd, the chairman at Oakwell, reacted with mystified bemusement, admitting that the offer of support to Elland Road had been made without his knowledge, apparently authorised by another member of Barnsley's board. The offer was withdrawn. 'I have nothing against Leeds United but this is their fight, not Barnsley's,' Shepherd told the *Yorkshire Post*.

In response to the writ, the Football League said little, a policy of silence which was rarely broken. Mawhinney merely promised to present a 'robust defence'. The FA were not thrilled by the thought of legal action against an organisation under their umbrella, but nor were they interested in engaging in a verbal scuffle with Bates. 'The decision on whether to refer the matter to the High Court is a matter for Leeds and not the FA,' a statement published by the governing body said. There was, however, a blatant obstacle which United appeared to have circumnavigated. In August, the club had put their name to an official document in which the club promised not to seek future redress from the Football League over their 15-point deduction. The League's understanding was that the waiver was legal and binding, and that the High Court writ served on them was in breach of that deal. Asked to justify his decision to sue, Bates told the *Yorkshire Evening Post*: 'The agreement we had saying we wouldn't take legal action was signed under duress. We were a couple of days from the start of the season and we wouldn't have been able to fulfil our fixtures without regaining our share in the Football League. In that situation, we either signed the document or we let ourselves be booted out of the League. But [European Union] law says Person A cannot prevent Person B from going to court if it's to right a wrongful decision.' Bates believed he had carte blanche to shred the agreement, a misconceived assumption as it would later transpire.

The issue of the 15-point deduction was an important sideshow to the season in progress, but a sideshow nonetheless. The statistical significance of the penalty was made clear by the League One table at the start of April, which showed Leeds 14 points short of second place. The division's other competitors had virtually forgotten about United's handicap, save for the occasional cries of protest heard from Elland Road, but they were awoken to it again by the sudden realisation of how drastically a ruling which revoked the punishment would alter the table. There were few who believed that Leeds would prevail, and few who believed their case was anything more than frivolous, but you never knew with Bates. United's chairman had faith in the argument drawn up by his legal team – a 27-page document submitted to the High Court – and nine months of preparation indicated that his challenge would not be without foundation. At a stroke, the return of 15 points would see Leeds regain the second automatic promotion position which Carlisle United held in their possession on 1 April, the day when the postponed match between Leeds and Doncaster Rovers was belatedly staged at the Keepmoat Stadium.

Gary McAllister had good reason to pay attention to the legal dispute, but equally good reason to distance himself from it in public. In a sense, it was nothing to do with him beyond his natural desire to see his club receive unreserved justice. He had come to Elland Road long after the penalty was imposed, and the instruction to him from Bates to complete United's promotion did not take the potential recovery of 15 points into account. McAllister's rhetoric never changed. 'We're leaving that side of things to our legal team and the chairman,' he would say. 'Our job as players and management staff is to get on with winning games. We're budgeting for zero points.' The strategy was rational and, to a degree, essential. Before their game at Doncaster – the first of seven remaining matches – United were eighth in League One with 58 points. The combined evidence of past seasons showed that a mark of around 75 might be required to guarantee a position inside League One's top six, a figure some six wins beyond Leeds' current position. A game at the Keepmoat Stadium was as difficult a fixture as McAllister could have looked for at the beginning of a decisive month but he had one advantage to fall back on – United's form and demeanour were considerably better than they had been in February, when a frozen pitch brought about the game's postponement.

McAllister believed his side's 2–0 victory over Walsall on 22 March saw the birth of their powerful run to the end of the season, but the 1–0 victory achieved in Doncaster seemed every bit as momentous. It was, perhaps, the night on which United were re-established as main players in League One. They trusted to good fortune on several occasions – never more so than at the start of the second half, when a Doncaster corner struck Bradley Johnson's arm and scuffed against Casper Ankergren's right-hand post – and while Leeds were unable to mirror the hosts' patient and fluid performance, the intensity of McAllister's players and their willingness to defend the 20th-minute goal provided by Alan Sheehan's brilliant free-kick – a direct left-footed strike from the corner of Doncaster's penalty area – depicted a team who were beginning to appreciate their potential. Sean O'Driscoll, Doncaster's manager, claimed his club could have won by a 'cricket score', a fair comment considering the number of opportunities they created, but the fact remained that Leeds had cashed in on a game which the bookmakers and many of their own supporters had assumed they would lose. No manner of ifs or buts could detract from a victory which was priceless in value and richly deserved on the basis of United's defiant attitude. Style – a trait associated with Doncaster – was of little relevance. As Jake LaMotta proved by becoming the first boxer to overcome the finesse of Sugar Ray Robinson, there is no substitute for punches that sting. Nor should you overlook the value of heart. I once met LaMotta in 2006 at the White Rose shopping centre in Leeds, half a mile away from Elland Road, where he was taking part in an organised book-signing session. The Italian-American was something of a contradiction – an 84-year-old with a hearing aid and desperately frail skin, but dressed in a flamboyant Stetson and armed with a quick tongue which proved he had lead left in his pencil. 'They'll say my chin could take a punch better than anyone else's in the world,' he said, when asked how the public would speak of him in later years. 'People will remember me as having the toughest chin of all time.' Robinson later served as best man at LaMotta's wedding; Leeds and Doncaster will never grow so close. But for all the punches landed on them, United's concentration and balance had held. 'This gives us a massive platform,' their young defender, Paul Huntington, admitted afterwards. 'You can't make excuses when you're in a position like this because the play-offs are there for the taking.'

Huntington spoke for the entire dressing room. Four days after the Tuesday night win in Doncaster, Leeds travelled to Leyton Orient and dismantled a team who, before kick-off, had been listed as possible candidates for a play-off position. The truth was that after a creditable but arduous season, Orient's progress was slowing to the pace of a resigned walk. They were pulled to pieces by a display which was as authoritative as any produced by Leeds under either McAllister or Wise, and the 2–0 scoreline in United's favour at the final whistle treated Orient kindly. Huntington scored the opening goal with a flicked header in the 16th minute, and Beckford took his tally for the season to 20 by rifling a cut-back from Dougie Freedman into the roof of Orient's net early in the second half. After a victory over Doncaster by what Rovers felt was a debatable split decision, the defeat of Orient was the equivalent of a vicious knockout. The only worry for McAllister was the sight of Beckford limping from the field at Brisbane Road with an injured ankle, a problem which he believed would prove minor. The striker wished to spend the Saturday night in London, which suggested the damage was not drastic. Surprisingly, it would take until the play-offs for the injury to heal fully, but 5 April was a time for considered and positive reflection. For the first time since McAllister's maiden game as manager, Leeds were ranked among League One's top six clubs. Martin Ling, the Orient manager, was sold on the idea that United might be moving in the direction of the Championship. 'Leeds will be in the play-offs now, without doubt,' he said. 'It was men against boys really. Let's be honest, the best team won and they showed the gulf in class.' They had also shown an impressive talent in applying tunnel vision to matters outside their control.

As the majority of McAllister's players began the journey home from London, the struggle between Leeds and the Football League was reaching a crescendo. The League had been given a fortnight to reply to the High Court writ served on them in February, but the response sent to Elland Road on the day of the deadline was not what Leeds had expected. Far from agreeing to grant Bates his day in court, the Football League offered to settle the disagreement through independent arbitration, to be staged privately and under FA rules. Bates was adamant that the deduction should be debated openly, allowing the public and in particular the media the chance to accurately analyse the issues involved. United's chairman hoped that a public hearing would serve to expose the flaws and malpractice which he claimed the Football League were guilty of. But proceeding to arbitration before the High Court was a sign of due process, and after 48 hours of consideration, Bates reluctantly accepted the proposal. The date for the start of arbitration proceedings was set for 16 April.

Leeds planned to apply the detailed contents of their High Court claim form to the arbitration tribunal and their argument – though complex in its entirety – was inherently simple. First, United did not accept that their insolvency had breached Football League rules or parliamentary law. Second, the club were not of the opinion that the Football League's rules relating to administration gave the body the power to impose a 15-point sanction on a club in the position that United had been on 3 August 2007. And third, the club would argue that they were powerless to prevent the collapse of their Company Voluntary Arrangement (CVA), which, when all was said and done, seemed to be the crux of the dispute. The League demanded a CVA from every insolvent club, but also required that insolvent clubs pay their football creditors in full. Her Majesty's Revenue and Customs (HMRC), meanwhile, detested the idea that tax funds went begging while players and managers received full reimbursement, and, as a matter of principle, were therefore unwilling to vote in favour of any CVA. Bates claimed that Leeds had been punished by the Football League for following the organisation's own rules on football debts, though HMRC's dissatisfaction with the CVA and their subsequent legal challenge against it was not solely concerned with their creditor status. It also paid close attention to the voting rights of three creditors who had helped to approve the agreement in June. Bates, however, sought to remind the League that his offer to creditors had been the highest and most valuable available to KPMG, something which Mawhinney and his board had accepted as fact. It was certainly a face-off that Leeds intended to win, without ever presuming that they would. With the agreement of both sides, a three-man arbitration panel was selected, comprising tribunal chairman Sir Philip Otton, Peter Leaver and Peter Cadman. Otton was a retired High Court judge whose name had entered the consciousness of professional football during the case involving Sheffield United and West Ham. He had been responsible for chairing that particular tribunal, and his biography revealed extensive legal experience alongside the occasional foray into the world of sporting litigation. Leaver was a former Premier League chief executive, and Cadman's background was that of prominent lawyer with many years of high-profile work behind him. Bates was satisfied with the panel's make-up, but as 16 April approached, the hatches came down. Both Leeds and the Football League had agreed to keep their dealings confidential until the arbitration panel revealed their verdict, and a nervous silence settled over the case.

To lighten the mood, Leeds announced on 3 April that McAllister had accepted a new contract with the club, a 12-month rolling deal which would begin immediately. Until the announcement, McAllister had been tied to an agreement that was due to expire at the end of the season, and though other issues were of more pressing importance than his own position, it was reassuring to see Leeds nail their colours to his mast. He had earned that support and justified it immediately with the convincing victory at Leyton Orient. Plans were drawn up to tie his assistant Steve Staunton and first-team coach Neil McDonald to similar terms. 'It took me all of two seconds to say yes to this,' McAllister said. 'There wasn't a great deal of negotiating. It's a show of faith in the club by me and it's a fantastic honour to be manager of Leeds United for an extended period.' United's manager had always anticipated that if the results under him were acceptable to Bates, his contractual position would take care of itself. Much the same thinking was applied by McAllister to the outcome of arbitration. But ignoring the case completely was often impossible, and the visit of Carlisle United to Elland Road for a 12.15 p.m. kick-off on 12 April was set against the backdrop of the pending legal duel set to begin in four days' time.

Carlisle had clung on to second position under pressure from Doncaster, and the Cumbrians were on the outskirts of securing automatic promotion with five steps of the 46-game season still to complete. Leeds remained 14 points further back, and were no threat to Carlisle – unless, that was, a decision from the arbitration panel altered League One's landscape. It did not take a graphic calculator to work out the mathematics involved. Carlisle's manager, John Ward, gave the impression of a man who was oblivious to the possible permutations, but there was no denying that the clubs who stood to suffer from a verdict in favour of Leeds were beginning to twitch. Doncaster sounded worried, to judge by the comments of their chairman John Ryan, and Carlisle were, too. Swansea City, meanwhile, could not be certain of winning the title despite their convincing lead at the top of the division. The situation was farcical, and though Leeds were ultimately blamed for the length of time taken to bring their claim to arbitration, it did not reflect well on the Football League's disciplinary system either. There was no excuse for allowing a matter of such gravitas to hang in the air for nine months. Wednesday, 16 April fell a mere fortnight before the end of the season and the credibility of League One was not enhanced by such ponderous progress. Every manager was desperate to shut out the conflict; some will have been more successful than others. It is ironic to record that the coach least affected by a brawl in his own back yard was McAllister himself.

A crowd of 28,530 were sucked into Elland Road for the game against Carlisle and were provided with outstanding value for money. The visitors dictated a first half in which Leeds lacked precise rhythm, and Scott Dobie gave Ward's team a 1–0 lead at the interval by tucking home a low cross from Simon Hackney. The opening 45 minutes – a period of intrigue rather than sensation – were the prelude to a gripping second half in which the clout provided by United's deep squad overwhelmed Carlisle. Dougie Freedman bundled an equaliser over the line in the 50th minute, punishing an error by goalkeeper Keiren Westwood, and Leeds established a narrow lead nine minutes later when Jonathan Howson arrived with convenient timing to thrash a rebound into the net. Within 60 seconds, Casper Ankergren dropped a corner at the feet of Danny Graham, who hooked home Carlisle's second goal, but the Cumbrians were hanging on by too thin a thread. When a free-kick from Neil Kilkenny sprung from a crowd of players who were blocking Westwood's view, Freedman pounced with a scintillating volley which strained the net in front of the Kop. The striker proved the decisive presence, and somewhat unexpectedly. He had not been expected to play against Carlisle, having been sent home from Leeds' hotel with sickness and diarrhoea 24 hours earlier, but he reappeared at breakfast on the morning of the game and was gratefully added to the squad by McAllister. Talk of Freedman's bowels raised a smile at the post-match press conference, but United's manager was more serious when he asked whether the constitution of rival clubs and players would hold with arbitration pending. 'What I've started thinking about is how other clubs are seeing it now and how they're feeling,' he said, before admitting that a resolution either way would also provide respite for him and his squad. 'As much as the players have been fully focused, if they pick up a paper and see that it's been dealt with, that will be a relief.'

Before the arbitration hearing could begin in earnest, Leeds were beaten 1–0 during a rain-drenched midweek match at Huddersfield Town. United's performance was not especially impressive but the game was complicated by the first-half dismissals of Jonathan Douglas and Jonathan Worthington, both shown red cards on the back of two yellows. The 10-a-side fixture that both teams were left to contest seemed to suit Huddersfield, who settled the West Yorkshire derby with a header from Andy Holdsworth 14 minutes before the final whistle. The result was frustrating but it did not hinder Leeds unduly. David Prutton seemed unconcerned. 'I'm not going to claim it's a good result,' he said, 'but it's a minor setback in the grand scheme of what we're trying to achieve. It's our first defeat in seven.' It was also a defeat that the supporters would be happy to accept in exchange for a telling victory off the field.

The arbitration panel selected to rule on the 15-point deduction convened at Keating Chambers on Essex Street in London on the morning of 16 April. The case had been set down for three days and the plan to conclude proceedings with final submissions on Friday, 18 April initially floated the possibility that a verdict might be forthcoming before Leeds played at Millwall the following afternoon. It soon became clear that the weight of evidence would force an extension of the hearing, and the case spilled into a fourth day on Monday, 21 April. Confusion was created momentarily by an announcement from Sir Philip Otton's office, revealing that a decision could take as long as four weeks to be reached, but the panic which greeted that suggestion soon brought a second statement confirming 1 May as the latest date for a full and final verdict. The timeline met the demands of Leeds, who had agreed to arbitration on the proviso that their case was considered and ruled upon before the end of the season, preventing any disruption to the final League One table or the organisation of the play-offs. But the exact timing of the verdict was a minor consideration for Bates, who had been prepared to wait for as long as necessary to take the Football League to task. In the end, the arbitration panel used every hour and minute available to them before issuing their decision to a watching world whose patience would have stretched no further.

So much attention had been garnered by the arbitration proceedings that United's excellent 2–0 win over Millwall was forced to vie for column inches as if it were an afterthought. In the predictably hostile surroundings of Bermondsey – an area of London to which the entire Metropolitan Police seemed to have decamped – Leeds repelled a lively performance from their hosts to arrive on the threshold of the play-offs with their 25th victory of the season. Millwall's Jem Karacan hit the crossbar at the start of the second half but David Prutton struck first in the 70th minute with a delightful volley from 20 yards, and Andrew Hughes ended the contest by adding the finishing touch to a lovely passing move which cut holes in the home. McAllister was gracious in praising Millwall's contribution, but a United squad who had grown in strength throughout the month of April were slowly squeezing the life from the few remaining clubs within reach of the top six. Their win at the New Den had shaken off the pursuit of Tranmere Rovers and Walsall; only Brighton could now outpace Leeds to sixth position, and the four-point lead held by United with two games to play did not say much for Albion's prospects. Leeds barely acknowledged the presence of the Sussex club behind them. A win at Yeovil Town six days later would render Brighton's intentions academic. 'It's a very good day for the club, and an important one as well,' said Hughes outside the New Den. 'We're nearly there. We just need one last effort.'

The Metropolitan Police had surprised United's travelling support by allowing the game between Leeds and Millwall to start at the traditional Saturday kick-off time of 3 p.m. The trusting approach conflicted with the attitude of many other constabularies asked to handle Yorkshire's Republican Army, and in Yeovil the sledgehammer was again taken to United's nut. On police advice, Leeds' last away fixture – a game for which their ticket allocation of 1,640 was a quarter of Huish Park's small capacity – was scheduled for a Friday night, creating a camel-train of travellers between Leeds and Somerset on 25 April. From the streets of Yorkshire to the door of Huish Park, the roads felt like a nose-to-tail procession of Leeds United supporters. There was the silver Ford Focus on the M621 with the club's crest splashed on its rear windscreen; the Transit van on the M1 by Sheffield carrying three passengers in the yellow colours of United's away shirt; Strensham Services at the top of the M5, which swarmed with supporters by 1p.m.; and the grey Vauxhall Astra on the A37 between Bristol and Yeovil with a scarf displaying white, blue and yellow stripes pulled across its back seat. On exiting the town on the morning after the game, the first car in front of me was a blue Mercedes with a Leeds scarf screwed up in the back window, no doubt as crumpled as the hungover body in the driver's seat. I arrived at the Travelodge at Podimore, on the northern edge of Yeovil, to find a window by the entrance blocked out by a huge flag bearing the letters 'LUFC', adjacent to a sign which read 'Extension newly opened. Rooms from £29 per night.' They was not short of takers. Yorkshire accents flew around on the steps of the hotel, and bottles of Stella Artois rolled. MasterCard would have lapped it up – a room for the night: £29; a bottle of Stella: £2.50; club merchandise: £9.99; entrance to Huish Park: priceless. Even at Yeovil's ground, three hours before kick-off, an opportunistic supporter had attached a flag bearing Leeds United's badge to the dull grey railings surrounding the training ground on the perimeter of the stadium. 'Bloody hell,' said a friendly steward, unusually old for the diamond stud in his ear. 'These Leeds fans are everywhere. If they've all got tickets, then Christ knows how. It's a busy night for us, I reckon.' His fears were not realised. The behaviour of United's supporters was impeccable, and a fourth-minute goal from Dougie Freedman was all it took to hand Leeds a 1–0 win over a tepid Yeovil side, and confirm beyond doubt that their season would finish in the play-offs, arbitration notwithstanding. Alan Sheehan's straight red card for a rash foul on Lee Peltier soured the evening slightly but his dismissal could not obscure the discussion of what the victory in Somerset meant. It was the 45th leg of a season which words at that moment could not adequately describe; a season for which superlatives were invented but could never do justice. You recalled the despondency felt on the day Leeds were relegated from the Championship, and the day they were clubbed by their 15-point deduction – recalled it, but could not truly feel it. The effect of United's triumphant endeavour from 11 August 2007 to 25 April 2008 had been to exorcise the negativity and infighting which had been so prevalent and so destructive at Elland Road 12 months earlier. It felt suddenly like watching a different club. McAllister took the credit he was due but, with perspective typical of an ambitious manager, dampened the sense of occasion. 'Everybody's pleased but it's a case of not over-celebrating,' he said. 'The achievement is minor for the fact that we're in the play-offs. The big target is to get out of this league.'

Arbitration had pledged to speed up that process by lifting United towards the one remaining automatic promotion position behind Swansea City, but the promise proved to be false. The populace of Leeds and beyond were brought to the edge of their seats by the news that a 5 p.m. announcement would be forthcoming from the tribunal panel on 1 May, the day of their self-imposed deadline and two days before the final weekend of the season. As television and radio journalists sifted urgently through the weighty 18-page ruling issued from the Chartered Institute of Arbitrators on Bloomsbury Square in London, word began to spread that United had lost their appeal. Worse still, they had lost their appeal emphatically. The tribunal upheld the 15-point deduction unequivocally, stating that 'the [Football League's] Board had all the requisite authority to exercise its powers and discretion to impose a Condition of a 15 point deduction. Moreover, the Insolvency Policy . . . properly construed, did not prevent the board imposing the condition.' That comment was no more than a postscript. The case presented by Leeds had already fallen at two previous hurdles after the panel decided that the legal waiver agreed between United and the Football League was binding, and that the delay in seeking arbitration was 'unreasonable and inexcusable' on the part of Leeds. The appeal was dismissed on those individual grounds alone, before the validity of the penalty was even considered. The tribunal did not confirm that United had *deserved* their punishment, but rather confirmed that the Football League had the right and the power to judge for themselves. In other words, it was the Football League's ball and you played the game by the rules as they saw them. For Bates, it was a defeat in any language, though he was not prepared to go quietly. He fought back against the criticism directed at Leeds over the period of nine months taken to resolve the argument, and described the issue of the legal waiver as 'a technicality'. He also repeated his previous request for the Football League to explain exactly which rule had been broken by Leeds. The tribunal's 18-page award document did not make that clear, though it had taken to describing the 15-point deduction as a condition rather than a 'sanction', as Mawhinney had called it in August. What became clear was that the punishment was in fact a compromise, agreed to by Leeds in preference to relegation to League Two or the complete cessation of their Football League membership. As the ruling made plain, the Football League considered all three eventualities when the matter of United's membership was discussed in July and early August of 2007. Leeds had taken the option of retaining their League One status while incurring a 15-point penalty, subject to a single appeal to their fellow clubs. Bates did record two victories, prompting recommendations from the three-man panel that the Football League review their insolvency policy and their appeals process. 'We might have lost the battle but we've won the war,' said Bates. His call for Mawhinney and the Football League board to resign en masse was ignored.

The only satisfaction to be taken from a day which had fallen so far short of Leeds United's expectations was the club's decision to draw a line under the dispute. 'The matter is now closed,' a statement from United read, ending nine months of bitter wrangling in five short words. The city grimaced as one, and then moved on. Forty-eight hours later, 38,256 spectators welcomed Leeds home for their one remaining match of the regular season at Elland Road, a staggering attendance which placed the mundane and perfunctory world of legal conflict in a suitably dark shadow. An arbitrational loss aside, Leeds were still the same buoyant entity they had been at Huish Park a week earlier. Perhaps it was appropriate – or even fated – that a season of such unprecedented strain would stand or fall in the play-offs. To quote John Milton:

'Long is the way and hard that out of hell leads up to light.'

Huish Park was an odd portrayal of heaven, but the stadium had been responsible for taking Leeds to the gates. How amusing it was that T-shirts sold by United at the start of the season had carried the question 'Where's Yeovil?' As I wrote in my match report for the *Yorkshire Evening Post* on 26 April, the enthralling answer was two stops from Wembley.

16

BACK TO THE PLAY-OFFS

THE MAJORITY OF PROFESSIONAL CLUBS MAINTAIN A LOVE–HATE relationship with the Football League's play-off system. Others, like Preston North End, stop a long way short of love. On six occasions Preston have qualified for the play-offs at the end of a league season, and on six occasions promotion has fallen into the hands of their competitors. In crude mathematical terms, the Lancashire club have staked 268 regular matches on the play-offs since 1993 – or 24,120 minutes if you prefer – and walked away with precisely nothing. Their record flagrantly ignores the laws of chance and cannot have failed to create a complex at Deepdale. Preston are a club for whom automatic promotion was invented, and for whom the play-offs are designed to torment. Leeds United's record is less humiliating, but it is nevertheless complete in its distinct lack of success – two play-off finals reached and two defeats incurred. The club's first involvement in 1987 came under a different format which pitched Leeds, then a member of England's second division, against Charlton Athletic in the final. Charlton had finished fourth from bottom in Division One and were effectively given a last and perhaps unwarranted chance to fend off relegation. They did so after a two-legged tie which required a replay at St Andrews, the home of Birmingham City. The result was naturally depressing for the players from Elland Road but they were afforded much credit for their involvement in an epic final. The reluctance with which United were pushed aside by Charlton was epitomised by their captain, Brendan Ormsby, who annihilated ligaments and cartilage in one knee while attempting to dispossess Garth Crooks. Twenty-one years on, Ormsby's joint still aches when he runs on concrete.

The story of 2006 was scarcely comparable, and 21 May 2006 was a day without redeeming features, save for the gathering of Leeds United's supporters inside Cardiff's Millennium Stadium, where their number was estimated at 50,000. If that guess was higher than the reality, it was not wrong by a significant margin. The attendance for the Championship play-off final was extraordinary but not, as it turned out, inspirational. United were beaten by a limited Watford team, and beaten heavily, in a woeful manner which has never been adequately rationalised. Whether through over-confidence or a crisis of confidence, the chance to reacclimatise themselves to the Premier League passed Leeds United by like a ship in the night. The parallel universe created in Wales on 21 May has been considered at length by many in Leeds. Four months later, Kevin Blackwell was sacked as the club's manager. Twelve months later, United were relegated and declared insolvent. That particular play-off final was called the '£30 million game' on account of the guaranteed income that lay in wait inside the Premier League. Leeds felt the cost of that lost revenue in so many different, painful ways.

Any mention of the play-offs in 2008 was therefore likely to cause a mild shudder among the fans who remembered the despondency of a long, damp and miserable road home from Cardiff. The scope for failure – deserved or otherwise – has always been vast in a promotion system which annually disappoints 75 per cent of the clubs who qualify for the semi-finals. Leeds had accepted that automatic promotion from League One was an unrealistic ambition weeks before their victory over Yeovil Town on 25 April, a fact confirmed by the negative outcome of arbitration. To Gary McAllister, confirmation of a place in the division's top six was an extremely positive development; such an outcome could not have been called a formality when he signed his initial contract at Elland Road. And there was, according to the statistics, a subtle difference between his version of Leeds United and that possessed by Blackwell two years earlier. In 2006, Leeds arrived at the play-offs with one victory from their final ten games; with a home fixture against Gillingham to come, McAllister was looking at a record of five wins from six matches. United might feel an ounce of trepidation at the sight of the semi-finals appearing over the horizon but the clamour among clubs eager to play them was unlikely to be deafening. 'We should be favourites to win the play-offs because we're the team in form,' said their winger, Bradley Johnson. With the exception of Nottingham Forest, who were spared from the lottery when they won the promotion jackpot on the final day of the season, the 21-year-old was right in claiming that no other club were showing better results.

In one respect, McAllister's approach to United's last fixture of the term mirrored that adopted by Blackwell two years earlier. Both men decided that what amounted to a dead rubber was a convenient point at which to bring forward the fringe members of their squads. Gillingham's season was at the point of imploding and a victory at Elland Road was of paramount importance to their laboured attempt to avoid relegation; but without favourable results affecting Cheltenham and Bournemouth, they would be downgraded to League Two status regardless. McAllister was aware of the impact that a weakened line-up might have on the complex situation at the foot of the division, but the issue of relegation was not his concern. Five alterations were made to the team who beat Yeovil, including the inclusion at right-back of 20-year-old League One debutant Scott Gardner. Fabian Delph – named on the bench by United's manager – was two days away from his 17th birthday. Among the absentees were Dougie Freedman, Jermaine Beckford, Jonathan Howson and Neil Kilkenny. The line-up may have pleased Gillingham but it might also have disappointed Ken Bates, who had unfinished business with Paul Scally, Gillingham's chairman. A firm supporter of the Football League's decision to impose a 15-point penalty on Leeds, Bates took great exception to Scally's stance, and his one-time friend was no longer a welcome face in the chairman's suite at Elland Road. After digesting the arbitration ruling against United, Bates admitted openly that he would take unbridled pleasure from the sight of Leeds relegating Gillingham on 3 May. 'It's ironic that, having voted to penalise us, Gillingham find their fate in our hands,' said Bates. 'It would be even more ironic if we win and are responsible for relegating them. Some might say it was poetic justice.' Gillingham were duly dropped from League One but, according to Scally, he and Bates did not exchange a single word over the course of the afternoon. As one chairman turned his attention to a play-off campaign which his club could not contemplate losing, and another considered the implications of falling a division, it was apparent that both men had bigger priorities than their extended and pointless feud. Scally did take the chance of a final word, however, in an interview with BBC Radio Five Live outside Elland Road. 'Ken Bates has disappointed me enormously,' he said. 'I'm stunned by the way he's behaved.' Their friendship had seen better days.

So too had Leeds, as McAllister was moved to admit after the final whistle. His players fell behind to a goal from Simeon Jackson in the 20th minute, presented to the striker by an uncharacteristic mistake from Paul Huntington. The young centre-back was disposed of while trying to dribble the ball out of his own box, and he could not cover United's goalline in time to divert Jackson's low shot to safety. There was little more to be said of the first half, other than to note that the loss of continuity among McAllister's players incurred by six changes had been immediate. Gillingham's vintage was not especially striking, but there was no mistaking a club with a stake to protect at Elland Road. An afternoon which began with beach balls flitting through the warm and spirited air above the Kop was threatening to deflate with speed, and to imply that the fixture was meaningless was not to say that the supporters in attendance has paid to watch an abject defeat. The size of the crowd at Elland Road was the story of the game, eclipsing every other attendance in the Football League during the previous nine months and an increase on the average assembly of 11 Premier League clubs, Tottenham Hotspur and Everton included. For almost two years, Leeds declined to use the upper tier of their East Stand to avoid incurring business rates of close to £100,000, but the club had quickly realised that their results in April were creating enough interest and optimism to make a sell-out possible. For the first time since their play-off semi-final at home to Preston in May 2006, the decision was made to open the top tier in anticipation of Gillingham's visit. Prices for the additional area of the stadium were drawn up with common sense, and tickets began to move with astonishing speed; the match sold out on the afternoon of Thursday, 24 April. The following week, United uncovered a further 850 tickets, which departed as quickly as they reached the counters of their ticket office. In a nice piece of public relations work – and on Bates' insistence – free match programmes were distributed to every supporter, and the communal spirit was amplified by an attendance which was officially declared at 38,256. The last time a League One stadium was so substantially filled, Margaret Thatcher was embarking on her first year in the office of Prime Minister. McAllister appreciated the pull of Elland Road and would regularly scan the Sunday newspapers to see which grounds or cities had attracted bigger crowds than Leeds. There were rarely many. Fewer still would have been capable of drawing in 38,000 for a game against Gillingham on which little hinged. In the 15 minutes given to him at half-time, McAllister reminded his team that it would be wrong to be presumptuous about the mood of a crowd who were not averse to making their feelings known. Mild booing had greeted the whistle signalling the interval, and although the dissent was pantomime-esque, it was enthusiastic enough to confirm that a response from the players would be appreciated. To the crowd's satisfaction, it came in the manner that Leeds know best – brutally. The equaliser was a goal of sheer class, produced on 69 minutes by a display of textbook technique from Johnson. The winger met a cross from Sebastien Carole on the very edge of Gillingham's box and, with a short stab of his left boot, thrashed a volley to the right of goalkeeper Derek Stillie. His awesome finish brought the curtain down on Gillingham, but Leeds had a goal left in them, and it was appropriate that Tresor Kandol signed off a season which his 89th-minute header at Tranmere's Prenton Park had set fire to in August. Sixty seconds remained on the clock again when the striker appeared in a position which smelled strongly of offside and sprinted into Stillie's box before lashing a shot into the roof of the net. The goal was less momentous than his invaluable intervention in Birkenhead, but it brought a smile to the collective face of Elland Road. It also underlined Gillingham's relegation, though Cheltenham's victory over Doncaster Rovers at Whaddon Road had already seen to that. McAllister was sympathetic, as professional coaches tend to be. 'Their manager can be very proud of his players,' he said. 'They gave it everything. But there are no words from me that are going to console them.' As for Scally, Bates did not even try.

The more compelling issue for the thousands who processed out of Elland Road was the identity of United's opponents in the play-offs. The afternoon may have been of no palpable significance to Leeds but it was decisive for several other clubs. Doncaster Rovers' defeat at Cheltenham had allowed Nottingham Forest to steal second position with a 3–2 win over Yeovil at the City Ground, and Carlisle United's unsteady run to the tape continued with a 1–1 draw at home to Bournemouth. The line-up for the play-offs was completed by Southend United, who, like Leeds, were in no danger of finishing lower than sixth but could not influence the tussle for automatic promotion either. Yet, as inconsequential as Kandol's late goal seemed, it had a definite effect on the League One table. United had climbed to fifth place in the final seconds of the season and would play Carlisle in the semi-finals, at Elland Road initially and then at Brunton Park during the second leg. Southend, meanwhile, were paired with Doncaster, a team stung by their failure to retain second position under pressure but undoubtedly the most dangerous team potentially on offer to Leeds in the play-offs. John Ryan, Doncaster's chairman, rated his club as the most proficient footballing team in the division, and he was not alone in saying so. But for Kandol's strike, a pressurised Yorkshire derby between Leeds and Doncaster would have ensued over two legs, and an out-of-form Carlisle side were easy to depict as a preferable alternative to the club from down the A1. McAllister and his players sounded confident. 'There weren't any teams I wanted to avoid,' said Bradley Johnson, 'but I'm happy with Carlisle.' In spite of their previous experience of the play-offs, and perhaps against their better judgement, United's supporters were quick to agree.

The Cumbrian club were intriguing opposition. A strong link between Brunton Park and Elland Road existed in Neil McDonald, the first-team coach at Leeds who had been made redundant by Carlisle in August, and in the most abnormal of circumstances. A 1–1 draw with Walsall on the very first day of the season had been the final act of his managerial reign in Cumbria, and he was dismissed from his post 48 hours later. A credible reason for a sacking which had nothing to do with results was never proffered by the club, and McDonald could only conclude that his face did not fit under Carlisle's owner, Fred Story. 'It was simply down to one man making a decision,' McDonald said. 'A decision I didn't agree with.' His return to Brunton Park promised to be interesting. More pensive, arguably, was Paul Huntington, who knew he would be the subject of deliberately hostile attention in Cumbria. The defender was a native of Carlisle, where he grew up and went to school before signing for Newcastle United as a trainee. There was no irritable history of note between Huntington and the city's professional club and, by his own admission, his behaviour during the tempestuous league game between Leeds and Carlisle on 12 April had been a mistake. He was caught gesturing in less than friendly terms to the visiting supporters at Elland Road, who reacted in kind. Complaints were made to police officers present at the stadium, and though neither the law nor the Football Association saw good reason to follow up the incident (the matter went unmentioned in the report submitted by the match referee, Gloucestershire's Lee Probert), the controversy became briefly sinister. Huntington's mobile phone number was distributed on Internet forums and among supporters travelling home from Yorkshire, and for a short while he was allegedly the target of death threats. Though doubtless idle, the threats were worth taking seriously. A rapid and full apology was issued by the 20-year-old, who admitted his culpability wholeheartedly. A misjudgement, McAllister called it, and Carlisle's manager, John Ward, saw fit to let the incident pass without special mention. Both men were old enough to recognise over-exuberance, but their common sense and understanding did not prevent a chilly welcome for Huntington in his hometown. Before either he or McDonald could concern themselves with Brunton Park, however, Carlisle would be exposed to the hostility of Elland Road.

There is a general misconception, belied by statistical fact, that home advantage is of greater value in the second leg of a play-off semi-final, but the fact that Leeds were required to fulfil the first fixture at Elland Road did not register with McAllister as a cause for concern. Brunton Park was the scene of League One's strongest home record, consisting of 17 victories, three draws and three defeats, and Leeds had lost their first game of the season on that very ground. But Elland Road was regarded as a potent weapon in its own right. There was accurate talk of another crowd in the region of 38,000 attending the first leg, and looser discussions about the size of victory that Leeds were capable of producing. With Jermaine Beckford available after an ankle injury, Leeds would have their full armoury on show, and some spoke of McAllister's players putting the tie beyond Carlisle before the aura of Brunton Park could influence proceedings. In the media room at Elland Road on the night of Monday, 12 May, the confidence was frightening. To a man, those present were predicting a Leeds win – many by a margin of 2–0, and some by a heavier scoreline. The optimism followed the logic that a team as out of form as Carlisle were would be swamped by the atmosphere and the occasion. For the past two years, it had been rare to hear such buoyancy among the press, and during the season in which United were relegated from the Championship – when defeat became the staple diet – blind faith in Leeds was almost unheard of. Bitten repeatedly, journalists were wise to the folly of clinging to hope. The soaring confidence was slightly unnerving, and a more realistic air hovered in the streets and car parks around Elland Road. The stadium had promoted the mood of a carnival for Gillingham's visit, but the quiet tone of the supporters waiting to reach their seats on 12 May was brooding. Behind the West Stand, tense smiles mixed with stern expressions, and the scene was set to the compulsive soundtrack of rotating turnstiles, the familiar click-clack sounding at the same rapid speed as the fans' heartbeats. It was an evening when nerves reacted of their own accord. McAllister had seen the scenario many times as a player, and he was anxious to dissuade his squad from giving too much credence to the power of the crowd. 'We've got to feed them rather than them feeding us,' McAllister said. 'It's not a case of us going out there and expecting the crowd to take us over the line.' The fans inside the stadium were nevertheless willing to provide that assistance if and when they were called upon. A total of 36,297 had reached the terraces in time to hear the sound of Tony Bates' first whistle, which was almost lost in a powerful wave a shiver-inducing noise. They say that your eyeballs shake at a certain level of decibels, and Elland Road on 12 May was proof of that science. The only spare seats were in patches of yellow in the tiny area dedicated to Carlisle, who had inexplicably failed to sell their allocation of 2,000 tickets. The live broadcast transmitted by Sky will have played a part, but the company's ever-reliable coverage seemed a distant second-best to the up-close-and-personal alternative.

Ward expected to be temporarily deafened by the noise from the terraces, but he was immune to intimidation. His team had played at Elland Road exactly 30 days earlier and had performed credibly in an atmosphere which was no less intense. Greg Abbott, his assistant, was even more in tune with his surroundings, having worked as a youth-team coach at Leeds before leaving to take up employment with Carlisle in 2006. In an unassuming way, the two men felt confident. Ward's formation bordered on 4-5-1, but his versatile midfielder Marc Bridge-Wilkinson was given the freedom to roam in pockets of space behind Danny Graham, Carlisle's only striker and a former loanee at Elland Road. 'It would be folly of me to say let's be careful when the players are thinking we can go and win this,' Ward said when questioned about the option of playing for a draw and banking on the reliability of Brunton Park. He did not even consider the possibility. Leeds shared the early rounds, and shots from Beckford and Dougie Freedman were flicked away at full stretch by Keiren Westwood, a goalkeeper whose reputation was spiralling upwards. Within days of the conclusion of the League One semi-final, Westwood was called into the Republic of Ireland's squad for a training camp in Portugal, his first involvement with an international team. Beckford's effort generated a save of supreme quality, diverted to safety by the faintest of touches from Westwood's fingertips. McAllister, in the dug-out, believed the shot was destined for the corner of the net. But his players in general were finding Carlisle's system difficult to read, and Bridge-Wilkinson had already hit the post with a vicious volley when a Simon Hackney shot struck the back of Graham and deflected past Casper Ankergren. Graham knew as little about the goal as United's keeper but was generously credited with a strike which, by then, had been coming. As half-time approached, McAllister had good reason to be concerned. The majority of his players were under-performing, and there was obvious irony in the realisation that the occasion on which Carlisle were expected to wilt was in fact unsettling Leeds. 'Sometimes a big crowd can affect you in the wrong way,' McAllister remarked before kick-off, with accurate foresight. He was at a loss to explain why the reliable team he had fashioned and grown to trust was regressing at such an unacceptable moment. Hackney had an inkling. 'I was told that they [Leeds] thought they weren't going to need the second leg,' he said. 'But don't underestimate us. We're a good team with good players.'

McAllister was finding that hard to dispute. Five minutes into the second half, Carlisle sliced through his midfield, and an exchange of passes between Hackney and Evan Horwood saw the latter's square ball turned into the net by an off-balance Bridge-Wilkinson, eight yards from goal. His finish was critical, and Elland Road took a united gulp. McAllister had not seen a clean sheet as a formality; on the contrary, he had specifically advised his players to resist the urge to panic if their tactics failed. But though he claimed that a 2–0 lead in Carlisle's favour would not have been decisive, he cannot have liked the odds of Leeds redressing that scoreline during the second leg, at a stadium which gave out away wins as regularly as banks give away money. In the moments after Bridge-Wilkinson's goal, United had the makings of a beaten team and their season flashed before the eyes of the crowd at Elland Road. 'We're in the shit now,' said a depressed and anonymous voice to the right of the press box, spelling out the scale of the crisis in five sharp words. Other cries heckled McAllister but they were isolated yells, and the solidarity of the crowd survived in those horrible minutes, held together by the amount of time remaining. Forty minutes were left at Elland Road, and a minimum of 90 would be played at Elland Road. A goal from Leeds would leave Carlisle winded; a goal from Leeds would change everything. McAllister's players dared not reach full-time without one. But their situation became desperate once the four minutes of injury time signalled by the fourth official came and went.

Bates, though, had halted the match in added time to book Andrew Hughes for a painful challenge on Paul Arnison, and the Staffordshire official readjusted his clock to allow the game to run into the 96th minute. With what amounted to the final attack of the night, Huntington – at the frantic behest of McAllister on the touchline – wrong-footed his marker on the halfway line and hooked a high punt into the depths of Carlisle's box. Westwood hesitated briefly before declining the chance to claim the delivery, and a kind ricochet knocked the ball into the path of Freedman, who seized the moment by turning his left foot into a low shot that raced over a crowded goalline. Elland Road froze with the uncertainty of a horde who did not trust their eyes, and then shook with delirium at the end of a defeat which must rank among the most wildly celebrated in Leeds. United's propensity for late goals had been acclaimed at the start of the season but Freedman's goal pushed the boundaries of late, and McAllister had a twinkle in his eye as he and Ward shook hands on the touchline. Not over, they thought simultaneously; not over by a stretch. Ward was composed and preferred to acknowledge a creditable victory rather than bemoan Freedman's sense of timing. In a live interview on Sky, both Graham and Westwood were also keen to stress that they were unmoved by the slight erosion of their lead. But though strengthened by a slight advantage, Carlisle were not entirely certain of whether they or Leeds were in possession of the impetus. Freedman's goal had created doubt where, in the minds of Carlisle's players, there had previously been confidence. United's squad left Elland Road with a spring in their step, and McAllister left behind a choice soundbite for the media to play with. 'It's game on,' he said, more convinced than ever that Leeds were fated to roll their dice in the play-off final.

The opportunity to draw breath was brief. Unlike Doncaster and Southend, whose semi-final was split over a full week, Leeds were due in Carlisle for the second leg on the night of Thursday, 15 May, an interlude of only three days. On his arrival at Elland Road, McAllister had revised the club's training schedule and implemented warm-downs on the day after a competitive match, a process of conditioning in line with certain Premier League clubs and which regularly called for players to attend Thorp Arch on Sunday mornings (McAllister insisted on a disciplined approach to professional football, and it was noticeable after his appointment that United's squad began attending home fixtures wearing suits, shirts and ties, as opposed to the training kit tolerated by Wise). As his players wandered into the training ground after a brief but welcome night's sleep, he was relieved to discover that the only concern of any note was the now familiar ailment being nursed by Beckford. The striker's ankle continued to ache, but McAllister would give him until Thursday lunchtime to reach a state of match fitness. The word from the physiotherapists was that his chances of playing in the second leg were promising. McAllister, however, had a difficult decision to make. He could count on one hand the players who had performed acceptably against Carlisle. If he was being brutally honest, he could find fault with all of them. He kept his thoughts to himself at a press conference on the Wednesday afternoon, little more than 24 hours before kick-off, but he was at a loss to explain the manner of their defeat. No lack of effort, he thought, but a sudden lack of quality. 'I was as surprised as anybody by the performance,' he admitted once the semi-final was settled. The dilemma on his mind was who, if anyone, would bear the cost of that performance. He slept on the matter on Wednesday evening, perhaps the longest night of his short tenure. There was little more he could do to influence the tie, and the plan for Thursday was limited to a relaxing walk with his players.

United's staff completed the short journey to Cumbria on Wednesday, but the supporters who followed them the next day were met by the most impressive traffic jam ever seen between Carlisle and Glasgow. The contingent from Leeds stumbled into a vast flock of Glasgow Rangers fans who were returning home from the UEFA Cup final in Manchester and had painted the M6 in red, white and blue. Estimates set the numbers of Scots in Manchester at well over 100,000, a minority of whom had been involved in full-scale riots in the city centre. A few of those with enough energy left found their way into Carlisle on Thursday, in time for a brawl with a handful of United's affiliates, but the scuffles were minor and flash-in-the-pan. The more sensible option for the Glaswegian foot soldiers was to head for home and nurse the hangovers and disappointment instigated by their club's 2–0 defeat to Zenit St Petersburg. The M6 was mobbed by the race for the border – the bulk of the traffic heading for Glasgow, and a portion doubtless aiming to catch the ferry between Stranraer and Belfast on the east coast of Northern Ireland – and the A6 into Carlisle was almost stationary. The summer weather had taken hold of Cumbria, and the busy roads added to the sense of anticipation. This was football's business end, the point of the season where irreparable damage is certain to be inflicted. McAllister, for the first time, was forced to accept that the final whistle at Brunton Park might officially mark the start of his summer holiday. It was a thought designed to inspire or terrify.

The silver coach carrying Leeds United's players rolled past the bronzed statue of Hugh McIlmoyle and up behind Brunton Park's aged main stand shortly after six o'clock, just as the sun was starting to dip. Carlisle's home is irregular in its design, and delights in lacking any sort of uniformity. The Petteril End, where 1,600 of United's fans would be held, is an uncovered stand, and the Unison Stand at the other end of the field consists of concrete terracing. The CBS Stand, meanwhile, tells a tale of laughably nonsensical planning. The right-hand side of structure is positioned 20 yards in front of one goalline – virtually level with the edge of the penalty box – leaving the left-hand side to run far beyond the opposite end of the field. Supporters in the furthest reaches of the CBS Stand effectively sit behind the Petteril End and further away from the field. The stand is a dubious heirloom of Carlisle's former chairman, Michael Knighton, who had grand plans to move the entire stadium by a matter of metres but completed only a quarter of the work. Quite why Brunton Park had become such a formidable ground to visit is something of a mystery. McDonald suggested that the length of the journey forced upon most clubs by a visit to Cumbria was a factor; one member of United's staff thought differently, explaining that the ground was a 'shithole'. Traditional might have been a fairer description. Either way, it was a stadium where nothing came for free. The attendance of journalists on 15 May was so large that most could not buy an electricity point.

The first matter of interest for the reporters present was the line-up named by McAllister. United's boss is a man who chooses his words with care, and he had wisely avoided any unnecessarily brutal criticism of his team's performance in the first leg. But the team sheet he supplied was a useful indicator of how badly his faith had been damaged. Against expectation – and reassuringly for the Leeds-minded writers – his line-up did not include a single change. It was a vote of confidence McAllister had not been obliged to give, and a second chance for players who had been honest about their own failure in the first leg. It was also a last chance: a draw or worse at Brunton Park would condemn Leeds without mercy or the promise of a reprieve.

The scenario, in a sense, was simple for McAllister – win or bust. Ward, on the other hand, had choices to make. Defending a 2–1 lead was not his style but it was clearly an option. Within 10 minutes of Alan Wiley's first whistle, that option was removed. David Prutton made the most of a poor goal kick from Casper Ankergren by heading the ball away from the touchline, and his flick set in motion a flow of passes which chipped a whole in Carlisle's stable defence. Jonathan Howson's pass released Dougie Freedman on the left wing, and the striker's cross was anticipated by Howson, who controlled the ball with his chest and drilled a volley with his left foot beneath the dive of Keiren Westwood. Game on. Carlisle's performance until then had not been without energy, but the effect of an early goal was obvious. Their passing was more ponderous than it had been at Elland Road, hampered further by a badly damaged pitch at Brunton Park. Carlisle had committed £30,000 to repairing the surface, but the money was not put forward in time to aid the semi-final. So concerned were the club about the state of the turf that a junior football tournament planned to be staged at the stadium during the bank holiday weekend at the start of May was postponed at short notice. Any damage was meaningful damage, and Ward admitted to anyone who asked that that surface did not suit his team's style. Their clearest opportunity before half-time fell to Marc Bridge-Wilkinson, whose low shot struck the legs of Ankergren. Until then, the Dane's evening had been nothing more than routine, which was exactly as McAllister intended. Without exception, every player who had fallen short of his requirements at Elland Road had regained their appetite at Brunton Park. The skip in their legs as they moved towards the tunnel after 45 minutes revealed of quiet contentment in their heads. The surge in spirit supplied by Freedman's belated finish three days earlier had been as strong as anticipated, and with the outcome of the semi-final completely unpredictable, Leeds began to assume the initiative. A low shot from Freedman was parried with one hand by Westwood, as reliable and consistent as ever, but even Carlisle's keeper could not have reacted to the header from Bradley Johnson which struck the outside of the post with 11 minutes remaining. Yet it spoke volumes about the attitude of Ward and McAllister than neither manager was drawn into a substitution before Wiley indicated a single minute of injury time. Both managers were prepared for extra time, and the jerky, often meaningless, signals issued from the touchline were the engrossed reactions of men consumed by the enormity of the passing seconds. A hush fell on Brunton Park as Shaun Procter-Green, the fourth official, beamed the additional 60 seconds from his board at the side of the field, revealing that the crowd were also ready for a further half-hour. In that lull, Leeds struck the jugular. Neil Kilkenny gave instructions for Jonathan Douglas to play the ball from the halfway line to Frazer Richardson on the right wing, but it was rolled instead to the Australian's feet on the edge of the centre circle. Kilkenny looked up and threaded the ball to Freedman, who called on his years as a professional footballer by laying a delicate pass into the path of Howson. With a deft sweep of his left foot, the teenager swung a shot across Westwood's body and into the only square of the goal Carlisle's keeper could not reach. Howson broke away to celebrate on the touchline, met by players who had spilled out of United's dug-out at the sight of the net rippling. Ward's team sank to their knees, struck by the cruel thought that Wiley's minute of injury time had passed. The blow was fatal, and not a single soul in Brunton Park doubted that Howson's goal was the equivalent of a ticket to Wembley. Wiley allowed the match to restart, but sounded the final whistle just in a flash, sending yellow shirts sprinting towards the Petteril End, which had lost any semblance of order. Carlisle decided before full-time to keep United's supporters inside the ground for reasons of safety, and the lock-in was unforgettable. Chased from the pitch briefly by an invasion of Carlisle's supporters, McAllister returned to throw triumphant punches towards an away end which would not have cleared even if the gates behind them had been opened. Given the chance, they might have stayed all night. In the tunnel, beaming smiles contrasted with the dejected features of a Carlisle squad who had no interest in hearing how much they had contributed to the semi-final. Credible though their effort was, patronising praise stood only one step away from unwarranted criticism. Ward's magnanimous reaction in those emotive moments was superb. 'You must have a drink with us,' he told McAllister with a mischievous smile. 'We've got loads of our cheapest red wine somewhere.' If Ward hadn't laughed he might well have cried, and restrained though McAllister so often was, the emotion of the game had clearly entered his blood. But in the short seconds it took for him to climb the stairs to the directors' box and begin his post-match interview, the level head returned. 'We move on again, slightly closer to the Championship,' he said. 'I don't want to be a killjoy but nothing's been achieved yet.'

An echo from McAllister's calming voice was heard in the emptying car park beside United's bus where, fresh from the shower and his hair still dripping, Freedman took a few minutes to reflect on the point in the road reached by his surrogate club. 'Wembley's at the back of my mind,' said the Glaswegian. 'The word promotion is what I'm thinking about.' The risk of presuming too much had already dawned on Freedman; Wembley, he realised, would still be required to produce a beaten finalist on 25 May, and defeat in a play-off final was no more of a memorable success than defeat at Brunton Park would have been. It was like his fellow Scot, Sean Connery, once said: 'Losers always whine about doing their best. Winners go home and fuck the prom queen.'

WEMBLEY

'**A**LL OR NOTHING', AS PLAY-OFF FINALS ARE PERENNIALLY
defined, is a slogan becoming of Wembley Stadium, the pride of
the Football Association and a theatre on which no expense was spared.
So fixated were the FA on creating 'shock and awe' inside England's
national arena that no part of its reconstruction was underfunded or
redesigned to match a budget. The figures involved in the prolonged
and hideously extravagant development of Wembley make the mind
boggle, and a microcosm of its astonishing scale is the fact that a
channel tunnel train could run unhindered through the twisted arch
which sweeps from east to west above the stadium. It is the definition
of a big ground, created exclusively for big games; built for matches
with the magnitude of the 2008 League One play-off final. Leeds
United had more illustrious fixtures on their resume – and, in the era
of the Premier League, none of greater repute than the Champions
League semi-final contested with Valencia seven years earlier – but the
average supporter was at a loss to decide whether any one-off game
had ever been bigger. The European Cup, Gary McAllister said, was
icing on a luxurious cake; League One provided nothing more than
stale bread and water, and a standard of living which would damage
Leeds United's health with increasing effect year after year. This was

the Champions League's antithesis, what McAllister called the 'nitty gritty'. Twelve months in the English third division had been 12 months too many, and there was no value to be found in a second season in League One. To claim otherwise would be nonsense. A more significant game than the Champions League semi-final? 'Probably,' he said.

There was a reluctance on his part to speak too highly of United's presence in the play-off final or to tempt fate by heaping praise upon his players. The Championship was close enough to touch but not yet within reach, and it is in those betwixt-and-between moments when anticipation is most dangerous. Arriving at Wembley, in McAllister's experience, was not the same as leaving with champagne soaked through your hair. He had played at the stadium twice in 1996 and walked away with few pleasant memories. In March of that year, a Leeds United team captained by McAllister were comprehensively beaten by Aston Villa in the League Cup final. Later that summer, his unsuccessful penalty – saved by the reactive elbow of David Seaman – resigned Scotland to 2–0 defeat to England during a heavily-hyped Euro '96 group fixture which neither country dared to lose. The poignant image of him with his hands on his head is still engraved in the minds of the tartan tribe who sat despondently behind Seaman's goal. But a personal failure though the international fixture was for McAllister, it had arguably been the more useful experience. 'If I score the penalty, Scotland win,' he said. 'There's no doubt in my mind about that. Our preparation for that game was excellent. The only thing I should have done was score.' For the players now under his wing it was a lesson worth learning, and an example of how small fractions can sway entire games. Scotland's performance on that scorching afternoon in 1996 had been admirable; Terry Venables, England's manager, admitted as much. But Wembley does not honour its losers, nor send them home with consolation. For beaten teams, the stadium is a cemetery.

Stark though that reality was, it did not detract from the general appreciation of how improbable United's appearance in the play-off final was. Their season had come to rest on a single game, but it was unjust to allow a solitary fixture to define the year behind McAllister's players. The more their progression was analysed, the more distinguished it became. Questions aimed at McAllister invariably touched on the 15-point deduction but he had come to realise that United's endurance went far beyond their battle with the Football League. This was a club who, on 4 May 2007, were forced to admit their insolvency. A club who, until the beginning of August, were incapable of signing a single professional player. And a club whose squad had been asked to work with two different managers and three assistants in the space of nine short months. The third point – which contradicted the idea that successful clubs require continuity – was often overlooked, but it was clearly the most unsettling factor that United's players had successfully managed to overcome. Dennis Wise's departure in January had been as unexpected as it was sudden, and the exit of Gustavo Poyet at the end of October proved similarly untimely. It was common in Leeds to hear people ask whether Wise's tenure had essentially run its course on the day Poyet left Elland Road for Tottenham Hotspur, and while there was nothing in the way of exact science to substantiate that claim, the statistics made interesting reading. In the period when Poyet held the post of assistant, United completed 13 League One matches without defeat. With Dave Bassett installed as Wise's number two, the club lost five of their next 15. Bassett felt victimised by the suggestion that his involvement was having a detrimental effect on the club's season – 'It's a cheap shot, and there are people who jump on the bandwagon. I expect they'll be saying that Gus Poyet did all the work behind the scenes and Dennis did nothing before I came' – and it was simplistic to say that the change of assistant manager was entirely responsible for the striking change in mood and consistency at Elland Road. Simplistic also to suggest that Poyet alone was the mastermind behind the club's results. Leeds did not *improve* with Bassett as their assistant – that much is true – but their tactics did not change noticeably either. A more honest appraisal would be to say that League One's clubs simply worked Leeds United out. Wise's direct strategy – so effective at first – became predictable insofar as opposition teams found Leeds increasingly easy to manipulate, and although a change of manager was enforced upon Ken Bates against his wishes, it was in truth a blessing in disguise.

McAllister's view of football was taken from a different angle to that of his predecessor, and after negotiating a nervous spell of immense transition during February, his revised strategy began to take hold. More fluent in their passing and more patient in their approach, United's performances at Leyton Orient and Carlisle United were as complete as anything which had gone before. In a season which became a tale of two managers, it was apparent that both men were as important as each other. Without McAllister's involvement, Wembley might have eluded Leeds; equally, it is doubtful whether anyone could have fostered the productive defiance generated by Wise in the early stages of the 2007–08 season. Horses for courses, as a trainer of thoroughbreds might say. David Prutton saw it like that. 'The change of managers was a bit unsettling,' he said. 'But in a way it was a good thing as well. The time might have been right to refresh the squad and to refresh the way we were playing. If you play one way all the time or adopt the same tactics game after game then eventually teams work you out. The style we've got at the moment is less predictable.'

Far more predictable was the chaotic scramble for tickets provoked by Leeds United's appearance at Wembley. A deluge of interest was inevitable, and also understandable. Their supporters had wallowed in more mediocrity and pity than most could remember, and it made little sense to endure the agony of the downward trend while missing the day on which United's redemption was planned. There was no incentive big enough to persuade the club's fans that they should be anywhere other than Wembley on 25 May. The only doubt was whether Wembley would supply tickets in great enough bulk to meet the demand. Both Leeds and Doncaster Rovers, who had been confirmed as League One's second finalists after a foreboding rout of Southend United, were awarded an allocation of 36,000 by the Football League. Leeds knew immediately that the numbers of supporters hunting for tickets would comfortably outstrip that figure. In 2006, around 50,000 seats at the Millennium Stadium were reserved for United's fans before the Championship play-off final in Cardiff. In total, Leeds received 100,000 individual ticket applications from anxious supporters, 50 per cent of whom were turned away. Nothing illustrated the breadth of their fanbase more vividly than a play-off final. The club's failure to organise an efficient scheme of ticket distribution for the 2006 final – causing heaving queues to snake wildly around their besieged ticket office – was roundly criticised, and a keen desire existed among senior staff at Elland Road to see passes for Wembley handed out with the minimum of stress and as little controversy as possible. There were few things as damaging to the club's image as the suggestion that they might be failing, mistreating or undervaluing their loyalty of their supporters. Their forward planning was so advanced that details of the procedure for selling tickets for Wembley were published on 9 May, three days before the first leg of Leeds' play-off semi-final against Carlisle United – a decision which the club said was pre-emptive of their qualification and not presumptuous. Advanced applications were requested from season ticket holders and affiliates of their official Members' Club, who were promised one ticket each, and the number received was big enough to crash the online booking service employed by Leeds. The expectation that all 25,000 would submit their forms with haste, however, was fanciful. On the afternoon of Tuesday, 20 May, as Leeds prepared to begin a general sale of sorts by allowing every season ticket holder and member to reserve a maximum three seats, fans began to gather in Fullerton Park, the plot of council owned wasteland adjacent to Elland Road and next to the club's ticket office. Some brought deckchairs and others brought sleeping bags, prepared for the long overnight wait ahead of them. Police officers were brought in to control the crowd and the atmosphere was good humoured until the sight of newly-arrived supporters invading the front of the queue dampened the mood at 6 o'clock on Wednesday morning. By the time the sun had risen fully, as many as 7,000 people were thought to have joined the wait for tickets, and the police struggled to keep control. Groups of supporters were trapped in painful crushes near the centre of the crowd, and a small number became badly dehydrated after standing for hours without food or water. At regular intervals, a trickle of fans was released towards the ticket office, but it was clear that a large number of those in Fullerton Park – some of whom had been present for well over 16 hours – would go home empty handed and thoroughly exhausted. It was not as Leeds United had intended. On hearing reports of the squabble, the more enterprising and resourceful individuals decided to relocate to Doncaster Rovers' stadium in an attempt to acquire tickets for the wrong end of Wembley. Better to be amongst the opposition, they reasoned, than not inside the ground at all. The earliest arrivals at the Keepmoat Stadium were rewarded with tickets, passing themselves off as Doncaster supporters, but the South Yorkshire club soon uncovered the truth. The gathering of Leeds fans outside their ground became so large that Rovers suspended sales after realising the extent of the threat to segregation inside Wembley. Ticket touts were also loitering with intent. Leeds United's entire allocation of 36,000 sold out at 7 p.m. on Wednesday, 21 May with a crowd of the club's supporters still standing forlorn and helpless on the dusty gravel of their car park. Even though Doncaster traded just over 22,000 of their own allowance, the Football League rejected the suggestion that a number of their remaining tickets might be passed to Elland Road. As a result of this, the uncompromising desire of fans to force their way into Wembley by any means was evident in the minutes before the play-off final kicked off, by which time three large pockets of Leeds' contingent had gathered in the western reaches of the stadium, an area which was in theory designated specifically to Doncaster. Stewards and police expecting a placid afternoon were forced to organise makeshift cordons around the rebel gatherings, who had splattered the red-and-white blanket of Doncaster shirts with clear patches of Leeds United yellow-and-white.

McAllister acknowledged the importance of the match to United's fanbase – as a member of the last Leeds squad to win the Division One title, he could see how demeaning the club's position was – but he was anxious to detach his players from the obsessional hunt for tickets and the mood of expectancy which had swept through Yorkshire like a deadly fever. As a last resort, it was inevitable that certain supporters would see the team as possible source of Wembley seats. On 21 May, having conducted his penultimate media briefing at Thorp Arch, McAllister and his squad boarded their bus and slipped silently out of the county. They journeyed south to Wigginton – a leafy and sleepy Hertfordshire village – where they took up residence in the nearby Champneys Health Resort. The location provided all the detachment that McAllister could have asked for, 35 miles from Wembley but a million miles from the intensity of that famous venue. Wrought iron gates, painted black with golden spikes, welcomed new arrivals onto vast acres of green and pleasant land, broken only by the resort itself a quarter-of-a-mile down a tree-lined tarmac track. Mobile phone reception was intermittent, and alcohol was sparse. A snooker table surrounded by rich leather sofas and a bust of Stanley Lief, Champneys' founder, stood on one side of the hotel's back door, and a croquet lawn lay on the other. It was a place where relaxation came naturally; McAllister himself had used the resort as a player. He knew the complex well and expected the tranquil surroundings to subdue the members of his squad who were beginning to grasp the enormity of the game awaiting them. 'We've heard what's been happening with tickets at Elland Road, and at Doncaster as well,' McAllister said. 'From that point of view, it's been a good decision to get down here in behind these iron gates, and into peaceful surroundings.' Leeds had been granted the use of Arsenal's training ground at London Colney – facilities not unlike their own in Wetherby – and on the Friday afternoon, United's squad took the short trip to Wembley to get their first impressions of the arena which would stand in final judgement of their season.

England's national stadium is regarded as one of the most impressive footballing venues in the world, though that statement is more a matter of fact than a compliment. At a cost of close to £1 billion, it ought to be. The time and money dedicated to remodelling Wembley were like nothing ever seen in England, and the project suffered excessive doses of delay, embarrassment and farce before the key to the gate was finally handed over to the Football Association in March 2007. The governing body were best placed to judge whether the finished product represented value for money but, criticism aside, the devotion to their crown jewel has produced a jaw-dropping venue. The suburb of Wembley in the north of London is run-down and featureless, an odd location, you might argue, for such an expensive construction, and the FA's pristine stadium takes pride of place in its heart. Outside Wembley Park, the underground station which leads down several flights of steps onto Olympic Way – or Wembley Way, as the football fraternity mistakenly call it – banners hung by the local council's tourism department urge onlookers to 'Discover Brent', which is not the ridiculous suggestion it sounds. The surrounding area may have plenty going for it, but the crowds who flock annually to Wembley Stadium wouldn't know. Were it not for the location of the FA's arena, most would never set foot in the borough. The ground itself has been built on a grand scale in every conceivable area of construction and hospitality. Wembley's unique arch is taller than the London Eye, and the oblong design of the stadium is one kilometre in circumference. More than 2,000 toilets have been furnished inside, and the combined length of Wembley's escalators would stretch around a 400 metre running track. Eighty-six steps down from the stadium's upper level, car parks the size of runways spill out in every direction around its base. It is also one of the few venues in Britain to offer hole-in-the-wall cash machines as standard (and viewing their food prices, it is not altogether a bad idea to offer customers the chance to re-fill their wallets). Even the statue of Bobby Moore situated at the entrance to Wembley is twice the actual height of England's late captain, standing six metres high on its plinth. With his arms crossed and his archaic boot placed on top of an old-fashioned ball, Moore is a gentle guardian of Wembley. He is also the embodiment of the standard that players who take to the turf of England's historical ground should aspire to. On one side of his memorial hangs a bronzed replica of his cap from the 1966 World Cup final; to the rear is fastened a plaque listing the many talents of Moore, the footballer and the man:

Immaculate Footballer – Imperial Defender – Immortal Hero Of 1966 – First Englishman To Raise The World Cup Aloft – Favourite Son Of London's East End – Finest Legend Of West Ham United – National Treasure – Master Of Wembley – Lord Of the Game – Captain Extraordinary – Gentleman For All Time.

Moore had an intricate and intimate knowledge of the original stadium but died in 1993 long before the Twin Towers were pulled down and the new venue completed. The majority of McAllister's players had experience of neither. The club's visit to Wembley two days early was a chance to acquaint the squad with the arena and prepare them mentally for the sight that would hit them when they walked from the tunnel minutes before kick-off. McAllister also wanted his squad to take to the pitch and ensure the boots they intended to use against Doncaster were suited to the condition of the turf. The length of the grass concerned him slightly, but he found that the groundstaff at Wembley were the groundstaff who had been employed by Leicester City while McAllister played at Filbert Street in the 1980s. They assured him that the surface would be trimmed. By unlucky chance, however, United's coach was delayed on the M25 as it picked its way through congested traffic and into north London around Friday lunchtime, and Leeds landed at Wembley at the very moment that Doncaster's players were entering the ground for a tour of their own. In a slightly awkward situation, both squads saw the joke, and McAllister and Sean O'Driscoll exchanged pleasantries before continuing with their respective excursions and then heading for home. 'It was all very friendly,' McAllister said with a smile, 'but I'm sure it will be different come Sunday.'

By the time he returned to the peaceful environment Champneys that afternoon, ready to stage a final press conference alongside Dougie Freedman, McAllister had settled on his starting line-up. It was always likely that he would trust once more in the 11 players who had resurrected United's season at Brunton Park, but the availability of Alan Sheehan after a three-match suspension was a development he could not ignore. As the only recognised left-back in the squad at Leeds – with the exception of youngster Ben Parker, who had been released on loan to Darlington by McAllister – Sheehan's absence from both play-off semi-finals did not automatically preclude him from an appearance at Wembley. Bradley Johnson had covered for Sheehan on the left side of defence for three successive matches, and had done so capably, but Johnson's natural talent was that of midfielder. A decision was there for McAllister to take, and 48 hours before the play-off final, his mind was fixed. 'I think the players have got an idea,' he said, hinting that the announcement of his line-up would contain few surprises. Ultimately, he would, as expected, pin his colours on the Brunton Park XI.

With kick-off so close, McAllister might have chosen to pull his players back from the full-blooded training sessions they were accustomed to, but he preferred to keep his squad on edge by encouraging their competitive streak on the practice field. No doubt O'Driscoll was doing the same. United's manager felt reassuringly calm, 'my confidence grows as the players' confidence grows, and the more I see the players perform, the more confident I feel in them.' But the word from Doncaster's camp was that butterflies among O'Driscoll's player were few in number. Individuals put forward for interviews carried with them a relaxed air, and the public musings of O'Driscoll suggested his tactics for Wembley were comprehensively thought-out and ready to employ. He looked permanently ready. And while his preparation will have been every inch as meticulous as McAllister's, the week preceding the play-off final did not impose the same level of scrutiny on Doncaster as it did on Leeds United. It was easier to fly beneath the radar at the Keepmoat Stadium than it was at Elland Road.

The media viewed the League One play-off final as a win-at-all-costs fixture for Leeds, implying indirectly and unfairly that Doncaster's involvement was enough of an achievement for O'Driscoll and his squad. The general public assumed that only one set of players could afford to contemplate defeat on Sunday, 25 May – it would not be those wearing white shirts – and the agenda from the start focused predominantly on what the result at Wembley would mean for Leeds United. The misapprehension was forgivable to a point – Doncaster had been a Nationwide Conference club in the season that Leeds infringed on the semi-finals of the Champions League – but O'Driscoll's squad were not also-rans. On the contrary, the neutral observer would routinely describe them as one of the most attractive and dominant teams in their division. Their potency had been adequately portrayed in their play-off semi-final against Southend United, who were beaten 5–1 at the Keepmoat Stadium after holding Doncaster to a goalless draw during the first leg at Roots Hall. The manner of Rovers' victory was no less exceptional than the 2–0 win produced by Leeds at Brunton Park, and if United were a team in form then O'Driscoll did not need to worry about the state of his own club. Though the bookmakers installed Leeds as favourites to win at Wembley as soon as the finalists were confirmed, the match was difficult to call. The only advantage assisting United was the undeniable sense that, from the moment Tresor Kandol's header passed through the legs of Danny Coyne at Prenton Park on 11 August, their escape from League One seemed meant to be. But Doncaster had no intention of presenting Leeds with a free ticket to the Championship, and had already demonstrated once during 2008 that they had the measure of United over 90 minutes. 'Everybody's got an opinion and I think they're a good side,' said a non-committal McAllister. 'We're aware of their strengths. Let's get the game on.' O'Driscoll insisted that his players train on a pitch with identical dimensions to Wembley's, adapting them to the large surface at the stadium, and he did not agree that Doncaster were arriving in the capital without pressure. 'There's a weight of expectation on both clubs and it will all come down to who has that little bit of luck, and who performs best on the day,' he said. 'The losers' dressing room will be a miserable place and we have to make sure we're not in it.' Leeds would be housed in Wembley's east changing room during Sunday's final, the same facilities occupied by Hull City the previous day. With the makings of an omen, Dean Windass walked out of the eastern dressing room and produced the spectacular moment of an unspectacular Championship play-off final to earn Hull a 1–0 win over Bristol City, and with it promotion to the Premiership. Later that evening, United's players left Hertfordshire and checked into The Landmark hotel in Marylebone, the closest five-star residence to Wembley and the penultimate stop of their punishing journey from pavement to penthouse. McAllister's work was almost done.

Superstitious supporters cannot help but look for portents on decisive occasions, and the changing room occupied by Hull was a promising, if tenuous, sign to those who believed in fate. The Saturday afternoon on which Hull's promotion was ratified – the first time in more than a century that City had earned the right to call themselves a top-flight club – was a day of glorious weather and intense heat. The warm wind swept over the wide expanses of concrete outside Wembley, and the sunshine contributed to an electric ambience on Olympic Way. The smell of fried onions mixed with cigarettes, lager, the occasional whiff of cannabis, and expectancy hung in the air. It was a day on which dreams were likely to be realised. The temperature at pitch-side cleared 30 degrees during the Championship final, and the game became the most picturesque event that Hull's supporters could have asked for, their amber colours sparkling triumphantly as the Football League's trophy past from hand-to-hand. It is often said that it is more aesthetically pleasing, and undoubtedly more satisfying, to win a play-off final than it is to finish second in your division and achieve promotion automatically, and Hull demonstrated why. In 50 years' time, they will reminisce on the Humber about the moment when Windass's volley crashed into the net, and the pain of the sunburn they returned home with. However much their day out cost, the investment was worth every penny. It was, then, more difficult for Leeds United's fans to feel instantly optimistic when they opened their curtains on the morning of 25 May to see driving rain thrashing into the pavements outside their hotels. The thousands who had travelled to Cardiff two years earlier recognised that weather immediately. United's defeat to Watford had wrecked what should have been a memorable afternoon in Wales, and the inhospitable showers that continued from first light to last ruined the day completely. There was nothing good to be said of the 2006 play-off final, and nothing good to be said of a day wasted in the soaking Welsh capital. The weather preceding United's return to the play-off final, on this occasion against Doncaster, was strangely reminiscent of the torrential conditions witnessed in Cardiff. Superstitious or not, the climate did not bode well, and where Hull's supporters had walked around topless, the invasion from Leeds came with thick jackets and large umbrellas. But McAllister was no meteorologist, and he could not control the weather. Yet again, all that mattered was the result.

The puddles were swimming around on Wembley High Road when a group of early arrivals swept us up from the depths of the suburb's Central Station and into the open air, a few minutes after 11a.m. The grey sky hung thick with cloud, but the spirited fans treated the uninviting conditions with disinterest. 'Where's the arch?' asked an excited young voice behind me, hoping to stumble onto a full-frontal view of Wembley Stadium but presented instead with a mundane row of shops and offices. The glaring contradiction of the FA's home is that it resides in an area which is inherently non-descript. On the road to Wembley is the central office of Brent Council and a department of the Inland Revenue. Pubs are scattered along the High Street – The Bear and JJ Moons on the right of the main road and Thirsty Eddie's on the left, all displaying printed messages in their windows inviting Doncaster Rovers supporters their doors and directing Leeds United's supporters elsewhere – and a small science college sits back from the road, in need of a lick of paint and a touch of modernisation. Wembley may be a billion-pound arena, but it will be many years before the surrounding area smacks of such lucre and luxury. Finally, between a solicitors' office and a curry house, the stadium's arch appeared in the distance, vying in height with the towering Ibis Hotel next door to the stadium. Wembley's piece de resistance looks impressive on television; in the flesh, it is positively enormous, a unmistakable icon of English football arcing through the air in the shape of a giant helix. Beneath the arch, Wembley's hospitality staff were queuing at the doors, waiting for bags to be searched and identification cards to be checked. Their black-and-white attire did not seem in tune with the drama of the game to come; most looked as if they were about to serve at a funeral. Though in the case of one or other of the clubs involved, the aftermath of game would not be far removed from the atmosphere of a wake.

At the front of the ground, rain trickled down the green legs and arms of Bobby Moore's effigy, and the cross of St George behind his head flickered viciously in the wind. Wembley had given warmer welcomes. But from the top of Olympic Way, the size of the crowd drawing in was already obvious. Organisers of the play-off final had divided the path leading to Moore's statue in two, funnelling Doncaster's supporters along one half and United's fans along the other. The sea of white was swelling rapidly, high above the collection of red-and-white shirts. Leeds had promised a colossal turn-out but even officials at Wembley were surprised by the weight of numbers crowding through their turnstiles. The League One play-off final is said to have broken the stadium's record for the number of fans housed in Wembley's corporate facilities for an individual match. The statistics included England's international fixtures and FA Cup finals. BBC Radio Five Live stated that 55,000 Leeds supporters had been present inside the ground for kick-off, a figure which was difficult to substantiate but which cannot have been far from the truth. United's half of the stadium was packed to breaking point, devoid of an empty seat. The end housing Doncaster was filled to a large extent, but swathes of unoccupied stands separated groups of their supporters. In amongst them, those in United's colours who had helped themselves to Rovers' ticket allocation gravitated towards one another and set up camp in three sweeping rows – one in the stadium's bottom tier, another in front of the giant scoreboard above the middle layer of seats, and a final congregation tucked away in the highest reaches of Wembley's terraces. Opposite them, the variety of flags gave a geographical census of Leeds' support. The local fans were represented by the names of Seacroft and Pontefract, both a stone's throw from Elland Road; others from further afield promoted the counties of Somerset and Hampshire. Irish tricolours flew alongside Union Flags, and hidden away high up in the stands hung a banner bearing the name of Armley White Horse, perhaps the most prolific flag on the Leeds United circuit. It had been present in Liberec and was present at Wembley having been on show every step of the odyssey from the obscurity of the Czech Republic to the spiritual home of English football. The owners of that banner had earned their seats a hundred times over, and unconditional though their support of Leeds seemed to be, it was many years since the club they followed reciprocated their spirit in the way that McAllister's squad had.

The first glimpse of his players came after 1p.m. on the giant screens at either end of Wembley, which showed the players walking in line from the steps of their bus to the changing room indoors. Tresor Kandol and Jermaine Beckford wore chunky headphones over their ears – their way of shutting out the animation around them – while their team-mates paced forward without a word to each other. Their concentrated expressions showed slight apprehension, but no more than was healthy. Nerves are good, McAllister would say, and proof that players had grasped the salient nature of the situation they were in. With a clear view from every one of its 90,000 seats, there is nowhere to hide at Wembley. But mixed with the nervous tension may also have been a tinge of relief that a game so heavily debated and anticipated had finally moved beyond the predictive stage. If ever a period of the football season showed how cheap talk could be, the week before a play-off final was it. This was their time, and theirs alone – do or die, kill or be killed. An hour-and-a-half later, his final words of wisdom imparted, McAllister had nothing left to say.

His team left their sanctuary and walked side-by-side with Doncaster's players towards the light at the end of the tunnel. As the squads reached the edge of the turf, flame-throwers either side of the halfway line launched balls of fire into the air, and fireworks screamed from their holders around the centre circle, leaving a curtain of smoke hovering in the air. The players lined up along strips of maroon carpet, a number standing stationary, others jumping from foot to foot, bouncing with suspense. Slowly, the sound of booing began to emanate from the ranks of United's supporters, rising suddenly into a fierce cacophony mixed with piercing whistles. From the side of the pitch stepped Lord Brian Mawhinney, preparing to carry out his traditional meet-and-greet routine with both teams. It was a glaring piece of humbug, and an attempt at cordiality which one half of the crowd did not appreciate. But each of United's players looked Mawhinney in the eye and shook his hand politely, conscious of the fact that in this stadium, on this day, the Football League chairman was not their enemy. Of greater concern was the line of players standing ten yards away from them, primed by O'Driscoll and ready to snap into life. Mawhinney moved on and disappeared from view, out of the picture at last. This was football as it was supposed to be: 11 versus 11, toe to toe, and not a single politician in sight.

McAllister took his seat and watched intently as Doncaster took his team by the throat. Twice in the opening ten minutes, the fine judgement of Casper Ankergren dispossessed players who had left United's defence coughing in their dust. His second intervention – a single-handed tap of the ball at the feet of James Coppinger – was produced in the knowledge that the slightest of misjudgements would have incurred a penalty and a straight red card. There was only so much that Leeds could ask of Ankergren, though, and shots from Richie Wellens and Jason Price – the former's striking the side-netting and the latter's arcing over the crossbar with the help of a deflection – reiterated how quickly Doncaster had settled in the zealous noise of Wembley. Leeds found their voice midway through the first half and slowly weakened their opponents' grip of possession, but a curling finish from Jonathan Howson which dipped beyond Neil Sullivan's goal was all that McAllister had to cling to. It was not enough, and nothing like the display of unerring resolve seen at Brunton Park ten days earlier. With the scoreline goalless, McAllister gathered his team's collective thoughts at half-time, but his counsel was silenced when his defence gave way in the 47th minute. A corner from Brian Stock dropped invitingly into Ankergren's box, and James Hayter met the ball with a diving header which flashed between United's goalkeeper and Neil Kilkenny, standing apart on the goalline. Hayter had not scored since January, but the reappearance of his finishing touch threatened Leeds with the gravest of consequences. Metaphorically, the stadium cracked in half, the western end awash with ecstasy and the eastern front a mass of rigid statues who feared the worst and could not intervene. McAllister replaced David Prutton with Tresor Kandol in the 69th minute, and Dougie Freedman – a bystander on his 34th birthday – left the field 13 minutes from the end of normal time, for once unable to pull Leeds back from the precipice. But McAllister knew that a final chance would come, and that no team was more effective at striking late than Leeds. It was their forte and, for months, their trademark. When the opportunity arrived, only three minutes remained and Doncaster's players were beginning to look searchingly towards Andy D'Urso, Wembley's referee, for the final whistle. Frazer Richardson's urgent throw-in sailed into Doncaster's box and deflected towards the penalty spot where Jonathan Douglas met the ball with a powerful volley. Sullivan stood transfixed as the shot curved away from him and towards his left-hand post, and the rising crowd of white behind his goal stood with their arms half-raised and their eyes looking desperately at the sky as the ball arced wide of the goal and smashed into the advertising boards in front of them. All around the stadium were expressions of despondency and expressions of defeat. D'Urso called for four minutes of injury-time, but United's supporters had abandoned hope. Football, once again, had abandoned them. The Championship was beckoning Doncaster, and few could begrudge O'Driscoll that calling after a match in which his side's imagination and creativity had overshadowed that shown by Leeds. A match which for Leeds was a game too far.

At the sound of D'Urso's final whistle, nine of McAllister's players dropped onto their backs, weighed down by the grim thought of how far they had come and by how fine a margin they had fallen short. Only Ankergren and Neil Kilkenny remained standing. United's supporters stood and applauded the team before fading away with haste, leaving behind a mass of empty seats, broken only by the tearful individuals who could not bring themselves to move. McAllister's players stood briefly to acknowledge Doncaster's squad as they climbed the steps of Wembley to receive the League One trophy, huddled together but lost in their own thoughts. At the first opportunity they took their leave of the field and left Doncaster alone in the winners' enclosure, bound for the silent misery of their dressing room.

A short while later, and inside the lower regions of Wembley, John Ryan worked his way towards a nearby television camera, his shirt sprayed with a mixture of lager and champagne. As the smiles and the platitudes rolled forth, Leeds United's players passed quietly behind him, their eyes red and their heads bowed. Requests for interviews were declined with a soft shake of the head until Casper Ankergren paused to address a small group of journalists who knew the answers to their questions before they asked. How did he feel? 'Devastated'. Where do Leeds United go from here? 'Good question'. Wasn't he proud of their season? 'Maybe in a few days we'll realise the achievement,' he said. 'It's been a great season for Leeds United. But right now we're standing here with nothing.'

Not quite nothing. Hidden behind their distraught faces, McAllister's players were leaving Wembley in possession of their pride and that of their club, an asset which Leeds United value above all others. Perhaps, as Ankergren had said, the passing of time would bring with it a sense of perspective, and remind his team-mates that there is honour in defeat. But at that dark moment in the shadows of Wembley there was none to be found, only devastated players with tears on their cheeks and broken dreams in their hands.

EPILOGUE

••

UNITED WE STAND

TEARS WERE SHED IN LEEDS UNITED'S DRESSING ROOM, each one lamenting the wasteland of defeat. Not only the players felt like crying. With all the sincerity he possessed and all the energy he could muster, Gary McAllister stared through the immediacy of a barren dressing room and offered profound thanks to his squad. There was no more to be said. On the bus home, the mood was identical, a contrast between the still and silent players and those unable to settle. At regular intervals, their coach would overtake a coach of Leeds supporters, themselves reflecting on the merciless outcome of another false dawn. Some who spotted McAllister's players clapped their hands. On every occasion, McAllister and Steve Staunton ordered their squad to rise from their seats and applaud the swarm of homeward travellers. A journey which started together on the banks of the Mersey was ending together on the tarmac of the M1. Leeds United, at last.